PEGASUS SHAKESPEARE BIBLIOGRAPHIES

Richard II,
Henry IV, Parts I and II,
and *Henry V*

An Annotated Bibliography of Shakespeare Studies
1777–1997

PEGASUS SHAKESPEARE BIBLIOGRAPHIES

General Editor

RICHARD L. NOCHIMSON

Richard II, *Henry IV, Parts I and II,* and *Henry V*

An Annotated Bibliography of Shakespeare Studies
1777–1997

Edited by

JOSEPH CANDIDO

Pegasus Press
UNIVERSITY OF NORTH CAROLINA
ASHEVILLE, NC
1998

© Copyright 1998
Pegasus Press
Asheville, NC

Library of Congress Cataloging-in-Publication Data

Candido, Joseph.
  Richard II, Henry IV, parts I and II : an annotated bibliography
of Shakespeare studies, 1777–1997 / edited by Joseph Candido
    p. cm. — (Pegasus Shakespeare bibliographies)
  Includes indexes.
  ISBN 1-889818-10-0 (acid-free paper)
  1. Shakespeare, William, 1564–1616. Richard II—Bibliography.
2. Shakespeare, William, 1564–1616. King Henry IV—Bibliography.
3. Richard II, King of England, 1367–1400—In literature—
Bibliography. 4. Henry IV, King of England, 1367–1413—In
literature—Bibliography. I. Title. II. Series
Z8812.R53C36 1998
[PR2820]
016.8223'3—dc21   98–25550
                                                            CIP

This book is made to last.
It is printed on acid-free paper
to library specifications.
The typeface is Garamond Antiqua.

Printed in the United States of America

CONTENTS

Preface vii

   List of Abbreviations ix

I. Editions of Shakespeare's Plays and Basic Reference Works

   A. Single-Volume Editions of Shakespeare's Plays 1

   B. Multi-Volume Editions of Shakespeare's Plays 4

   C. Basic Reference Works for Shakespeare Studies 6

II. The Plays of the Second Tetralogy as a Group

   A. Influences; Sources; Historical and Intellectual Backgrounds; Topicality 14

   B. Language and Linguistics 19

   C. Criticism 22

   D. Performance Criticism; Film and Television Versions ... 39

   E. Collections of Essays 42

   F. Bibliographies 42

III. *Richard II*

   A. Editions 44

   B. Dating and Textual Studies 46

   C. Influences; Sources; Historical and Intellectual Backgrounds; Topicality 46

   D. Language and Linguistics 49

   E. Criticism 52

   F. Stage History; Performance Criticism 59

   G. Pedagogy and Collections of Essays 62

   H. Bibliographies 64

IV. *1* and *2 Henry IV*

    A. Editions   65

        (*1 Henry IV*)   65

        (*2 Henry IV*)   68

    B. Dating and Textual Studies   70

    C. Influences; Sources; Historical and Intellectual Backgrounds; Topicality   71

    D. Language and Linguistics   75

    E. Criticism   77

    F. Stage History; Performance Criticism   87

    G. Collections of Essays   90

    H. Bibliographies   91

V. *Henry V*

    A. Editions   93

    B. Dating and Textual Studies   96

    C. Influences; Sources; Historical and Intellectual Backgrounds; Topicality   97

    D. Language and Linguistics   101

    E. Criticism   102

    F. Stage History; Productions; Performance Criticism; Film Versions   111

    G. Collections of Essays   115

    H. Bibliography   116

Index I: Authors and Editors (Sections II, III, IV, and V)   117

Index II: Subjects (Sections II, III, IV, and V)   120

PREFACE

The twelve volumes of this series, of which this is the third, are designed to provide a guide to secondary materials on Shakespeare not only for scholars but also for graduate and undergraduate students and for college and high school teachers. In nine of the twelve volumes, entries will refer to materials that focus on individual works by Shakespeare; a total of twenty-five plays, plus *The Rape of Lucrece,* will be covered in these volumes. The remaining three volumes will present materials that treat Shakespeare in more general ways. This is a highly selective bibliography. While making sure to represent different approaches to the study of Shakespeare, the editors are including only work that is either of high quality or of great influence.

In this volume, entries for the works included are numbered consecutively throughout the volume. Within each subsection, entries are organized alphabetically by author.

Each entry contains the basic factual information and a brief annotation. Since inclusion of a book, article, or edition in this bibliography implies a positive evaluation, the annotations are designed to be descriptive primarily rather than evaluative. The intention is to convey to the reader the contents of the work being annotated. Readers will find that where evaluative comments could not be resisted they appear at the end of an annotation.

The organization of this volume is as follows.

Section I, which will be essentially the same in all twelve volumes, contains those editions and general reference works that in the collective opinion of the editors are most basic to the study of Shakespeare. The annotations in this section have been written by the following series editors: Jean E. Howard, Clifford C. Huffman, John S. Mebane (who has undertaken the updating as well as the composing of the annotations in subsections A and B), Richard L. Nochimson, Hugh M. Richmond, Barbara H. Traister, and John W. Velz.

Section II is devoted to the plays of the second tetralogy as a group, and Sections III, IV, and V are devoted to *Richard II, 1* and *2 Henry IV,* and *Henry V* respectively. Each of these sections is divided into subsections (six for Section II and eight each for Sections III, IV, and V); the kinds of works represented by these subsections are described in the table of contents. Many items, of course, cannot be neatly categorized under the heading of a single subsection. When an item could easily fall into more than one subsection, the editor of this volume has placed the item in the most appropriate subsection, and has cross-referenced it at the end of the other relevant subsections. For example, J. Dover Wilson's *The Fortunes of Falstaff* (no. 195) appears in Section IV under "Criticism," and it is cross-referenced at the end of the subsections on "Influences" and "Stage History." Readers should consult the cross-references at the end of each subsection as well as the subject index (where items are listed by item number only), to see the full range of material relevant to a particular area or topic. Since, in effect, all items in this bibliography could be considered forms of "criticism," no cross-references are listed at the end of that subsection.

No item in this bibliography is given more than one bibliographical entry. The only exception to this rule is that in Section I entries do appear for the eight most valuable multi-volume editions of Shakespeare's works—for example, the New Variorum Edition of Shakespeare. Where appropriate, volumes from those editions are also described individually in the subsections on "Editions" in Sections III, IV, and V.

Sections II, III, IV, and V include a subsection for "Collections of Essays." The items in these subsections include collections of both previously published and original materials. Selected materials in these collections are annotated elsewhere in the volume; these are listed by cross-references in the collection annotations, and the individual entries, in turn, refer to the collection entries. The collection entries also contain brief descriptions of other relevant critical or scholarly material in each volume.

Within the entries, numbers prefaced by "no." indicate cross-references; numbers in parentheses indicate either the page numbers in the book or article where a specific topic is discussed or quoted, or the act, scene, and line numbers of the passage discussed, divided by periods (e.g., 5.5.45–50). For convenience, unless specified otherwise, the act, scene, and line designations are taken from *The Riverside Shakespeare* (no. 2).

Abbreviations used are listed on the next page.

Acknowledgments

The editors wish to thank their wives as well as those colleagues and friends who helped with the compiling of this bibliography.

Joseph Candido
University of Arkansas,
Fayetteville

Richard L. Nochimson
Yeshiva University

August 1997

Abbreviations

anon.	anonymous
c.	circa
chap., chaps.	chapter(s)
Co.	company
comp., comps.	compiler(s)
ed., eds.	edited by/editor(s)
e.g.	for example
et al.	and others
etc.	and so forth
F	folio
ff.	and following
i.e.	that is
MS	manuscript
no., nos.	number(s)
n.s.	new series
p., pp.	page(s)
pub.	published
Q	quarto
repr.	reprint/reprinted
trans.	translated
Univ.	University
vol., vols.	volume(s)

I. EDITIONS AND REFERENCE WORKS

A. Single-Volume Editions.

1. Bevington, David, ed. *The Complete Works of Shakespeare.* Updated 4th edition. New York: Addison Wesley Longman, 1997.

Bevington's *Complete Works* includes 38 plays and the nondramatic poems. Introductions, aimed at a broad audience, focus upon questions of interpretation. The general introduction discusses social, intellectual, and theatrical history; Shakespeare's biography and his career as a dramatist; his language and versification; editions and editors of Shakespeare; and the history of Shakespearean criticism. Appendices include discussions of canon, dates, and early texts; brief summaries of sources; and performance history. There are genealogical charts, maps, and a selected bibliography. Emendations of the copy text are recorded only in an appendix; they are not bracketed in the texts of the plays. Spelling is modernized unless an exception is necessary for scansion, to indicate a pun, or for other reasons discussed in the preface. Notes appear at the bottom of the column. Speech prefixes are expanded. Illustrations include photographs from recent performances. Features ranging from the clarity and high quality of the introductions to the readability of the typeface combine to make the texts in this edition admirably accessible to students and general readers. Available with this edition are the BBC's CD-ROM programs on *Macbeth* and *A Midsummer Night's Dream*. These multimedia resources provide the full text and complete audio recordings; footnotes; word and image searches; sources; comments and audio-visual aids on plot, themes, language, performance history, historical background, and characterization; print capability; and clips from film and video performances. A *Teacher's Guide* to the CD provides suggestions for assignments and classroom use.

2. Evans, G. Blakemore, et al., eds. *The Riverside Shakespeare.* 2nd edition. Boston: Houghton Mifflin, 1997.

This edition includes 39 plays, the nondramatic poems, and segments of *Sir Thomas More*. Introductions by Herschel Baker (histories), Frank Kermode (tragedies), Hallett Smith (romances and nondramatic poems), Anne Barton (comedies), and J. J. M. Tobin ("A Funeral Elegy" by W. S. and *Edward III*) discuss dates, sources, and major interpretive issues. Harry Levin's general introduction discusses Shakespeare's biography, artistic development, and reputation; intellectual backgrounds; Renaissance playhouses and theatrical conventions; Elizabethan English; and stylistic techniques. Heather Dubrow provides an analytical survey of twentieth-century Shakespeare criticism. Evans provides an introduction to textual criticism. Appendices include a history of Shakespearean performance by Charles H. Shattuck and William T. Liston; substantial excerpts from historical documents related to Shakespeare's life and works, including some early responses to the plays; "Annals, 1552–1616," a listing in four parallel columns of events in political history, Shakespeare's biography, theater history, and nondramatic literature; a selected bibliography; indexes; and a glossary. Emendations of the copy text are enclosed in square brackets, and each play is followed by a summary discussion of editorial problems and by textual notes listing the sources of all emendations. Spelling is modernized except for "a selection of Elizabethan spelling forms that reflect ... contemporary pronunciation" (67). Notes appear at the bottom of the column. The volume includes numerous illustrations, including color plates. While the *Riverside* has many features aimed at general readers, the impressive textual apparatus, Evans's fine discussion of textual criticism, and the collection of documents make this edition of special interest to advanced graduate students and to scholars.

2a. Greenblatt, Stephen, Walter Cohen, Jean E. Howard, and Katharine Eisaman Maus, eds. *The Norton Shakespeare, Based on the Oxford Edition.* New York: Norton, 1997.

This edition includes 38 plays (including quarto, folio, and conflated texts of *King Lear*) and the nondramatic poems, including works of uncertain authorship not included in other single-volume editions. The texts (except for "A Funeral Elegy," ed. Donald Foster) are updated versions of those in the modern-spelling, single-volume *Oxford Shakespeare* (1988) produced by general editors Stanley Wells and Gary Taylor with John Jowett and William Montgomery. The *Oxford* edition is based on revisionary editorial principles, including the belief that some texts previously regarded as having limited authority are in reality records (at times highly imperfect) of early authorial versions later revised in the theater. The revised versions are usually chosen as control texts. In the *Oxford*, passages from earlier versions are often reprinted in appendices; the *Norton* prints these passages from earlier versions, indented, within the texts. *The Norton Shakespeare* provides marginal glosses and numerous explanatory notes; the latter are numbered in the text and appear at the bottom of each page. Textual variants are listed after each work. Stage directions added after the 1623 Folio appear in brackets. Greenblatt's general introduction discusses Renaissance economic, social, religious, and political life; Shakespeare's biography; textual criticism; and aspects of Shakespeare's art, including "The Paradoxes of Identity" in characterization and analysis of the "overpowering exuberance and generosity" (63) of Shakespeare's language. Introductions to individual works discuss a range of historical and aesthetic issues. Appendices include Andrew Gurr's "The Shakespearean Stage"; a collection of documents; a chronicle of events in political and literary history; a bibliography; and a glossary. This edition combines traditional scholarship with a focus on such recent concerns as the status of women and "The English and Otherness." Also available is *The Norton Shakespeare Workshop*, ed. Mark Rose, a set of interactive multimedia programs on a CD-ROM that can be purchased either separately or in a package with *The Norton Shakespeare*. The *Workshop* provides searchable texts of *A Midsummer Night's Dream*; *The Merchant of Venice*; *Henry IV, Part Two*; *Othello*; *Hamlet*; *The Tempest*; and sonnets 55 and 138. Students can find analyses of selected passages; sources; essays that illustrate the play's critical and performance history; clips from classic and from specially commissioned performances; selections of music inspired by the plays; and tools for developing paper topics.

3. **Hinman, Charlton**, ed. *The Norton Facsimile: The First Folio of Shakespeare*. 2nd edition. Introduction by Peter Blayney. New York: W. W. Norton, 1996.

The First Folio of 1623 is a collection of 36 plays made by Shakespeare's fellow actors, Heminge and Condell. *Pericles*, *The Two Noble Kinsmen*, and the nondramatic poems are not included. Heminge and Condell claim to have provided "perfect" texts, distinguishing them from what they describe as "stolne, and surreptitious copies, maimed, and deformed by the frauds and stealthes of injurious impostors" (A3). While some of the previously published quartos are regarded today as superior versions, the First Folio indeed provides the most authoritative texts for the majority of Shakespeare's plays. It also includes commendatory poems by four authors, including Ben Jonson, and the Droeshout portrait of Shakespeare. During the two years that the 1623 edition was in press, corrections were made continually, and the uncorrected pages became mingled with corrected ones. In addition, imperfections of various sorts render portions of numerous pages difficult or impossible to read. Hinman has examined the 80 copies of the First Folio in the Folger Shakespeare Library and selected the clearest versions of what appear to be the finally corrected pages. In the left and right margins, he provides for reference his system of "through line numbering," by which he numbers each typographical line throughout the text of a play (the verse and prose of the play as well as all other material such as scene headings and stage directions); in a page from *King John*, for example, which includes what might otherwise be referred to as 3.1.324 through 3.3.74 (this form of reference appears in the bottom margin), the through line numbers run from 1257 to 1380. Appendix A presents some variant states of the Folio text, and Appendix B lists the Folger copies used in compiling this edition. Hinman's introduction discusses the nature and authority of the Folio, the printing and proofreading process, and the procedures followed in editing the facsimile, explaining, among other points, the advantages of "through line numbering." Blayney's introduction updates Hinman's discussions of such matters as the status of quarto texts, the types of play-manuscripts available to printers, and the printing and proofreading processes. Blayney also discusses the theory that, since different versions of a given play may represent authorial or collaborative revisions, in such cases there is no "ideal text." No interpretive introductions or glosses are provided. While some valuable facsimiles of quarto versions are available, the Hinman First Folio is clearly an excellent place to begin one's encounter with early printed texts that are not mediated by centuries of editorial tradition.

B. Multi-Volume Editions.

4. Barnet, Sylvan, general ed. *The Signet Classic Shakespeare.* New York: Penguin.

Originally edited in the 1960s, the 30-volume Signet series includes 38 plays and the nondramatic poems. Collections entitled *Four Great Comedies* and *Four Great Tragedies* are available. Each volume includes a general introduction and discussions of Shakespeare's biography, Elizabethan theaters, and editorial principles of the series. Spelling is generally modernized, and speech prefixes are expanded. Explanatory notes appear at the bottom of each page. Appendices contain textual notes, discussion of (and often excerpts from) sources, several critical essays, and a brief annotated bibliography. The bibliographies and selections of critical essays were updated in the 1980s. Although introductions in this series are written for beginning students, the substantial selection of distinguished critical essays is useful for more advanced students as well.

5. Bevington, David, ed. David Scott Kastan, James Hammersmith, and Robert Kean Turner, associate eds. *The Bantam Shakespeare.* New York: Bantam, 1988.

In 1988, 37 plays and the nondramatic poems were published in the 29 volumes of *The Bantam Shakespeare.* Collections entitled *Four Comedies* and *Four Tragedies* are available. Texts, explanatory notes (at the bottom of each page), and interpretive introductions are similar to those of Bevington's *Complete Works of Shakespeare* (see no. 1). Included in the Bantam series are brief performance histories of individual plays and Joseph Papp's forewords on Shakespeare's enduring appeal. Each volume includes a one-page biography of Shakespeare and an introduction to Elizabethan playhouses. Appendices include concise discussions of dates and early texts, textual notes, substantial excerpts from sources, and a brief annotated bibliography. While this series necessarily excludes some of the historical information found in the *Complete Works*, the forewords by an eminent producer/director and the well-written performance histories are engaging features, especially appropriate for students and general readers.

6. Brockbank, Philip, founding general ed. Brian Gibbons, general ed. A. R. Braunmuller and R. C. Hood, associate general eds. *The New Cambridge Shakespeare.* Cambridge: Cambridge Univ. Press, 1982–.

So far, 26 volumes in the New Cambridge series of 39 plays (including *The Reign of Edward III*) and the nondramatic poems have appeared. Introductions discuss date, sources, critical history and interpretive issues, staging, and performance history (with numerous illustrations). Discussion of the text precedes each play, and more detailed textual analysis sometimes appears in an appendix. All volumes include a selected bibliography. Spelling is generally modernized; speech prefixes are expanded. Textual notes signaling departures from the copy text and extensive explanatory notes appear at the bottom of each page. Designed for students and scholars, *The New Cambridge Shakespeare* provides more detailed attention to stagecraft and performance history than most other edi-

EDITIONS AND REFERENCE WORKS 5

tions. This series succeeds *The New Shakespeare*, edited by Arthur Quiller-Couch and John Dover Wilson.

7. Knowles, Richard, and Paul Werstine, general eds. *A New Variorum Edition of Shakespeare.* New York: Modern Language Association.

From 1871 to 1928 H. H. Furness, Sr., and H. H. Furness, Jr., published 19 works of the Variorum Shakespeare. Since 1933, nine new editions have appeared in the MLA series. The completed 40-volume variorum will contain 38 plays and the nondramatic poems. Each volume provides an old-spelling text and a collation of significant emendations from previous editions. Explanatory notes (printed below the textual notes at the bottom of each page) try to record all important previous annotation. Appendices include discussions of a play's text and date. Recent volumes survey the history of criticism and performance and refer to a substantial bibliography; early volumes include excerpts from previous criticism. Sources and analogues are discussed and reprinted. As compilations of scholarship, criticism, and textual analysis, these volumes represent a significant resource for scholars and teachers.

8. Mowat, Barbara A., and Paul Werstine, eds. *The New Folger Library Shakespeare.* New York: Pocket Books, Washington Square Press, 1992–.

Nineteen volumes of the New Folger series, which replaces *The Folger Library General Reader's Shakespeare*, appeared between 1992 and 1997. Several new titles will come out each year until the series of 38 plays and the nondramatic poems is complete. Each volume provides a brief initial comment on the play followed by basic introductions to Shakespeare's language and style, his biography, Elizabethan theaters, early editions, and the editorial principles of the series. Half brackets enclose emendations of the copy text; in some volumes square or pointed brackets indicate the sources of passages that appear (for example) only in the folio or an earlier quarto. Explanatory notes appear on pages facing the text, textual notes in an appendix. Spelling is selectively modernized, and speech prefixes are expanded. For each play a different critic offers the "Modern Perspective" that follows the text. A brief annotated bibliography focuses mostly on recent approaches to the play; standard works on language, biography, theatrical setting, and early texts also appear. While this series aims at the broadest possible audience, the clarity and helpfulness of its introductions and explanatory notes make it especially well suited for beginning students.

9. Proudfoot, Richard, Ann Thompson, and David Scott Kastan, general eds. *The Arden Shakespeare.* Walton-on-Thames, Surrey: Nelson House.

The 40-volume *Arden Shakespeare* includes 38 plays and 2 volumes of the nondramatic poems. The edition is continually updated; although some current volumes are from the 1950s, six plays and the Sonnets have appeared in revised third editions in recent years. Introductions provide extensive discussion of dates, texts, editorial principles, sources, and a wide range of interpretive issues. Extensive textual and explanatory notes appear at the bottom of each page. Appendices typically include additional textual analysis, excerpts from sources, and (sometimes) settings for songs. The Arden series often includes scholarship and criticism that is essential for advanced students and scholars. The complete second edition of the Arden series is available on CD-ROM from Primary Source Media. The CD-ROMs enable one to view the edited texts simultaneously with materials from the following: early quarto and folio editions; Bullough's *Narrative and Dramatic Sources* (no. 14); Abbott's *Shakespearian Grammar*; Onions's *Shakespeare Glossary* (no. 20); Partridge's *Shakespeare's Bawdy*; and a 4,600-item bibliography.

10. Spencer, T. J. B., general ed. Stanley Wells, associate ed. *The New Penguin Shakespeare*. London: Penguin Books.

The 39-volume New Penguin series now includes 36 plays and the nondramatic poems; *Titus Andronicus* and *Cymbeline* are planned. Dates range from the 1960s through the 1980s. Introductions discuss a range of interpretive issues and are followed by brief bibliographical essays. Explanatory notes appear in an appendix, followed by textual analysis, selective textual notes, and (sometimes) settings for songs. Spelling is generally modernized, and speech prefixes are expanded. Emendations of the copy text are not bracketed. The New Penguin will appeal to those who wish the pages of the text to be free of annotation.

11. Wells, Stanley, general ed. Advisory eds. S. Schoenbaum, G. R. Proudfoot, and F. W. Sternfeld. *The Oxford Shakespeare*. Oxford: Oxford Univ. Press.

Between 1982 and 1996, 23 plays (plus collections entitled *Comedies*, *Histories*, and *Tragedies*) were published in the multi-volume *Oxford Shakespeare*. The completed series will include 38 plays and the nondramatic poems. Introductions provide detailed discussion of dates, sources, textual criticism, questions of interpretation, and performance history. Textual notes and extensive commentary appear at the bottom of each page. The commentary and introduction are indexed. Spelling is modernized, and speech prefixes are expanded. The Oxford series is based on revisionary editorial principles, including the belief that some texts previously regarded as of little value are in reality records (at times highly imperfect) of early authorial versions later revised in the theater. The revised versions are usually chosen as copy texts, and appendices sometimes include passages from earlier printed versions. Some appendices include musical settings for songs. Partly because of its editorial principles, this series is of special interest to scholars and advanced students.

C. Basic Reference Works for Shakespeare Studies.

12. Beckerman, Bernard. *Shakespeare at the Globe: 1599–1609*. New York: Macmillan, 1962.

This study of the 29 extant plays (including 15 by Shakespeare) produced at the Globe in its first decade yields information about the playhouse and how Shakespeare's company performed in it. The first chapter, on the repertory system, is based on analysis of Henslowe's diary. Subsequent chapters about the stage itself, acting styles, the dramatic form of plays and of scenes within plays, and the staging derive from study of the Globe repertory. Detailed appendices provide statistics on which Beckerman's analysis partly depends. Beckerman concludes that the style in which these plays were presented was neither symbolic nor what modern audiences would call realistic. Rather, he suggests, passion by the actors was presented within a framework of staging and scenic conventions in various styles according to the needs of particular plays.

13. Bentley, G. E. *The Jacobean and Caroline Stage.* 7 vols. Oxford: Clarendon Press, 1941–68.

Bentley designed his survey of British drama to carry on that of Chambers (see no. 15) and cover the years 1616–42. Vol. 1's 11 chapters provide detailed information about 11 adult and children's acting companies (1–342); vol. 2 surveys information about actors, listed alphabetically (343–629), with relevant documents reprinted and annotated (630–96), with an index (697–748). Vols. 3, 4, and 5 are an alphabetical list, by author, with bibliographical material and commentary, of "all plays, masques, shows, and dramatic entertainments which were written or first performed in England between 1616 ... and ... 1642" (3.v), from "M.A." to Richard Zouche, with a final section (5. 1281–1456) on anonymous and untitled plays. Vol. 6 considers theater buildings (private, 3–117; public, 121–252; court, 255–88; and two that were only projected, 291–309). Vol. 7 gathers together, as appendices to vol. 6, "scattered material concerning Lenten performances and Sunday performances" and arranges chronologically "a large number of dramatic and semi-dramatic events" of interest to students of dramatic literature and theater history (6.v); it includes a general index for vols. 1–7 (129–390) which has numerous references (344–45) to Shakespeare and his plays.

14. Bullough, Geoffrey. *Narrative and Dramatic Sources of Shakespeare.* 8 vols. London and New York: Routledge & Kegan Paul and Columbia Univ. Press, 1957–75.

This work is a comprehensive compendium of the texts of Shakespeare's sources for 37 plays and several poems. Bullough includes analogues as well as sources and "possible sources" as well as "probable sources." All texts are in English, old spelling Elizabethan when extant, and in some other cases in the compiler's translation. Bullough includes a separate introduction for each play. In the early volumes, interpretation is largely left to the reader; introductions in the later volumes include more interpretation and tend to be longer. There have been complaints of occasional errors in transcription; the major caveat, however, about using this learned, thorough, and imaginative work concerns what Bullough could not conceivably print—the passages in his sources that Shakespeare presumably read but either chose to omit or neglected to include.

15. Chambers, E. K. *The Elizabethan Stage.* 4 vols. Oxford: Clarendon Press, 1923. Revised 1945; with corrections 1967.

In vol. 1, Chambers provides detailed information about the court (1–234):

the monarchs, their households, the Revels Office, pageantry, the mask, and the court play. In the section entitled "The Control of the Stage" (236–388), he covers the struggles between the city of London and the court and between Humanism and Puritanism, and treats the status of actors and the socio-economic realities of actors' lives. In vol. 2, Chambers focuses on the history of 38 different acting companies (children, adult, and foreign) (1–294), gives details, such as are known, about an alphabetical list of actors (295–350), and treats the playhouses (16 public and 2 private theaters), including discussion of their structure and management (351–557). In vol. 3, Chambers surveys the conditions of staging in the court and theaters (1–154), the printing of plays (157–200), and then offers a bibliographical survey, including brief biographies, of playwrights alphabetically arranged, from William Alabaster through Christopher Yelverton (201–518). In vol. 4, Chambers concludes that bibliography with anonymous work (1–74) and presents 13 appendices that reprint or summarize relevant historical documents. Chambers concludes this work with four indices (to plays, persons, places, and subjects) to the four volumes (409–67). In these four volumes, Chambers presents an encyclopedia of all aspects of English drama during the reigns of Elizabeth I and James I up to the date of Shakespeare's death in 1616. A subsequent and detailed index to this entire work was compiled by Beatrice White, *An Index to "The Elizabethan Stage" and "William Shakespeare" by Sir Edmund Chambers*. Oxford: Oxford Univ. Press, 1934.

16. Chambers, E. K. *William Shakespeare: A Study of Facts and Problems.* 2 vols. Oxford: Clarendon Press, 1930. Repr., 1931.

This work is an encyclopedia of information relating to Shakespeare. The principal topics of the first volume are the dramatist's family origins, his relations to the theater and its professionals, the nature of the texts of his plays—including their preparation for performance and publication, and also questions of authenticity and chronology (relevant tables about the quartos and metrics are in the second volume). The data available (and plausible conjectures) concerning all texts attributed to Shakespeare, including poems and uncertain attributions, are then laid out title by title. The second volume cites the significant Shakespeare records then available, including contemporary allusions, performance data, legends, and even forgeries (the last two items are more fully covered in Schoenbaum's *Shakespeare's Lives*). There are comprehensive indices and a substantial bibliography. While it is sometimes necessary to update this book by correlation with Schoenbaum's *Documentary Life* (see no. 22) and other more recent texts, Chambers's scholarship has been supplemented rather than invalidated by more recent research, and his work remains a convenient starting point for pursuit of background data on Shakespeare's life and works.

17. Doran, Madeleine. *Endeavors of Art: A Study of Form in Elizabethan Drama.* Madison: Univ. of Wisconsin Press, 1954.

Doran reconstructs the Elizabethan assumptions about many aspects of dramatic form, defined broadly enough to include genre, eloquence and copiousness, character, and "moral aim." A detailed exploration of classical, medieval, and Renaissance backgrounds makes this a study in historical criticism; however, the cultural context laid out is aesthetic, not ideational. Doran examines the problems of form faced by Shakespeare and his contemporaries—problems of genre, of character, of plot construction—in an attempt to explain the success (or, sometimes, lack of success) of the major dramatists in "achieving form adequate to meaning" (23). Doran's unpretentious, readable study is justly famous as the first book on the aesthetics of Renaissance drama to understand the entire context, to perceive the Renaissance assumptions about dramatic art as a fusion of classical and medieval influences.

18. Gurr, Andrew. *Playgoing in Shakespeare's London.* Cambridge: Cambridge Univ. Press, 1987.

Gurr focuses on the identity, class, and changing tastes of London playgoers from the opening of the Red Lion in 1567 to the closing of the theaters in 1642. He examines the locations, physical features, price scales, and repertories of the various playhouses, distinguishing particularly between "halls" and "amphitheatres" and rejecting the more common labels "private" and "public." Turning from the theaters, Gurr examines the playgoers, asking such questions as whether they ventured to the playhouses primarily to "hear" a text or to "see" a spectacle. In a final chapter entitled "The evolution of tastes," he discusses assorted playgoing fashions: from the craze for Tarlton's clowning to the taste for pastoral and romance in the last years of Charles I. Two appendices list identifiable playgoers and references to playgoing during the time period.

19. Gurr, Andrew. *The Shakespearean Stage 1574–1642.* 3rd edition. Cambridge: Cambridge Univ. Press, 1992.

Gurr summarizes a vast amount of scholarship concerning the material conditions of Elizabethan, Jacobean, and Caroline theatrical production. Each of his six chapters provides a wealth of detailed information on theatrical life. The first gives an overview of the place of the theater in urban London from the 1570s until 1642, including an examination of the social status of playwrights, the differences and similarities between the repertories at the open-air amphitheaters (public) and at the indoor playhouses (private), and the changing role of court patronage of theater. Chapter two describes the typical composition of London theater companies and their regulation by the Crown. It also gives an historical account of the theatrical companies that at various times dominated the London theatrical scene. In his third chapter, Gurr looks at actors, discussing the famous clowns of the Elizabethan era, prominent tragic actors such as Burbage and Alleyn, and the repertory system within which they worked. The fourth chapter summarizes what is known about the playhouses, including information gleaned from the recent excavation of the remains of the Rose Theater, as well as accounts of the Globe Theater, The Fortune, the hall playhouses, and the Banqueting Hall. Chapter five discusses staging conventions and the differences between public and private theaters, and among the various particular theaters, in their use of song, music, clowning, and jigging. Also examined are stage properties and costumes. The final chapter analyzes information about audiences: who went to which kinds of playhouse and how they behaved. Gurr argues that women and all social classes were represented in theatrical audiences, with an increasing tendency in the seventeenth century for the private theaters to cater to a wealthier clientele who demanded a more sophisticated repertory with more new plays. This valuable book concludes with an appendix indicating at which playhouses and by which companies various plays were staged.

20. Onions, C. T. *A Shakespeare Glossary.* Oxford: Clarendon Press, 1911. 2nd edition revised, 1919. Repr., with corrections, 1946; with enlarged Addenda, 1958. Enlarged and revised by Robert D. Eagleson, 1986; corrected, 1988.

Onions's dictionary of Elizabethan vocabulary as it applies to Shakespeare was an offshoot of his work on the *Oxford English Dictionary.* Eagleson updates the third edition with new entries, using modern research (now aided by citations from the Riverside edition [see no. 2], keyed by the Spevack *Concordance* [see no. 23]), while conserving much from Onions's adaptation of *OED* entries to distinguish Shakespearean uses from those of his contemporaries and from modern standard meanings. The glossary covers only expressions that differ from modern usage, as with "cousin" or "noise." It includes some proper names with distinctive associations, such as "Machiavel," and explains unfamiliar stage directions: "sennet" (a trumpet signal). Many allusions are more fully elucidated, as with the origin of "hobby-horse" in morris dances, or the bearing of "wayward" on *Macbeth*'s "weird sisters." This text, which demonstrates the importance of historical awareness of language for accuracy in the close reading of Shakespeare, now has a brief bibliography of relevant texts but still lacks guidance about Elizabethan pronunciation.

21. Rothwell, Kenneth S., and Annabelle Henkin Melzer. *Shakespeare on Screen: An International Filmography and Videography.* New York: Neal-Schuman, 1990.

This list of film and video versions of Shakespeare seeks to be comprehensive, covering the years 1899–1989, except that it excludes most silent films, referring the reader to Robert Hamilton Ball's *Shakespeare on Silent Film* (1968). It does include "modernizations, spinoffs, musical and dance versions, abridgements, travesties and excerpts" (x). The introduction, by Rothwell, offers an overview of screen versions of Shakespeare (1–17). The body of the work, with over 675 entries (21–316), is organized by play, listed alphabetically, and within each play chronologically. Represented are 37 plays and the *Sonnets. Pericles* and *Timon of Athens* appear only in the BBC versions in "The Shakespeare Plays" series. For *Hamlet* we have 87 entries. Included also are another 74 entries (317–35) for documentaries and other "unclassifiable" films and videos that present Shakespeare in some form, such as John Barton's "Playing Shakespeare" series and James Ivory's film, "Shakespeare Wallah." The sometimes quite extensive entries include information about and evaluation of the production, and an attempt to provide information about distribution and availability. The work concludes with a useful selected bibliography with brief annotations (337–45), a series of helpful indexes (349-98), and a list of the names and addresses of distributors, dealers, and archives (399-404).

22. Schoenbaum, S. *William Shakespeare: A Compact Documentary Life.* Oxford: Oxford Univ. Press, 1977. Repr., with corrections, 1978.

An abridged version of Schoenbaum's massive documentary study of Shakespeare published by Oxford in 1975, the *Compact Documentary Life* traces all textual evidence about Shakespeare chronologically from his grandfather's generation up to the deaths of Shakespeare's surviving family members. Legends for which there is no specific documentation—such as the deer-poaching incident—are examined for probability on the basis of surviving materials. Where appropriate, Schoenbaum juxtaposes biographical details with specific passages in Shakespeare's works. Amply illustrated and annotated, this work, unlike Schoenbaum's earlier, larger version and his later (1981) *William Shakespeare: Records and Images*, refers to documents but generally does not reprint them.

23. Spevack, Marvin. *The Harvard Concordance to Shakespeare.* Cambridge: Belknap Press of Harvard Univ. Press, 1973.

This text covers the total of 29,066 words (including proper names) used by Shakespeare in his plays and poems, in the modern-spelling text of *The Riverside Shakespeare* (see no. 2). Stage directions appear in another volume. Contexts are omitted for the first 43 words in order of frequency, mostly pronouns, prepositions, conjunctions, auxiliary verbs, and articles. Individual entries distinguish between prose and verse, and between total and relative frequencies. The modern spelling is not enforced with proper names or significant Elizabethan divergencies: "embassador-ambassador." While the cited context of each use is normally the line of text in which it appears, other limits occur when the sense requires further wording. This concordance helps to locate specific passages and also invites subtler research uses, such as study of the recurrence of words in each play: thus the continuity of *Henry VIII* from *Richard III* appears in their shared distinctive use of certain religious terms. Similarly, accumulated references show the divergence or consistency of meaning or associations for particular terms (Shakespeare's references to dogs are unfavorable). In using this text, one must remember that variant spellings or forms of speech may conceal recurrences of words with the same root or meaning (guilt, gilt, guilts, guilty, guiltily, guiltless), while similar spellings of the same word may have contrasting senses (your grace [the Duke] of York, the grace of God, external grace). The contexts provided ensure awareness of most complications, but rarely provide the complete syntactical setting required for exact interpretation of a word. The magnitude of the effort involved in this concordance indicates the research gain from electronic procedures, which also permit many permutations of its data, as seen in the eight volumes of Spevack's *A Complete and Systematic Concordance to the Works of Shakespeare* (1968-70).

24. Styan, J. L. *Shakespeare's Stagecraft.* Cambridge: Cambridge Univ. Press, 1967. Repr., with corrections, 1971.

Styan's book explores how Shakespeare's plays would have worked, theatrically, on the Elizabethan stage. Beginning with a discussion of the kind of stage for which Shakespeare wrote and of the conventions of performance that obtained on that stage, Styan then devotes the bulk of his attention to Shakespeare's handling of the visual and aural dimensions of performance. He argues that the scripts guide actors in communicating aurally, visually, and kinetically with an audience. Topics considered include gesture, entrances and exits, the use of downstage and upstage playing areas, eavesdropping encounters, the visual orchestration of scenes involving one or several or many characters, the manipulation of rhythm and tempo, and variations among stage voices. The final chapter, "Total Theater," discusses the inseparability of all the elements of Shakespeare's stagecraft in the shaping of a theatrical event aimed at provoking and engaging the audience's fullest response. The book makes a strong case for studying Shakespeare's plays as flexible blueprints for performance that skillfully utilize and transform the stagecraft conventions of the Elizabethan theater.

25. Wells, Stanley, ed. *The Cambridge Companion to Shakespeare Studies.* Cambridge: Cambridge Univ. Press, 1986. Repr., 1991.

Wells has assembled 19 other scholars to write on different aspects of Shakespeare studies; most of the essays include endnotes and a reading list. S. Schoenbaum writes about Shakespeare's life (chap. 1), W. R. Elton places him in the context of the thought of his age (chap. 2), Peter Thomson discusses contemporaneous playhouses and actors (chap. 5), and Alan C. Dessen places Shakespeare in the context of his age's theater conventions (chap. 6). Essays more on Shakespeare's writing are Robert Ellrodt's on the nondramatic poetry (chap. 3), Inga-Stina Ewbank's on his use of the arts of language (chap. 4), and the pairing of David Daniell's on the traditions of comedy (chap. 7) and G. K. Hunter's on the traditions of tragedy (chap. 8). R. L. Smallwood focuses on the ten plays about English history (chap. 9). MacD. P. Jackson discusses canonical and textual questions (chap. 10). The last chapters cover stage history and the history of literary criticism. Russell Jackson reviews stage history from 1660 to 1900 (chap. 11), Roger Warren carries this review into the twentieth century (chap. 14), and Robert Hapgood extends the coverage to film and television (chap. 15). Harry Levin surveys the dominant critical approaches from 1660 to 1904 (chap. 12), and in chap. 13 three scholars discuss twentieth-century trends in the study of the comedies (Lawrence Danson), tragedies (Kenneth Muir), and histories (Edward Berry). Terence Hawkes defines some of the newer critical approaches (chap. 16), and Dieter Mehl concludes the volume with a discursive list of important Shakespearean reference books (chap. 17). This book replaces the earlier *A New Companion to Shakespeare Studies* edited by S. Schoenbaum and K. Muir in 1971.

Note on Bibliographies

In addition to the above works, readers should be aware of the various bibliographies of Shakespeare studies. Among the most valuable are Stanley Wells, *Shakespeare: A Bibliographical Guide*, Oxford: Clarendon Press, 1990; David M. Bergeron and Geraldo U. De Sousa, *Shakespeare: A Study and Research Guide*, 3rd edition, Lawrence: Univ. Press of Kansas, 1995; Larry S. Champion, *The Essential Shakespeare: An Annotated Bibliography of Major Modern Studies*, 2nd edition, New York: Hall, 1993. Thorough bibliographies for each of a gradually increasing number of plays have been appearing since 1980 in the Garland Shakespeare Bibliographies, general editor William L. Godshalk. An important specialized bibliography is John W. Velz, *Shakespeare and the Classical Tradition: A Critical Guide to Commentary, 1660-1960*, Minneapolis: Univ. of Minnesota Press, 1968. In the special area of Shakespearean pedagogy, a useful (although brief) bibliography appears in Peggy O'Brien, "'And Gladly Teach': Books, Articles, and a Bibliography on the Teaching of Shakespeare," *Shakespeare Quarterly* 46 (1995): 165-72. For information on new materials on the study of Shakespeare, readers should consult the annual bibliographies published by *Shakespeare Quarterly*, *PMLA* (*The MLA International Bibliography*), the Modern Humanities Research Association (*Annual Bibliography of English Language and Literature*), and the English Association (*The Year's Work in English Studies*). Ph.D. theses on Shakespeare are listed in *Dissertation Abstracts International*.

II. THE PLAYS OF THE SECOND TETRALOGY AS A GROUP

A. Influences; Sources; Historical and Intellectual Backgrounds; Topicality.

26. Belsey, Catherine, "Making Histories Then and Now: Shakespeare From *Richard II* to *Henry V*." In *Uses of History: Marxism, Postmodernism, and the Renaissance*, ed. Francis Parker, Peter Hulme, and Margaret Iverson, 24–46. Manchester: Manchester Univ. Press; New York: St. Martin's Press, 1991. Repr., in part, in Holderness (no. 85).

Belsey reads the second tetralogy from a postmodern perspective "as history," repudiating the "nostalgic," "right wing" perspectives of historicist scholars such as Tillyard (no. 35). At the heart of Belsey's essay is a skepticism about "grand narratives" of history written to preserve order (32); thus she sees the second tetralogy as a story of change, reflective of the instability of meaning, that begins in nostalgia (*Richard II*) and ends in indeterminacy (*Henry V*). She argues that Richard II forges a gap between names and things (e.g., kingship and its referent, majesty), thus creating an ideological world in which Bolingbroke can succeed, but also a world of uncertainties and conflicts of meaning which are also conflicts of power and identity. For Belsey, these conflicts spill over into *Henry V*, particularly in Henry's discussion with Williams on the eve of Agincourt (4.1), where the people (embodied in Williams) confront the crown; here, as elsewhere in the plays, Shakespeare rejects linguistic transparency in favor of political struggle.

27. Campbell, Lily B. *Shakespeare's "Histories": Mirrors of Elizabethan Policy*. San Marino: The Huntington Library, 1947. Repr. London: Methuen, 1964. Repr., in part, in Waith (no. 86) and in Berman (no. 259).

Campbell discusses the second tetralogy (as well as *Richard III* and the anonymous *Troublesome Reign of King John*) against the backdrop of Elizabethan notions of history, historiography, and politics, seeing the plays as "mirrors" of contemporary political concerns. In her examination of *Richard II* (168–212), she takes up the question of the deposition of a monarch, discusses behavioral parallels between Richard and Queen Elizabeth, and contends that Shakespeare probably did not write the play with anything like support for the Essex rebellion in mind; indeed, the drama treats the issue of rebellion so fairly that it might just as well have served as a warning against it. Campbell treats the *Henry IV* plays together (213–54) as an illustration of the folly of rebellion; the revolt of the Percies mirrors the Northern Rebellion in 1569, and Hal, in his eagerness to be king and attraction to bad habits and dubious company, mirrors the later behavior of James I. She sees Falstaff's behavior as a commentary on contemporary abuses in the military profession as well as the sad plight of the Elizabethan soldier. In discussing *Henry V* (255–305), Campbell affirms the epic qualities of the play and the heroism of Henry, and relates these to such contemporary issues as the morality of war and the various theories regarding its art and practice; she finds topical allusions in the involvement of the clergy in Henry's war in France (Elizabeth relied upon church funds in her preparations for war), and in Henry's conversation with his soldiers (4.1), which mirrors issues involved in the surrender of the town of Deventer to the Spanish in 1587. Campbell's arguments are marbled throughout with detailed allusion to Elizabethan political, historical, and moral writings.

28. Cox, John D. "The Elizabethan Hal." In *Shakespeare and the Dramaturgy of Power*, 104–27. Princeton: Princeton Univ. Press, 1989.

Cox examines Shakespeare's plays both in the context of medieval drama and from the perspective of New Historicism, and devotes full attention to the comedies, tragedies, and romances as well as to the histories. In his chapter on Hal, Cox argues that church/state relations as depicted in the second tetralogy are substantially Elizabethan rather than pre-Reformation in practice, particularly as regards the matter of secular control of church property (*Henry V* [1.1]); Hal/Henry V, too, possesses a thoroughly Elizabethan sense of self—opaque and theatrical in its grasp for power—that reminds us of his father and of Queen Elizabeth. Cox sees Hal/Henry V as disingenuous and opaque even in his soliloquies throughout the *Henry* plays, and connects him in this regard with Essex, and even Elizabeth, as similar purveyors of self-interested humility and vulnerability. For Cox, such theatrical opacity raises serious questions about the nature of the self; and he goes on to explore how Hal's creation of his own morality-play reformation (including his supposed vulnerability to the temptations of Falstaff) parallels Essex's use of the *ars moriendi* tradition at his own execution and Elizabeth's use of political myths of vulnerability to serve her own political ends. Cox concludes by examining the influence of the actor Richard Tarlton on the formation of the character of Falstaff, and the influence of the Renaissance epic and romantic comedy on the formation of *Henry V*.

29. Greenblatt, Stephen. "Invisible Bullets." In *Shakespearean Negotiations: The Circulation of Social Energy in Renaissance England*, 21–65. Berkeley: Univ. of California Press, 1988. Repr. in Bloom (no. 204).

Greenblatt's New Historicist study approaches literary art as the product of various social, cultural, and materialist phenomena (i.e., "negotiations") that shape its character and significance. He argues in "Invisible Bullets" that an understanding of the relationship between orthodoxy and subversion in Thomas Harriot's *A Brief and True Report of the New Found Land of Virginia* (1588) can provide "an interpretive model" useful in considering Shakespeare's history plays (23). Greenblatt sees Harriot's text as endorsing the use of coercive religious belief to control a colonized populace (a principle that can ironically subvert Christianity by affirming it), and further probes how authoritarian social structures seek to contain those subversive elements that are paradoxically embedded within them. He argues that the ideal image of Hal projected in the second tetralogy "involves as its positive condition the constant production of its own radical subversion and the powerful containment of that subversion" (41), and traces this idea in numerous episodes throughout the *Henry* plays, viewing Hal/Henry V as an agent of "falsification" whose behavior undermines the very values he seeks to uphold (42). Greenblatt's skeptical and detailed reading of the Prince, power, and society—which posits a world where "moral authority rests upon a hypocrisy so deep that the hypocrites themselves believe it" (55)—is one of the signature pieces of the New Historicism.

30. Holderness, Graham. *Shakespeare's History.* Dublin: Gill and Macmillan; New York: St. Martin's Press, 1985. Repr., in part, in Holderness (no. 85).

Holderness's study of the second tetralogy is divided into two parts: part one (1–144) attempts to describe the "*production* of Shakespeare's historiography, its origins, its qualities, and its ideological capacities," and part two (147–226) examines the plays' "*reproduction* in different phases of British society's historical development" (4)—i.e., the cultural afterlife of the plays. In part one Holderness attacks Tillyard (no. 35) for seeing Shakespeare in light of a single Elizabethan ideology, and argues instead that the histories are historiographical attempts to reconstruct the full complexity of medieval feudal society. He sees *Richard II* as depicting the conflict between the crown and feudal barons and also between royal sovereignty and an ancient code of chivalry. In *1* and *2 Henry IV* he regards Falstaff's tavern world as analogous to a medieval carnival, particularly as it embodies a counterideology that contains utopian fantasies of freedom, equality, and abundance; these oppositional energies, however, get suppressed in *Henry V* and are replaced by a nationalized and militarized feudal ideology. Part two takes the British school system to task for misappropriating Shakespeare in its attempt to create a unified national culture—an "ideological hegemony" (150) clearly apparent in Laurence Olivier's 1944 film of *Henry V* as well as in the cultural and literary influence of Matthew Arnold. Holderness dismisses the 1951 "Festival of Britain" production of the histories as ideologically conservative, but praises Jane Howell's BBC-TV versions of the plays of the first tetralogy as demonstrating the truth that Shakespeare's histories are analogous to Brechtian dramas of alienation. The book is frankly polemical, strongly indebted both to Marxist and poststructuralist thought. Over three-quarters of the study is reprinted in Holderness's *Shakespeare Recycled: The Making of Historical Drama* (Hempstead: Harvester Wheatsheaf; New York: Barnes & Noble, 1992), with the addition of a feminist reading of *Richard II* (73–88) and a discussion of Kenneth Branagh's film of *Henry V* (190–210).

31. Kelly, Henry Ansgar. *Divine Providence in the England of Shakespeare's Histories.* Cambridge, Mass.: Harvard Univ. Press, 1970.

In examining the various "myths" of history as they appear in the chronicles of Polydore Vergil, Hall, and Holinshed, as well as in the poetry of the period, especially Daniel's *Civil Wars*, Kelly argues for a "Lancaster" myth and a "York" myth, as well as the "Tudor" myth propounded by Tillyard (no. 35). Kelly both draws upon and qualifies the notion of the providential view of history expressed by Tillyard, finding the so-called Tudor myth "an ex post facto Platonic form" (298) not rigidly endorsed by Shakespeare's histories, since each play "creates its own moral ethos and mythos" (306). Kelly treats the second tetralogy as a sequence (203-45), and finds no evidence in the plays of providential punishment; *Richard II* reflects both the Lancastrian and Yorkist perspectives on history, and neither view has God's approval, since events result from human action rather than divine intervention. Kelly reads *1* and *2 Henry IV* as similarly lacking in criticism for the deposition of Richard II, and affirms that in neither play does Shakespeare depict the Lancastrians as punished by God. Kelly sees *Henry V* as a play representing a just king with genuine piety rightfully claiming France; the victory at Agincourt is the work of God, but the ensuing turmoil of Henry VI's reign is "a new situation with causes of its own" (245), not the result of divine retribution.

32. Reese, M. M. *The Cease of Majesty: A Study of Shakespeare's History Plays.* London: Edward Arnold, 1961. Repr., in part, in Waith (no. 86) and in Berman (no. 259).

This study examines the histories (excluding *Henry VIII*) against the backdrop of Tudor historical, political, and social thought—the homilies, *The Mirror for Magistrates, Gorboduc,* Tudor historians, etc.—and particularly the providential notion of history as a movement from discord to harmony as presented by Hall. Reese includes three essays on the second tetralogy: "*Richard II*" (225-60); "*Henry IV*" (286-317); and "*Henry V*" (317-32). He sees Richard II as morally and temperamentally unsuited for kingship, a man whose failures permeate the whole society; Bolingbroke, too, is a man of moral deficiencies, whose actions are "the diseased product of a diseased condition" (230). For Reese, the *Henry IV* plays depict neither the rebels nor the adherents of the king in a favorable light; only Hal is capable of redeeming this "total loss of majesty" (292), and he does so by rejecting three temptations and the figures who embody them: riot and misrule (Falstaff), false chivalry (Hotspur), and political expediency (Henry IV). Reese views *Henry V* without irony as a dramatic epic celebrating the mirror of all Christian kings: the choruses help set the epic tone; the war in France is just; the evocation of Falstaff (2.3) merely underscores Henry's greater virtue; and the meeting with the soldiers on the eve of Agincourt (4.1) shows Henry to be a fitting monarch. He sees Shakespeare bringing the tetralogy to a close "with a heartening picture of a society cured of its sickness and united under a prince whose own redemptive experience corresponded with that of his people" (332). Reese's detailed argument touches upon virtually every major episode in the plays, and remains one of the standard orthodox readings of the second tetralogy.

33. Ribner, Irving. "Shakespeare's Second Tetralogy." In *The English History*

Play in the Age of Shakespeare, 151-93. Princeton: Princeton Univ. Press, 1957. Revised edition, New York: Barnes & Noble; London: Methuen, 1965.

This study treats all ten of Shakespeare's English histories, either in detail or in passing, in the context of the development of the English chronicle play as a genre. Ribner sees *Richard II* as following the pattern of the morality play, but not simplistically endorsing Tudor notions against rebellion, since Richard is depicted as a lawful yet ineffective ruler and Bolingbroke as the opposite; the play thus skeptically examines the doctrine of divine right. For Ribner, the *Henry IV* plays depict Shakespeare's endorsement of Henry IV's reign despite its illegality, since the king promotes "the good of England" (166); they also stress the education of a king (Hal), who moves impressively from soldier to statesman, rejecting the attractions of vice (Falstaff) in favor of the needful austerities of law (the Lord Chief Justice). Ribner takes the heroic qualities of *Henry V* and its protagonist very seriously; the king is a sort of "Christian Tamburlaine" (185), virtuous in action and in morality, who emerges as the ideal king: "a typical Renaissance mirror for princes" (192). Citations are to the revised edition.

34. Tennenhouse, Leonard. "Strategies of State and Political Plays: *A Midsummer Night's Dream, Henry IV, Henry V, Henry VIII.*" In *Political Shakespeare: New Essays in Cultural Materialism,* ed. Jonathan Dollimore and Alan Sinfield, 109-28. Ithaca: Cornell Univ. Press, 1985. Repr., in part, in Holderness (no. 85).

Tennenhouse seeks a political explanation for why history plays except for *Henry VIII,* romantic comedy, and Petrarchan poetry dramatically decreased in popularity after 1599, and locates it in differing attitudes on the parts of Elizabethans and Jacobeans regarding carnivalesque displays of state power (the practice was looked upon with far more suspicion in James's reign than in Elizabeth's). He claims that since history plays like *Henry IV* and *Henry V* show the politically effective monarch (in the manner of Elizabeth) containing figures of misrule, they are far more analogous to the practices of Elizabeth's court than that of James; in Shakespeare's *Henry* plays "the figures of carnival ultimately authorise the State as the State appears to take on the vigour of festival" (123), since by containing misrule Hal/Henry V also invests the state with an ideal identity. For Tennenhouse, *Henry VIII* is decidedly more "Jacobean" in its politics than Shakespeare's *Henry IV* plays and *Henry V,* because it flattens out misrule by subjugating it to genealogical "continuity" rather than allowing it to be contained by a new and effective monarch (125). Tennenhouse's essay is absorbed into his book *Power on Display: The Politics of Shakespeare's Genres* (New York: Methuen, 1986), where he also discusses *Richard II* (76-81); here he sees Bolingbroke as the carnivalesque figure who can successfully "incorporate disruptive cultural elements within the official rituals of state" (81).

35. Tillyard, E. M. W. "The Second Tetralogy." In *Shakespeare's History Plays,* 234-314. London: Chatto and Windus, 1944. The book is repr. often and, in part, in Waith (no. 86). The essay is repr., in part, in Brooke (no. 141), in

Cubeta (no. 143), in Newlin (no. 144), in Bevington (no. 202), in Hunter (no. 205), and in Berman (no. 259).

This study treats all of Shakespeare's English histories (excluding *Henry VIII* but including *Macbeth*) in the context of their cosmic, historical, and literary backgrounds. In his discussion of the second tetralogy, Tillyard emphasizes the informing concept of the "Tudor Myth," a belief in a cosmic and providential pattern of history that culminates gloriously in the accession of the House of Tudor; he also stresses the plays' epic qualities, the importance of Respublica (i.e., England) as their central focus, and their political orthodoxy. Tillyard regards *Richard II* as highly ceremonial and symbolic, the embodiment of a declining medievalism that contrasts with the more modern political world of the *Henry IV* plays. He sees *1* and *2 Henry IV* as a single play built on the pattern of the moralities, extolling the virtues of Prince Hal as a man "of large powers, Olympian loftiness, and high sophistication" (269) who represents Shakespeare's idea of the perfect ruler. In this context Hotspur emerges as a figure deserving of ridicule, Henry IV as a father who fails to understand his son's complexity, and Falstaff as the traditional Vice (and fool) who embodies the archetypal principle of disorder. Tillyard maintains that for *Henry V* Shakespeare needed to depict a great hero/king in order to bring his epic of England to a close, but that this need ran counter to the competing need to present Henry as the hearty good-mixer of legend; the result was a new Henry, combining both elements, but inconsistent with the Hal of the *Henry IV* plays. For Tillyard, *Henry V* stands oddly apart from the *Henry IV* plays, and its inferior quality reflects Shakespeare's loss of interest in his dramatic epic. Tillyard's critical argument throughout is highly allusive, and refers frequently to the backgrounds of the plays. The book is a seminal study of the histories, often serving as the starting place for later critical reevaluations.

See also nos. 49, 52, 53, 54, 56, 58, 64, 65, 67, 68, 69, 70, 71, 73, 83.

B. Language and Linguistics.

36. Barton, Anne. "Shakespeare and the Limits of Language." *Shakespeare Survey* 24 (1971): 19–30.

Barton is interested in those moments when Shakespeare (in opposition to his age's faith in the efficacy of words) expresses something akin to a modern distrust for language; and she explores this idea in plays as diverse as *Love's Labor's Lost*, *King Lear*, *Coriolanus*, *Pericles*, *The Tempest*, and Marlowe's *Tamburlaine*. She contends that both Richard II in the deposition scene (4.1) and Falstaff in the related "deposition" scene in the tavern in *1 Henry IV* (2.4) fail in their attempts to alter harsh realities into more attractive ones through imaginative language; the same conflict of imagination against fact, words against political reality, is evoked in Henry V's meeting with Pistol in *Henry V* on the eve of Agincourt (4.1.35–63). In each case, claims Barton, we are drawn toward the imaginative, but hard realities always win out (21–23).

37. Calderwood, James L. *Metadrama in Shakespeare's Henriad: "Richard II" to "Henry V."* Berkeley: Univ. of California Press, 1979. Repr., in part, in Holderness (no. 85), in Bloom (no. 140), and in Bloom (no. 260).

Calderwood's metadramatic approach to the second tetralogy focuses upon the nature of dramatic form, the role of the dramatist, theatrical mimesis, and the self-reflexive aspects of these plays. He examines throughout Shakespeare's engagement with the materials of his own art. The book consists of eight related chapters (and an appendix) on the second tetralogy, suggesting that its main metadramatic interest is in the "fall of speech" (5) and its gradual recovery. Calderwood maintains that in *Richard II* the king's royal semantics metaphorically reflect Shakespeare's own artistic investment in a language of ontological rightness that is literally "debased" by Bolingbroke's secularization of language, a condition in which linguistic relationships are ephemeral and unstable. According to Calderwood, Hal, too, becomes associated with Shakespeare, since both are interior dramatists trying to restore value and meaning to kingship and the language that expresses it; and this redemption of the word (on the part of both Hal/Henry V and Shakespeare) proceeds through the *Henry IV* plays and into *Henry V*, where language recovers a new pragmatic value. Lying behind Calderwood's argument is a perspective that emphasizes Shakespeare's dilemma as a poet writing plays at a time when language was undergoing revolutionary changes.

38. Hapgood, Robert. "Shakespeare's Thematic Modes of Speech: *Richard II* to *Henry V*." *Shakespeare Survey* 20 (1967): 41–49.

This essay examines the characteristic "modes" of speech used by characters in the second tetralogy: in *Richard II* it is denunciation, in *1 Henry IV* retrospection, in *2 Henry IV* false report (often indirect and corrupt), and in *Henry V* dispute. For Hapgood these modes, and their respective "anti-modes" (acquiescence, anticipation, forthrightness, and conciliation) combine to form a coherent sequence of speech throughout the plays, moving from disorder, to chaos, and finally to a restoration of order.

39. Lanham, Richard A. "The Dramatic Present: Shakespeare's *Henriad*." In *The Motives of Eloquence: Literary Rhetoric in the Renaissance*, 190–209. New Haven: Yale Univ. Press, 1976.

Lanham's book treats the relationship between rhetoric and the formation of the self in a wide variety of literary texts from Plato through Shakespeare. His essay on the second tetralogy approaches the plays through *Henry V*. For Lanham, the choruses suggest a history of "the rhetorical view of life" (191) in which style plays an important role in augmenting history. Lanham finds in *Henry V* wide-ranging elements "from certifiable fact to pure romance" that contribute to a "complex structure of styles and attitudes toward style" (199), and claims that in order to understand the *Henriad* properly we must approach the plays with no preconceived notions of "fact" or "style." He briefly examines the stylistic and thematic features of *Richard II* and the *Henry IV* plays, seeing these and *Henry V* as vitally concerned with the combination of role-playing, rhetoric, and the self-conscious fashioning of the self. In this context, *Richard II* becomes a play about the political uses of rhetoric and ceremony, which Bolingbroke manages more effectively than Richard; the *Henry IV* plays concern themselves with "how to hold and ensel a myth" (204), with particular attention to the personality of Hal, who learns how to play a royal role without being absorbed by it.

40. **Macdonald, Ronald R.** "Uneasy Lies: Language and History in Shakespeare's Lancastrian Tetralogy." *Shakespeare Quarterly* 35 (1984): 22–39. Repr. in Bevington (no. 202).

Macdonald is concerned with the linguistic conventions that sustain monarchy and "attempt to manage certain fundamental contradictions" that threaten its disruption (23). His argument proceeds as follows: in *Richard II* the language of anointed kingship is an idiom helpless to control the political world it describes, but Richard attains a certain self-conscious mastery over this bankrupt idiom when he at last seems to glimpse his own real weakness; in *1 Henry IV* the same sort of linguistic contradiction appears in the play's large number of contravened oaths and empty boasts, while in *2 Henry IV* (also a play in which words are at odds with a reality speakers are powerless to control) political success comes by "learning the languages of others and inventing a language of your own" (34) in a world where language shifts and meanings alter. Underlying Macdonald's whole argument is the idea that in order for words to have any real force their supposedly transcendant power must be denied; but this denial, after the deposition of Richard II, ensures that anointed kingship will always be an "uneasy lie" (39).

41. **Porter, Joseph A.** *The Drama of Speech Acts: Shakespeare's Lancastrian Tetralogy.* Berkeley: Univ. of California Press, 1979.

Porter draws upon the speech-act theory of J. L. Austin (specifically the idea that language has a performative and dramatic quality) in arguing that one of the chief unifying elements of the second tetralogy is its continuing emphasis on language and verbal action. He includes a full chapter on each play, a chapter on methodology, and a chapter detailing his conclusions. Porter sees *Richard II* as the clash of two opposed linguistic perspectives: a univocal, absolutist notion of language (Richard), and a more relativistic notion of practical tongues and silences (Bolingbroke); this conflict is apparent, for example, in the action of naming, which for Richard is sacred and absolute, but for Bolingbroke is secular and dependent upon honor earned in a social context. For Porter, the *Henry IV* plays depict a polyglot linguistic world, where no single dialect or mode of expression dominates; hence these plays record a shift from an essentially undramatic and "univocal" linguistic environment to a dramatic one where contradictory voices proliferate (what Porter calls the "Babel theme"). In this context, the rise of Hal/Henry V is of crucial importance, for, as a sort of linguistic polyglot himself, he has the capacity to unify the linguistic chaos that characterizes his father's reign; in *Henry V*, under his linguistic aegis, language becomes an example of a manageable order, conveying not merely action but also meaningful interaction. Throughout the book, Porter links speech acts to other matters such as the plays' progress from a medieval to a modern world and the metaphor of the Fall. His discussion is detailed and evidential, and gives full attention to virtually every important episode in the plays.

42. Vickers, Brian. "The World of Falstaff." In *The Artistry of Shakespeare's Prose*, 89–170. London: Methuen, 1968.

Vickers treats *1* and *2 Henry IV*, *Henry V*, and *The Merry Wives of Windsor* as a group of plays united by the presence of Falstaff and "a unique continuity of character and mood" (91). He notes in *1 Henry IV* the association of Falstaff's prose with a sense of equivocation and "doubleness" (94)—a mode of speech and of living from which Hal distances himself by his own prose mockeries of it, and which Hal uses at times only to "explore the great lower classes" (103); in *2 Henry IV* Falstaff's relative isolation from the Prince both removes his "moral censor" (119) and signals his general decline in our sympathies. Vickers sees Falstaff triumphing rhetorically only once in *2 Henry IV*, in his first confrontation with the Lord Chief Justice (1.2), while after this episode his prose devolves into an "incomparably specious manipulation of logic and rhetoric in the service of appetite" (140) that Hal is right to reject. The discussion of *Henry V* locates a "wonderfully mixed feeling" (159) in the Hostess's description of Falstaff's death (2.3) that produces a touching epitaph for the fat knight. Throughout his study of *Henry V*, Vickers concentrates on the individualizing patterns of virtually every prose speaker in the play, in particular Henry's on the eve of Agincourt (4.1) and in the wooing scene (5.2), where the king's rhetorical brilliance reflects excellence in the private as well as in the public sphere. Vickers's thorough, evidential, and meticulously argued essay is a seminal treatment of Shakespeare's prose style in the *Henry* plays.

See also nos. 62, 66, 68, 69, 74, 75, 76.

C. Criticism.

43. Bamber, Linda. "*1 Henry VI* to *Henry V*: Toward Tragedy." In *Comic Women, Tragic Men: A Study of Gender and Genre in Shakespeare*, 135-67. Stanford: Stanford Univ. Press, 1982. Repr., in part, in Holderness (no. 85).

Bamber's approach is to resist the practice of feminist critics who try to assimilate Shakespeare "into the system of feminist ideas"; rather she seeks to locate "feminism in the critic—not in the author or even the work" (2). As regards the histories, she sees women in the early plays (e.g., Joan of Arc) as defined in terms of their "masculine-historical struggle for power," while women in the later histories (e.g., Queen Isabel) embody an idea of the feminine that is fully differentiated from such masculinity—"private, slow, full of sorrow" (135). Bamber sees Isabel in the garden scene of *Richard II* (3.4) creating "a sense of a female principle apart from history," and in so doing Isabel anticipates the "feminine Otherness" of females in the tragedies that invests these figures with a female identity apart from that of men (140-41). She maintains that female characters in the histories after Isabel, like Lady Percy and Katherine of France, "neither participate in history nor challenge it" (142); indeed, it is only Falstaff who provides the greatest challenge to the hero's place in history. Bamber examines the wooing scene in *Henry V* (5.2) in some detail, finding Kate to be a negligible presence and Henry the perpetrator of "a piece of good-natured guerrilla theater before an audience of one" (145). She also finds in the histories a developing separation between fathers and sons that parallels the separation between the male self and the female other, and traces this idea from the *Henry VI* plays through the relationship of Hal and his father in the *Henry IV* plays. Bamber sees in these two patterns of separation a "movement toward tragedy" (153). The essay is a seminal reading of the significance of women in the histories.

44. Blanpied, John W. *Time and the Artist in Shakespeare's English Histories.* Newark: Univ. of Delaware Press; London: Associated Univ. Presses, 1983. Repr., in part, in Bloom (no. 204).

Blanpied approaches Shakespeare's English histories (excluding *Henry VIII*) as a nine-part sequence concerned with the evolving relationship of subject to medium and history to drama. He contends that Shakespeare approaches historical drama as a conscious artist concerned with the *idea* of history as a category of experience. The interest here in Shakespeare as "actor" in his own histories also embraces the kingly character and other figures of power as being either "antic" or "Machiavel." In a discussion that includes separate chapters on each of the plays of the second tetralogy (chaps. 8-11 [120-245]), Blanpied attempts to show how Shakespeare identifies with Richard II by parodying his own artistic pretensions in the character of the king, since both struggle with issues of imaginative freedom and control. He contends that in *1 Henry IV* a sort of muted tragedy emerges (elicited by Falstaff's comic energies) that underscores "the inability of Henry and Hal to attend truly to the vacancy between them" because of their mutual commitment to the future (178); similar issues appear in *2 Henry IV*, a play that "can be said to dramatize the ghosts" of its predecessor (187). According to Blanpied, in *Henry V* the audience must engage in a rigorous improvisational relationship with the action that unites it with the play; in this sense *Henry V* is a truly "ceremonial" drama "because it boldly commits itself to our capacities to understand and be changed by it" (245). The book is densely (sometimes floridly) argued, often providing lengthy discussions of selected passages.

45. Burckhardt, Sigurd. "'Swoll'n With Some Other Grief': Shakespeare's Prince Hal Trilogy." In *Shakespearean Meanings*, 144-205. Princeton: Princeton Univ. Press, 1968. Repr., in part, in Bevington (no. 202).

This book (published posthumously) consists of nine separate essays and an appendix. In his chapter on the *Henry* plays Burckhardt addresses the problem of disorder, citing Prince John's treachery at Gaultree Forest in *2 Henry IV* (4.2) and Hal's relative absence from that play as typical of the disappointed expectations it repeatedly presents, especially in wake of the more reassuring *1 Henry IV*. On the matter of royal succession, Burckhardt sees Richard's deposition as the destruction of a world view based upon natural (inherent) law in favor of one based upon positive (manmade) law; the result is a debunking of the providential view of history found in the first tetralogy and in Hall. In Burckhardt's view, Shakespeare was confronted with two incompatible models of succession, primogeniture and combat; and his grappling with these competing models forced him into an ethical and artistic compromise in *Henry V*, where Henry and Shakespeare settle for neither model entirely, but discover "what lesser means of ordering are possible" (199). Throughout, Burckhardt emphasizes Shakespeare's movement from a concept of order centered in God to one founded in human experience; in this context Henry's wooing of Katherine (*Henry V*, 5.2) becomes the transposition of the combat model "into terms where success means succession, where victory generates a *line*" (202).

46. Carr, Virginia M. [Virginia Vaughan]. "Once More Into the Henriad: A 'Two-Eyed' View." *Journal of English and Germanic Philology* 77 (1978): 530–45.

The argument here is that the second tetralogy presents an ongoing dialectic between two opposed notions of kingship: a medieval ("ceremonial") view and a modern ("Machiavellian") one. The author maintains that in *Richard II* the ceremonial model loses its validity since in the person of Richard it becomes divorced from substance, while in the *Henry IV* plays the loss of ceremonial meaning is apparent in the moral chaos and confusion that characterize Bolingbroke's reign. She concludes that Henry V, the only king able to embrace both sets of values, eschews a one-sided view of reality for a more viable (if more unsettling) "two-eyed" view that uneasily integrates ceremony with political effectiveness, and thus forces him (and us) to accept ambivalence as a fact of political life.

47. Champion, Larry S. *Perspective in Shakespeare's English Histories.* Athens, Ga.: Univ. of Georgia Press, 1980.

Champion discusses all ten of Shakespeare's English histories in pursuing the notion that these plays offer a structural variety and "complexity of perspective" (5) that create an essentially ambivalent view of history. He treats *Richard II* together with *Richard III* (54–91) as plays that focus upon a single tragic figure; the former elicits conflicting and shifting responses from the audience regarding its protagonist, and compounds this sense of ambivalence by portraying Bolingbroke, whom we neither fully admire nor despise, as a chameleon-like foil to Richard. Champion discusses the *Henry IV* plays and *Henry V* along with *King John* (92–165) as examples of the dramatist's mature art; in *1 Henry IV* the absence of a dominant character and the broadening of structural and social perspective intensify the ambivalence that we feel about characters like Henry IV, Hal, Falstaff, and Hotspur, while in *2 Henry IV*, which is even more diffuse in perspective than its predecessor, we observe "a panoramic scene depicting the fortunes of a wide variety of individuals caught in the political uncertainties and the economic and social instabilities which characterize Henry IV's reign" (129).

As regards *Henry V*, Champion cites the use of multiple plot lines, diverse settings, the presence of the Chorus, etc., as further broadenings of dramatic perspective; Henry, too, is a part of this growing complexity, since we view him from a variety of contradictory perspectives throughout the play. Champion sees *Henry V* as the play in which Shakespeare's sense of "historical perspective" (164) reaches a new level of sophistication, for here ambivalence is so subtly expressed that the audience must actively decide whether the play is "the most complex or among the most simplistic of the histories" (165).

48. Champion, Larry S. *"The Noise of Threatening Drum": Dramatic Strategy and Political Ideology in Shakespeare and the English Chronicle Plays.* Newark: Univ. of Delaware Press; London: Associated Univ. Presses, 1990.

Champion's assumption is that Elizabethan history plays (Shakespearean and non-Shakespearean) encourage a multiplicity of ideological responses from their socially and politically heterogeneous audience. He argues that when regarded from one perspective these plays seem to uphold establishment notions of absolutism, but when regarded from another they seem to undermine this view, severely questioning existing power structures. The book consists of nine chapters, the first seven treating various Elizabethan histories (*The Famous Victories of Henry V*; *Edward III*; *Sir John Oldcastle*; *Thomas, Lord Cromwell*; *Edmund Ironside*; and Shakespeare's *Henry VI* plays and *King John*) and the last two devoted to the second tetralogy. In chap. 8, "*Richard II*" (99–109), Champion argues that the play debunks the concept of divine right through Richard's pragmatic mockery of it as king—especially in his behavior during the duel between Bolingbroke and Mowbray (1.1)—and further that it allows the audience no clear identification with a single political tenet such as providentialism. Chapter 9, "The *Henriad*" (110–28), elaborates on the question of divided audience response, emphasizing how the last three plays of the tetralogy expose official Tudor ideology as a cynical instrument of power. For Champion, Bolingbroke and, particularly, Hal/Henry V are superb role-players—Machiavellian, calculating, and adroitly exploitive. The discussion throughout alludes to literary and historical sources, particularly Holinshed.

49. Dean, Leonard F. "From *Richard II* to *Henry V*: A Closer View." In *Shakespeare: Modern Essays in Criticism*, revised edition, ed. Leonard F. Dean, 188–205. New York: Oxford Univ. Press, 1967. Repr., in part, in Cubeta (no. 143).

In maintaining that the second tetralogy does not simplistically endorse Tudor ideology, Dean argues for a movement in these plays toward an ironic view of history. He argues that in *Richard II* this irony appears in the juxtaposition of conflicting ethical values such as weakness and transcendence; only Hal/Henry V is free of the "enveloping ironies" (196) that continue into the *Henry IV* plays and *Henry V*, and which lead in *Henry V* to a "rich heroic composition" (201), at times approaching tragedy, but always enlisting our sympathy for the new king. The essay first appeared in *Studies in Honor of DeWitt T. Starnes*, ed. Thomas P. Harrison and James H. Sledd, 37–52. Austin:

Univ. of Texas Press, 1967, and was added to Dean's revised collection of essays in the same year.

50. **Dorius, R. J.** "A Little More Than a Little." *Shakespeare Quarterly* 11 (1960): 13-26. Repr. in Waith (no. 86); and in Bevington (no. 202).

Dorius begins by differentiating between the kings of Shakespeare's tragedies and those of the English histories; he sees the latter as concerned less with the nature of man than with political realities. Turning to the second tetralogy, Dorius emphasizes the importance of prudence and economy (and their opposites—carelessness, excess, waste, and disease) in defining the nature of kingship, commonwealth, and political man. The largest portion of the essay is devoted to *Richard II*; here Dorius shows how prudence and excess are related to ideas of time, gardening, and sickness—all combining to depict Richard as a failed monarch who leaves the realm "fat and very sick" (22). In his brief treatment of the *Henry IV* plays, Dorius pays special attention to Falstaff as a representative of all the moral and behavioral negatives Prince Hal must overcome if he is to rule effectively.

51. **Edwards, Philip.** "Person and Office in Shakespeare's Plays." *Proceedings of the British Academy* 56 (1970) [pub. 1972]: 93-109.

This essay (first delivered as the British Academy's Shakespeare lecture on 29 April 1970) treats the second tetralogy along with *Julius Caesar*, *Coriolanus*, and *King Lear*. In his discussion of the second tetralogy (99-107), Edwards asserts that Richard II's involvement in his dual identity as king and man is no mere enactment of a role, but rather a sacramental fact of being that he slowly learns for himself. Contrarily, Edwards regards Bolingbroke and, especially, Hal/Henry V as royal actors separate from their public roles, figures in whom person and office have no essential connection.

52. **Fischer, Sandra K.** "'He Means to Pay': Value and Metaphor in the Lancastrian Tetralogy." *Shakespeare Quarterly* 40 (1989): 149-64.

Fischer stresses the importance of "economic contracts and their metaphorical applications in the process of history" (153), particularly as depicted in the metaphor of indebtedness. She traces the use of this idea and related metaphorical language throughout the second tetralogy, from Richard II's failure to grasp the changed political economy of his world to Bolingbroke's and Hal's success in the *Henry IV* plays (and the latter's in *Henry V*) based upon their sophisticated economic attitude toward power and the progress of history. The discussion alludes instructively to the historical background of the plays, most notably Holinshed's use of the "econo-contractual metaphor" (155) as an informing principle for Shakespeare.

53. **Forker, Charles R.** *Fancy's Images: Contexts, Settings, and Perspectives in Shakespeare and His Contemporaries.* Carbondale and Edwardsville: Southern Illinois Univ. Press, 1990.

This book, which ranges widely over Shakespeare's dramatic career and concludes with an essay on incest, narcissism, and identity in Renaissance drama, contains two essays on the history plays: "Shakespeare's Chronicle Plays as Historical-Pastoral" (79-95), and "The Idea of Time in Shakespeare's Second Historical Tetralogy" (126-38). In the first essay, Forker argues that Shakespeare's use of pastoral in the histories points to ironic contrasts between public and private life and between order and chaos: in *Richard II* pastoral suggests the king's escape from responsibility, his love of beauty and artifice, and ironic analogies to Eden; in *1* and *2 Henry IV* it suggests the ancient parallel between court and country; and in *Henry V* it suggests the violation of natural law. In the second essay, Forker identifies two historical perspectives in the plays: 1) a cyclical view, derived from classical antiquity, that history repeats itself; and 2) a teleological view, derived from medieval Christianity, that human history has clear beginnings and ends. He sees these two views as superimposed upon each other, and traces them in key scenes throughout the tetralogy in order to chart the "indeterminancy of response" (129) they give us to characters and events; also, in keeping with this dual perspective, he sees the second tetralogy as encompassing both tragedy and comedy. Forker relates the idea of time to the rhythmic motion of the plays, and instructively examines how Shakespeare's alternation between "immediate" and "remote" measurements of time connects "present urgencies with a more distant awareness of both past and future" (135-36).

54. Frye, Northrop. "The Bolingbroke Plays (*Richard II, Henry IV*)." In *Northrop Frye on Shakespeare*, ed. Robert Sandler, 51-81. New Haven: Yale Univ. Press, 1986.

The essays in this book derive from tapes of Frye's undergraduate lectures on Shakespeare recorded by Robert Sandler; these were then recast into essay form by Frye. In addition to the essay on the histories, there are also essays on *Romeo and Juliet, A Midsummer Night's Dream, Hamlet, King Lear, Antony and Cleopatra, Measure for Measure, The Winter's Tale,* and *The Tempest*. After briefly treating the historical background of the histories, Frye examines the importance of Richard II as the "Lord's anointed" (55) and treats the concept of divine right in *Richard II* and its relation to the clash between *de jure* power (Richard) and *de facto* power (Bolingbroke), which Frye sees as a governing principle of the play. He also emphasizes the question of identity and its connections to a dramatic sense of self, as well as the importance of Cain's murder of Abel (an archetype of civil war) and the Wheel of Fortune as presiding metaphors in *Richard II*. Throughout, Frye concentrates on various thematic strands in the play (e.g., "the theme of the beggar and the king, and the theme of setting the word against the word" [67]) and Shakespeare's integration of these themes into a unified whole. Frye sees Hal as the central figure of the *Henry IV* plays, flanked by Falstaff (a parody father) and Hotspur (a parody brother), and provides evidential discussions of the former as a figure of "self-serving rationality" (75) who is nonetheless genuinely fond of Hal, and of the latter as a figure "always running away from something" (73). The essay concludes with a brief discussion of *2 Henry IV* as a "tough, gritty, cynical play" (81) in which the rejection of Falstaff (5.5) serves to embody the play's values and action.

55. Goddard, Harold C. *The Meaning of Shakespeare*. Chicago: Univ. of Chicago Press, 1951. Repr., in part, in Bloom (no. 203) and in Bloom (no. 204).

Goddard writes separate essays on all 37 of Shakespeare's plays, considering Shakespeare primarily as a poet and thinker rather than as a playwright. He sees *Richard II* (148-60) as the psychological study of a "poetically gifted but mentally dishonest and frightened man" (151) who clings to an outmoded notion of divine right; both Richard's fearful sentimentalism and Bolingbroke's "doctrine of the strong man" (159), however, pale in comparison with the gardener's intimations of democracy (3.4), which Goddard sees as a solution to the political problems of the play. Treating the *Henry IV* plays as a single dramatic unit (161-214), Goddard argues that either Henry, Hal, or Falstaff may be regarded as the central figure; each is a character with two distinct natures, and this sense of the double nature of man is also reflected in the play's alternation between tavern and court. For Goddard, Hal/ Henry V is a figure who, in rejecting the imaginative side of Falstaff, fails to rise above the merely political success of his father. Goddard sees *Henry V* as deeply ironic (215-68), arguing that the choruses, the churchmen, and the comic figures all reinforce the deflationary aspects of the play; the king is savage and sophistic, a guilt-ridden and diminished figure who grows more like his father as the play proceeds. Goddard's notion that Shakespeare was a thinker who could placate conventional minds even as he spoke more skeptically to those who truly could "enter his spirit" (vii) informs the whole discussion, particularly his influential reading of *Henry V*.

56. Goldberg, Jonathan. "Desiring Hal." In *Sodometries: Renaissance Texts, Modern Sexualities*, 145-75. Stanford: Stanford Univ. Press, 1992.

Goldberg's book examines the relationship between sodomy and repressive power structures (Elizabethan and modern). Arguing (after Foucault) that sodomy is not a self-evident category in the Renaissance but a "confused" one that exists only relationally (1-26), Goldberg looks at these confusions in works by Spenser, Shakespeare, Marlowe, and William Bradford. In the essay on Hal, he examines critics' "desired identification" with the prince, seeing it as a sort of "misogynist heterosexuality always in danger of homophobia" (147-48). Goldberg treats a variety of episodes in *1* and *2 Henry IV* involving Hal, Falstaff, and Hotspur, as well as the wooing of Katherine in *Henry V* (5.2), in arguing that these plays constantly transgress the boundaries they seem to be producing between illegitimate and legitimate male/male relations, especially as these are bound up with such matters as misogyny, the fear of male effeminacy, and emulative male-relationships.

57. Hapgood, Robert. "Falstaff's Vocation." *Shakespeare Quarterly* 16 (1965): 91-98.

The argument here is that the pattern of the robber who is also robbed contributes both to the unity of the second tetralogy and to its moral complexities. Seeing Falstaff as a thematic touchstone for the plays, Hapgood briefly traces the literary and cultural backgrounds of the figure. He then argues that, starting with Richard II's theft of Bolingbroke's inheritance in *Richard II* (2.1) and continuing through Henry V's campaign in France in *Henry V*, the plays present repeated instances of thieves robbing each other, and that this persistent motif qualifies and complicates our sympathies for Richard, Henry IV, Hotspur, and Hal/Henry V.

58. Hawkins, Sherman. "Structural Pattern in Shakespeare's Histories." *Studies in Philology* 88 (1991): 16–45.

Hawkins regards the two tetralogies as distinct yet linked units mirroring each other by parallel and contrast in something analogous to the form of a diptych. Specifically he sees the first tetralogy as presenting the tragic downward evolution of a tyrant (Richard III) while the second focuses upon the epic upward progress of a hero (Henry V). He identifies amid these overarching structures numerous other structural and thematic parallels, suggesting that Shakespeare planned the second tetralogy "as counterpart and contrast to the first" (25). The argument draws upon classical as well as Renaissance models (Plato, Aristotle, Lucan, Xenophon, Plutarch, Hall, Marlowe, and Spenser), and includes much detailed analysis of structural patterns in the plays individually and as parts of a tetralogy. Hawkins concludes that the structural pattern he locates was for Shakespeare both habitual *and* intentional—"a major feat of architectonic imagination" (45).

59. Hodgdon, Barbara. *The End Crowns All: Closure and Contradiction in Shakespeare's History.* Princeton: Princeton Univ. Press, 1991.

Drawing heavily upon stage and film productions as well as quarto and folio texts of the plays, Hodgdon addresses the problem of closure in all ten of Shakespeare's English histories, emphasizing the complex array of meanings a play can assume in performance. Chapters 5, 6, and 7 (127–211) are devoted to *Richard II*, *1* and *2 Henry IV*, and *Henry V* respectively. Hodgdon sees the ending of *Richard II* as disturbingly incorporating Richard's "myth" and Bolingbroke's "history" in the fiction of the King's Two Bodies, an idea "rewritten" (150) in the *Henry IV* plays as the father's two bodies as problematically represented in Falstaff and Henry IV. For Hodgdon, part one ends with the refusal to exclude a father figure (Falstaff), who is rejected at the end of part two (5.5) by a new king bitterly severing all his former fatherly ties. Hodgdon reads the ending of *Henry V* as subversively exploring the "fissures in the play's own representational politics" (187), and sees the play as a proto-Brechtian form.

60. Howard, Jean E., and Phyllis Rackin. *Engendering a Nation: A Feminist Account of Shakespeare's English Histories.* New York: Routledge, 1997.

The thesis of this book is that the historical transition in England from dynastic kingdom to modern nation was vitally connected to a shifting cultural understanding of gender and social roles, and that the complex elements of this cultural transition were clearly apparent in Elizabethan history plays, particularly Shakespeare's. Part one (1–40), which takes up such questions as the nature of the Elizabethan history play, women's place in culture and historical drama, and the theatre as a cultural institution, begins with a consideration of *Henry V*; the authors contend that the play reduces women to "signifiers of patriarchal power and possession" (6)—a point made in Kenneth Branagh's 1989 film of the play (but avoided in Laurence Olivier's 1944 film) by the language lesson episode (3.4), where the princess is depicted as a closeted woman preparing to be vanquished by English aggressiveness. Part two (41–133) consists of separate chapters on *1 Henry VI*, *2 Henry VI*, *3 Henry VI*, *Richard III*, and *King John*. Part three (135–215) consists of separate chapters on *Richard II*, *1* and *2 Henry IV*, and *Henry V*. As regards *Richard II*, the authors see Richard as embodying stereotypically feminine qualities such as weeping, an aversion for war, and a taste for luxury, and Bolingbroke as embodying stereotypically masculine qualities such as personal merit and political competence; this "gendered opposition" they see reflected in the anxieties of an Elizabethan aristocracy that "felt emasculated by conversion from a militarized to a consuming class" (143)—a situation exacerbated by the presence of a female monarch on the throne. For the authors, Bolingbroke and Richard represent two rival forms of theatricality, the former astutely political, and the latter powerfully expressive. The essay on *1* and *2 Henry IV* characterizes the plays as "an aggregate of heterogeneous people and places" (160) where dynastic authority, patrimonial inheritance, and even the desire for a wife get discredited; in this "decentered" world (164) women acquire subversive power only in marginalized places such as Eastcheap or Wales. Perceiving strong feminine qualities in Falstaff, the authors associate him with female threats to manhood and military honor—the same threats evoked by the alien world of female power and magic (Wales) and the presence of Elizabeth on the English throne. Throughout the discussion Howard and Rackin associate Eastcheap "with the attractions as well as the dangers of the playhouse" (175), and also with criminalized and comic women (i.e., Doll and Mistress Quickly) on whom male anxieties about social order can be conveniently displaced. The discussion of *Henry V* emphasizes the play's topicality and modernity for Elizabethan playgoers, since it presents a world where a man secures his status by performative masculinity and personal achievement; here the authors equate Henry V, Hotspur, and Petruchio as male dominators of various "Kates," thus identifying "the subjugation of wives as a middle-class project" (193), and, in Henry V's case, a masculine domination represented in specifically erotic terms. Howard and Rackin examine the play in detail, affirming that "military conquest provides the arena and sexual conquest the warrant for establishing the male protagonist's authority, and female characters are defined primarily in terms of their sexuality" (198); in this world "the hierarchies of status and nation are supported rather than threatened by sexual violence" (199). The book is meticulously and evidentially argued.

61. Kahn, Coppélia. "'The Shadow of the Male': Masculine Identity in the History Plays." In *Man's Estate: Masculine Identity in Shakespeare*, 47–81. Berkeley: Univ. of California Press, 1981. Repr., in part, in Holderness (no. 85).

Kahn's book, which also includes essays on *Venus and Adonis, Romeo and Juliet* and *The Taming of the Shrew*, cuckoldry and marriage, *Coriolanus* and *Macbeth*, and the Shakespearean family, explores such psychological issues as sexual identity, family relationships, and gender roles in the plays. Her discussion of the histories sees the two tetralogies as emphasizing the importance of the father in male self-definition, either as "a figure from whom men strive to separate themselves or [as a figure] with whom they merge" (47). For Kahn, *Richard II* depicts a struggle between maternal and paternal images of kingship (as seen in Richard and Bolingbroke respectively), and, when Richard's identification with mother England collapses, so does his identity. Kahn regards the *Henry IV* plays as depicting a prince whose attraction to Falstaff constitutes a rebellion against his father, but who actually resembles his real father in many ways and eventually chooses to embrace his inherited identity in order to insure his lineal succession. She finds questions of male identity in *Henry V* to be far less complex than those in the preceding plays; here Henry, in his reliance upon "simple, idealized male comradeships" (81), forges a male identity evocative of those in the first tetralogy.

62. Kernan, Alvin [B.] "From Ritual to History: The English History Play." In *The Revels History of Drama in English: Volume III 1576–1613*, J. Leeds Barroll, Alexander Leggatt, Richard Hosley, and Alvin Kernan, joint authors, 262–99. London: Methuen, 1975. Repr., in part, in Cubeta (no. 143).

Kernan sees the second tetralogy as a unified dramatic epic tracing the passage from an essentially medieval, ceremonial, and psychologically stable world (*Richard II*) to a modern, historical, and psychologically contingent one (*Henry V*). The essay makes detailed allusion to the many connecting strands throughout the plays (of language, action, character, incident, etc.) that reinforce this unity and suggest a coherent movement. First published in the *Yale Review* 49 (1969): 3–32 under the title "The Henriad: Shakespeare's Major History Plays," and often reprinted, Kernan's essay is one of the standard defenses of the artistic and thematic integrity of the second tetralogy.

63. Maclean, Hugh. "Time and Horsemanship in Shakespeare's Histories." *University of Toronto Quarterly* 35 (1966): 229–45.

The focus here is upon Hal/Henry V's successful use of time in contrast to the misuse of it by others in the second tetralogy (most notably Richard II, Henry IV, Hotspur, and Falstaff), with particular reference to the motif of horsemanship in this context. Maclean is concerned to counter ironic or deflationary interpretations of the character of Henry V. In so doing, he demonstrates how Hal/Henry V is the sole figure in the sequence from *Richard II* to *Henry V* (and even including *Richard III*) who has the ability "to *move in time*, and to grasp its nature—neither to oppose it nor submissively to be overmastered by it" (231).

64. Manheim, Michael. *The Weak King Dilemma in the Shakespearean History*

Play. Syracuse: Syracuse Univ. Press, 1973.

In exploring the problem of the weak king in the Elizabethan and Shakespearean history play, Manheim alludes to all ten of Shakespeare's histories; *Richard II* (53-75) and *Henry V* (161-82), however, are the only two plays of the second tetralogy to which he devotes full essays. Manheim argues that *Richard II* belongs more properly with the anonymous *Woodstock* and Marlowe's *Edward II* than with the plays of the second tetralogy, since all three plays treat the question of loyalty to a weak king. He then traces the movement of our shifting sympathies toward Richard as well as our ambivalence toward Bolingbroke, and concludes that the play leaves us unresolved regarding the emerging Machiavellianism of the day. Manheim examines *Henry V* in this ideological context, arguing that here Machiavellianism (in the person of the king) appears without irony as an attractive alternative to weakness. For Manheim, Henry V is a master of artifice and illusion, but such is the best we can expect from him or from any effective ruler; indeed, "successful monarchy is as much involved with effect and artifice as Shakespeare's theatre itself" (182).

65. Ornstein, Robert. *A Kingdom for a Stage: The Achievement of Shakespeare's History Plays.* Cambridge, Mass.: Harvard Univ. Press, 1972. Repr., in part, in Holderness (no. 85) and in Newlin (no. 144).

In treating all ten of Shakespeare's English histories, Ornstein argues that these plays do not reflexively defend Tudor notions of orthodoxy, but instead emphasize "the fabric of personal and social relationships" (222) upon which social order is based. Each play of the second tetralogy is discussed in a separate chapter (102-202). Ornstein sees *Richard II* as a play of neither heroes nor villains, but as the story of a weak and vain tyrant necessarily deposed in order to preserve the state; *1 Henry IV* is remarkable for its unity of plot, but behind the "logic" of its events is the partisan and self-interested "illogic of human motive" (128), which Ornstein sees in the behavior of virtually every major character (particularly the ironic, poised, and self-absorbed Prince Hal). Ornstein regards *2 Henry IV* as considerably more lifeless and drab than *1 Henry IV*; it depicts declining moral values, loneliness and isolation, disintegrating relationships, and a prince whose studied conventionality insures his political success. This success Ornstein treats at length in his discussion of *Henry V*, which he sees as a "thoughtful and serious" play (175); here the king appears as a scrupulous thinker, far superior in moral sensitivity to those around him, showing a deep need for self-justification yet also driven by a desire for glory. For Ornstein, the Chorus serves as Shakespeare's "surrogate" (186)—a figure through whom the dramatist reflects seriously on art and history. Ornstein's discussion focuses repeatedly upon the multifaceted nature of the plays of the second tetralogy and of their major characters.

66. Pater, Walter. "Shakespeare's English Kings." In *Appreciations: With an Essay on Style*, 185-204. London: Macmillan, 1889. Repr. often. The essay is repr., in part, in Muir (no. 94), in Brooke (no. 141), and in Newlin (no. 144).

Pater sees the English histories as a study in "the irony of kingship—average human nature, flung with a wonderfully pathetic effect into the vortex of great events" (185–86). He finds Richard II to be the most touching example of this sort of irony, Bolingbroke/Henry IV to be a consummate expression of opportunistic "kingcraft" (189), and Hal/Henry V, whose speeches cogently enunciate the ironies of royalty, to be "the *greatest* of Shakespeare's kings" (190). Pater has extremely high praise for the poetical lyricism of Richard, seeing such poetical beauty as the expression of a sensitive, eloquent, and genuinely royal nature abounding in emotional appeal. The essay amounts to an unabashed paean to the affective powers of both *Richard II* and its title figure; indeed for Pater, *Richard II* "belongs to a small group of plays, where, by happy birth and consistent evolution, dramatic form approaches to something like the unity of a lyrical ballad" (203).

67. Prior, Moody E. *The Drama of Power: Studies in Shakespeare's History Plays.* Evanston, Ill.: Northwestern Univ. Press, 1973.

Prior's book amounts to a complete reevaluation of the two tetralogies and their relationship to each other. It consists of 16 separate chapters, 10 of which (chaps. 4, 7, 8, 9, 10, 11, 12, 13, 14, and 16) treat the second tetralogy. Emphasizing the independence of the separate plays, Prior modifies the idea of the two tetralogies: the three *Henry VI* plays make up a trilogy followed by a play of very different character (*Richard III*), just as *Richard II* and the *Henry IV* plays make up a second trilogy, again followed by a different kind of play (*Henry V*). He sees each of the five plays beginning with *Richard III* and ending with *Henry V* as taking up "a particular problem of kingship in relation to legitimacy, authority, and the exercise and influence of sovereign power" (8), whereas the *Henry VI* plays make up "the great prologue"—"the rich ore out of which the later plays are refined" (9). After reviewing Shakespeare's narrative and intellectual sources, Prior concludes that the dramatist was exposed to a variety of attitudes and a diversity of historiographical influences, some Christian and providential, others more pragmatic and utilitarian. What follows below is a summary of Prior's ideas on the second tetralogy represented in the ten chapters cited above.

As regards *Richard II*, Prior notes that the idea of divine right was not codified before the seventeenth century, but was consistent with such Tudor beliefs as obedience to the monarch and the idea of the king as God's representative; thus he sees the origin of royal power and the limits of its authority as issues central to the play. Prior sees Bolingbroke as a deft politician, since he is able to claim the throne "without damaging the mystique of divinely ordained sovereignty and the authority which comes with legitimately acquired power" (150–51), and discusses the play as a new kind of tragedy in which Richard searches for meaning in his fall. He refuses to see Richard as a figure of "impressive proportions" (179), but he does see him as one who searches for "consolation and identity as he grasps and relinquishes various ways of acting out his true tragedy" (182). Prior's focus in the *Henry IV* plays is on such issues as the politics of usurpation, the idea of Honor, the morality of power, and the making of a king. He sees Bolingbroke as a "capable if not very appealing usurper" (193) who succeeds in restoring order to the kingdom; Hotspur and Falstaff as embodiments of opposing views on Honor; Prince John as degrading the concept and the Lord Chief Justice as enlarging the idea and making it attractive to Hal; and Hal (though, like his father, a manipulator of others) as a figure who undergoes a genuine reformation and finally emerges as an ideal prince. Prior regards *Henry V* as a play in which the will of God is acknowledged as governing events; here a nation stands united under a popular king who is not called upon to defend his title, a figure who is the most straightforward and candidly political of Shakespeare's monarchs. For Prior, Henry is the mirror of all Christian kings, a man, like Richard III, "of mythic proportions, not drawn within the normal human scale" (184); thus the play is very different from the three dramas on national disorder that precede it, especially the *Henry IV* plays, which Prior sees as "the last serious study of kingship in the cycle" (341). The book contains detailed readings of virtually all the plays' key episodes.

68. Pye, Christopher. *The Regal Phantasm: Shakespeare and the Politics of Spectacle.* London: Routledge, 1990.

This New Historicist study treats the relationship between theatricality and power by focusing on *Henry V*, *Richard II*, and *Macbeth*, as well as on the "spectacle of the monarch's presence, and the spectacle of punishment ritually played out on the scaffold" (2). Pye's concern throughout is to stress the role of the theatre in linking politics with aesthetics. In "Mock Sovereignty: *Henry V*" (13–42), he examines the connection between absolute power and opaque theatricality as located in the notion of the king's two bodies; since *Henry V*, depending on how one regards the play in the context of Shakespeare's two tetralogies, can come either first (before the *Henry VI* plays) or last (after the *Henry IV* plays) in the sequence, Henry can be seen theatrically as his own inheritor—a duality that solidifies his claim to power. Pye sees Henry's power as deriving from mockery and deceit, and regards the wooing of Katherine (5.2) as containing a homoerotic subtext—in the figure of the barred maid who is also a boy actor—that relates directly to the presence of Elizabeth on the English throne. In "The Betrayal of the Gaze: *Richard II*" (82–105), Pye argues that Richard strives to master his own demise, and that this theatrical spectacle "is elaborated within the play through a specific optical trope—anamorphosis—which bears on the formation of subject and sovereign alike" (11). In treating Richard's orchestration of his own deposition, Pye draws upon the idea, derived from Greenblatt (no. 29), that power ironically depends upon its own subversion.

69. Quinones, Ricardo J. "Shakespeare's Histories." In *The Renaissance Discovery of Time*, 290–360. Cambridge: Mass.: Harvard Univ. Press, 1972. Repr., in part, in Bloom (no. 203).

Quinones's study treats developing notions of Renaissance time in Dante, Petrarch, Rabelais, Montaigne, Spenser, Shakespeare, and Milton. In his chapter on the histories, he notes the association of time with the garden and the family; in *Richard II*, these three motifs coalesce to chart the inevitable course of the self-inflicted decline of Richard—a man who wasted time and is in turn wasted by it. Quinones argues that in the *Henry IV* plays Hal's ability to order, clarify, and exploit experience is reflected in the imagery of time, and emphasizes the point by suggesting that Shakespeare's manipulations of time in *1 Henry IV* show Hotspur's activities to be "a disrupted sequence of heightened moments," while Hal's are "more continuous" and communal, reflecting just the sort of "controlling powers that Shakespeare valued in his more life-seeking monarchs" (341). In this context, Falstaff becomes the "prime creation of a negligent greatness" (341), whose excesses and temporal mismanagement are gradually exposed as the *Henry IV* plays proceed. Quinones sees time as important in the histories as a means of endorsing Shakespeare's political ethic—good government, prudence, responsibility, and decorum. The essay is a classical, and often ignored, rejoinder to negative or skeptical readings of Shakespeare's representation of political man.

70. **Rabkin, Norman.** "The Polity." In *Shakespeare and the Common Understanding*, 80–149. New York: Free Press, 1967. Repr. Chicago: Univ. of Chicago Press, 1984.

Rabkin treats the second tetralogy in the context of other plays dealing with political ideas (most notably *Measure for Measure, Julius Caesar,* and *Coriolanus*). In his discussion of the English histories (80–101) and throughout the book, he emphasizes that Shakespeare's plays are "built on visions of complementarity" (27) that underscore the unresolvable complexities of life. He considers *Richard II* to be a problem play that centers on the contradiction of a divinely ordained king who is politically inept and that extends to wider ambivalences about political virtue resulting from man's tragic divisions between ethical responsibilities and the need for amoral gratification. Stressing the importance of Falstaff in the *Henry IV* plays as a moral dilemma for the prince, Rabkin argues that Hal must reject the fat knight and all that he represents in order to fulfill his political destiny. The king's political triumph in *Henry V* is seen in ironic terms, thus making the play the most melancholy of the histories.

71. **Richmond, H. M.** *Shakespeare's Political Plays.* New York: Random House, 1967. Repr. Gloucester, Mass.: Peter Smith, 1977.

This book treats the first and second tetralogies, *King John, Julius Caesar,* and *Coriolanus*. In his discussion of the second tetralogy (123–58), Richmond argues for a political rather than a tragic dimension to *Richard II*, seeing the play as presenting the decline from an innocent medieval ideal of society to one of Machiavellian pragmatism as evidenced in Bolingbroke, the "new type of amoral personality" (140). Seeing the remaining plays of the tetralogy as exploring whether or not such a personality is compatible with the Christian ideal of kingship, Richmond argues that *1* and *2 Henry IV* reveal the unhappy effects of Henry's reign, most notably in a general sense of societal greed and in the irresponsible behavior of Hal, Falstaff, and Hotspur. But Richmond also emphasizes the moral complexity of Falstaff and Hotspur, seeing each as embodying emotional qualities lacking in Hal; Falstaff, in particular, achieves a sort of moral superiority in *1 Henry IV* by recognizing his own defects. Richmond sees in *2 Henry IV* "the disintegration of healthy standards of conduct" (162), and Hal/Henry V as showing "a manipulative capacity equal to his father's" (171); moreover, the pattern continues into *Henry V*, where the king practices deceit and hypocrisy for crude political ends. But here, Richmond contends, Henry does manage to learn moderation as a result of his near-defeat in France; and he finally emerges as a man whose success is based "not on the romantic bellicosity of a clever young hero masquerading as the ideal king, but on the ultimate steadiness attained by a mature man who knows his failures and, regretting them, puts his trust in Providence" (200).

72. Rossiter, A. P. *Angel with Horns: Fifteen Lectures on Shakespeare*, ed. Graham Storey. London: Longmans, Green; New York: Theatre Arts Books, 1961. "*Richard II*" is repr. in Brooke (no. 141); "Ambivalence" is repr., in part, in Berman (no. 259).

This book consists of Rossiter's lectures on Shakespeare given at Cambridge in the 1950s, two of which, "*Richard II*" (23–39) and "Ambivalence: The Dialectic of the Histories" (40–64), treat the second tetralogy. Rossiter sees *Richard II* as a play of discontinuities—in its characterization of Richard, its political ideas, and its style of verse; the play lacks unity, and characters' motives for action are often ambiguous. For Rossiter, the play is an "*obscure tragedy*, in which men are compelled, constrained, baffled and bent by circumstances in which their actions do *not* express their characters" (37). In his second essay, Rossiter defines "ambivalence" as a situation that exists when "two opposed value judgements are subsumed" and are equally "valid" for the work in which they occur; thus we can appreciate the whole only when we take a "two-eyed" view of it (51). He finds this sort of duality particularly centered in Falstaff, but strangely absent from *Henry V*, where Shakespeare produces a play that demands a "one-eyed" approach, since in this world of jingoistic patriotism there is no place for so "ambivalent" a figure as Falstaff. Rossiter claims that the essence of Shakespeare's insight into English history is not in *Henry V*; rather it is located in the more "ambivalent" and "comic" history of the *Henry IV* plays.

73. Stewart, J. I. M. "The Birth and Death of Falstaff." In *Character and Motive in Shakespeare: Some Recent Appraisals Examined*, 111–39. London: Longmans, Green and Co., 1949. Repr., in part, in Hunter (no. 205).

This book consists of a series of loosely connected essays approaching Shakespeare from the perspective of early twentieth-century psychological criticism. In his essay on Falstaff, Stewart examines the merits of various critical approaches to the character. He sees in the evolution of Falstaff in *1* and *2 Henry IV* and in the description of his death in *Henry V* (2.3) analogies to ancient myths involving the death of an aged king who must be ritually slain in order to regenerate the land; Henry V, by a displacement common in ritual, rejects and kills Falstaff (the father-substitute) instead of his real father, with whom Falstaff has been implicitly compared throughout *1* and *2 Henry IV*.

74. Traversi, Derek A. *Shakespeare: From "Richard II" to "Henry V."* Stanford: Stanford Univ. Press, 1957. Repr., in part, in Waith (no. 86), in Muir (no. 94), in Berman (no. 259), and in Quinn (no. 261).

Traversi's study of the second tetralogy approaches the plays as an integrated unit chronicling the interruption of divinely ordained rule, the disastrous consequences of that interruption, and finally the restoration of order on a more secure, albeit more limited, basis. He sees *Richard II* as a play of opposed personalities and ideas as represented in Richard (feudal, emotional, anointed, yet morally flawed) and Bolingbroke (modern, pragmatic, rational, yet not divinely ordained); the play thus dramatizes the passing from a world of certainties to one of political expediency. Traversi focuses upon Hal in his discussion of the *Henry IV* plays, seeing the prince as inheriting from his father a quality of detachment that is necessary for political success in the new political environment Henry IV has created; he also emphasizes Hal's necessary separateness from Falstaff and Hotspur, since both embody limitations the prince must put aside if he is to rule effectively. For Traversi, *Henry V* focuses upon the conditions of kingship, particularly the sacrifice of common humanity that being an effective ruler entails; in the king we notice a tension between passion and self-control, and this tension reflects a moral contradiction at the heart of kingship itself. Traversi's interpretive method is essentially New Critical; in treating virtually every important episode in the plays, he gives detailed close readings of imagery, poetical texture, and structural or thematic importance.

75. Van Doren, Mark. *Shakespeare.* New York: Henry Holt and Co., 1939. Repr. often. Repr., in part, in Bevington (no. 202), in Berman (no. 259), and in Quinn (no. 261).

Van Doren's book consists of individual essays on all of Shakespeare's plays. He sees *Richard II* (84–95) as a play in which Shakespeare fully indulges his penchant for musically intoxicating language, and Richard as a self-conscious "great minor poet" (84) who luxuriates in gorgeous sentiment but fails to attain real tragic stature. Van Doren treats the *Henry IV* plays as a single dramatic unit and as a superb dramatic achievement (116–35). Relegating Hal and Henry IV to the background of the action (and ignoring political matters almost completely), he focuses instead upon Hotspur and Falstaff, whom he regards as appealing embodiments of the high-spiritedness and vivacity that pervades the plays. Van Doren disparages both *Henry V* and its protagonist (170–79); its style, treatment of subject matter, and overt patriotism are all evidence of artistic failure, and even Henry himself, instead of the ideal ruler the play proclaims him to be, is no more than "a mere good fellow, a hearty undergraduate with enormous initials on his chest" (176).

76. Webber, Joan. "The Renewal of the King's Symbolic Role: From *Richard II* to *Henry V*." *Texas Studies in Literature and Language* 4 (1963): 530–38.

Webber is concerned with the nature of kingship, particularly its relationship to language and reality. She argues that Richard II's problem is that his language is powerless to affect human action, while Bolingbroke has precisely the opposite problem—he is a man of action who lacks the skill in language and ceremony to justify his office or behavior. Seeing these two imperfect kings as the backdrop against which Hal/Henry V undertakes a process of royal self-discovery, Webber contends that the prince begins by trying out a series of linguistic roles in the *Henry IV* plays as a form of auto-didacticism through which he grows into his symbolic role as monarch; in *Henry V* the triumphant king is able to unite England into a functioning whole, thus renewing the symbolic role of the king lost in *Richard II*.

77. **Winny, James.** *The Player King: A Theme of Shakespeare's Histories.* London: Chatto and Windus, 1968.

Winny devotes virtually his entire book to the second tetralogy, arguing that the plays are imaginative constructs rather than political or historical tracts, and stressing their "imaginative basis in metaphors of moral conflict within the individual" (41), particularly those relating to the matter of individual identity. In his full discussion of the second tetralogy (48–214), he examines *Richard II* as a play about a man obsessed with surface experience, denied contact with his own inward reality by his complete absorption in his identity as king; the play also explores the ironies implicit in the recurring pattern of a father disgraced by a morally degenerate son—a condition that Bolingbroke feels doubly, both as son and as father, by virtue of his infamous deposition of Richard *and* the behavior of the scapegrace Hal. For Winny, the *Henry IV* plays underscore the theme of identity through their reliance upon duplicity and false appearances; Bolingbroke, for example, is more cynical and self-serving than he is in *Richard II*, a "royal counterfeit" who adopts "a facade of moral respectability which hardens into a character he himself accepts as authentic" (93). Winny treats Falstaff as a satirical double for Henry, a figure who constantly reminds us of the falseness of the king's character, since both are old, morally vacuous, and diseased in body and spirit; he finds Hal to be the antithesis of Bolingbroke, presenting virtue in the guise of vice, and finally redeeming his father's tainted kingship at the end of *2 Henry IV*, while Hotspur and the rebels are variations on the theme of duplicity, concealing self-interest under the facade of idealism and honor. Winny treats *Henry V* as an inferior play which depicts its hero romantically rather than realistically; he sees shifts in the drama between uncertainty and decisiveness that reflect not only Henry's dilemma, but also Shakespeare's in attempting to give "full reality" to a play he recognized as inferior (210).

78. **Yeats, W[illiam] B[utler].** "At Stratford-on-Avon." In *Ideas of Good and Evil*, 142–67. London: A. H. Bullen; New York: The Macmillan Co., 1903. Repr. New York: Russell & Russell, 1967. The essay is repr., in part, in Brooke (no. 141), in Newlin (no. 144), and in Berman (no. 259).

This essay, written in May 1901, was prompted by Yeats's having seen all of Shakespeare's English histories (excluding *Henry VIII*), performed at Stratford;

it attempts to debunk what Yeats perceives as a mistaken notion among nineteenth-century critics that Shakespeare saw Richard II as a sentimental failure and Henry V as a model of heroism and success. Yeats claims that Shakespeare preferred the lyrical and imaginative dignity of Richard to the more common political competence of Henry, calling Richard an "uninspired Hamlet" and a "vessel of porcelain" and Henry a "ripened Fortinbras" and a "vessel of clay" (162-63). For Yeats, Henry represents all that is aesthetically impoverished in modern life; he has "the gross vices, the coarse nerves, of one who is to rule among violent people" and is "as remorseless and undistinguished as some natural force" (163). The essay is highly impressionistic, having as its explicit subtext the disparagement of conventional political and aesthetic values in favor of a more passionate and visionary approach to life.

D. Performance Criticism; Film and Television Versions.

79. Crowl, Samuel. *Shakespeare Observed: Studies in Performance on Stage and Screen.* Athens, Ohio: Ohio Univ. Press, 1992.

This book, which attempts to "develop a dialogue between stage and film productions of Shakespeare and the critical discourse surrounding his plays" (14), contains three separate essays on the plays of the second tetralogy. In "The Long Good-bye: Welles and Falstaff" (35-50), Crowl treats Orson Welles's film *Chimes at Midnight,* noting its emphasis upon the thematic importance of Falstaff to the *Henry* plays, and especially his role as a rival father who (like Bolingbroke) threatens to submerge Hal's identity. The essay makes many evidential allusions to the film in arguing that through its "farewell motif" (43) Welles creates a sense of loss and lament that characterizes the Falstaff/Hal relationship. In "Minding Giddy Business: Michael Bogdanov's *The Wars of the Roses*" (142-64), Crowl provides a highly detailed analysis of Bogdanov's seven-play production of the two tetralogies, which Crowl saw in Chicago in 1988, as a postmodern critique of the plays that disturbingly questions their traditional meanings. The essay, which focuses primarily on the *Henry IV* plays and *Henry V,* gives many useful details of setting, costume, acting styles, etc. In "Fathers and Sons: Kenneth Branagh's *Henry V*" (165-74), Crowl treats Branagh's 1989 film both in the context of Olivier's 1944 film and as emerging from Branagh's performance in the role of Henry in Adrian Noble's 1984-85 Royal Shakespeare Company production. The "fathers" referred to in Crowl's title are Olivier and Noble—figures whom Branagh must both acknowledge and transcend in his film production. Crowl provides a highly detailed description of the Branagh film (with frequent allusion to the Olivier and Noble productions) to show how it takes Henry's piety *and* sense of guilt seriously, and both builds upon and departs from the practices of its two influential predecessors.

80. Goldman, Michael. *Shakespeare and the Energies of Drama.* Princeton: Princeton Univ. Press, 1972.

Goldman is interested in how we experience plays in the theatre, and writes essays on *Romeo and Juliet, Hamlet, King Lear, Coriolanus, The Winter's Tale* and *The Tempest, 1* and *2 Henry IV*, and *Henry V* from this perspective. In chap. 4, "Falstaff Asleep" (45-57), he argues that Falstaff's presence in the histories reminds us of "the needs and achievements of the body" (45). After examining the sense of revelry and pathos Falstaff evokes throughout the *Henry IV* plays, Goldman concludes with the scene in which Falstaff sleeps (*1 Henry IV*, 2.4.529ff.), finding him here to be the central figure in a poignant tableau, expressive both of self-indulgence and of vulnerability, that unites his theatrical body with ours. In chap. 5, "*Henry V*: The Strain of Rule" (58-73), he argues that the play conveys the idea of strenuous energy—in the speeches of the Chorus and of the king, in the wooing scene (5.2), and particularly in Henry's enactment of the contrary roles of king and man. In Goldman's view, our overriding experience of the play gives us a sense of "the effort of greatness ... the demands on the self that being a king involves" (73).

81. Jorgens, Jack J. *Shakespeare on Film*. Bloomington: Indiana Univ. Press, 1977.

Jorgens's book contains two chapters on films treating the second tetralogy. In "Orson Welles's *Chimes at Midnight (Falstaff)*" (106-21), he argues that the *Henry IV* plays depict the transition from a medieval to a Renaissance world, and that Welles's film captures "the tensions, contrasts, and discontinuities" of this "double perspective" (109). He examines the film in detail, suggesting that its cinematography suffuses it with nostalgia and a sense of loss rather than with broad hilarity; he stresses the idea of parallel and contrast in the film, particularly the idea of "farewell" (114). The argument is sensitive to the thematic nuances of both the film and the *Henry IV* plays. In "Laurence Olivier's *Henry V*" (122-35), Jorgens emphasizes the changes Olivier makes in Shakespeare's text in order to heighten the contrast between the English and the French and to soften Henry's character and that of the characters in the low plot. He sees the film as both engaging the complications of Henry's character and presenting him as an admirable figure who matures in the course of the action. There is particularly high praise for the structural unity of the film, which follows the pattern of "a movement outward followed by a return" (131). Jorgens ends his discussion by comparing the film with *Chimes at Midnight*, and concludes that the two works reveal "two different cinematic sensibilities at work" (135). Jorgens's book is a standard and highly influential study of Shakespearean film.

82. Pilkington, Ace G. *Screening Shakespeare from "Richard II" to "Henry V."* Newark: Univ. of Delaware Press; London: Associated Univ. Presses, 1991.

The aim of this book is "to demonstrate that films can be read and reread and that they are subject to the same kind of detailed and accurate examination which has traditionally been given to printed texts" (20). Pilkington is concerned with moving film criticism beyond conventional "reviewing" to the sort of analysis that includes "point-by-point comparisons of shooting scripts and release scripts and examinations of the expressed intentions of directors and actors" (21). He pursues this agenda in full and detailed chapters on each of the following screen productions: the BBC *Richard II* (1978); the BBC *1* and *2 Henry IV* (1979); the BBC *Henry V* (1979); Laurence Olivier's *Henry V* (1944); and Orson Welles's *Chimes at Midnight* (1966). The book provides highly detailed "readings" of virtually every important scene in these screen productions, often alluding to literary criticism as well as performance criticism to shed light on dramatic action. Pilkington includes a useful list of "Works Cited," followed by an extensive "Filmography" that provides full credit and cast lists for each of the productions (189-204). The volume is extremely useful for any study of Shakespeare on screen.

83. Rackin, Phyllis. *Stages of History: Shakespeare's English Chronicles.* Ithaca: Cornell Univ. Press, 1990.

Rackin treats the history plays as scripts for performance rather than as texts for reading; in so doing, she also takes up such questions as their relationship to Tudor historiography, the nature of historical causation, Shakespeare's use of anachronism and nostalgia, female subversion of patriarchal structures, and the subversive power of the underclass. The plays of the second tetralogy are not accorded a single chapter, but are examined throughout the book in the context of the other histories. Rackin emphasizes the sense of ambiguity and duplicity that characterizes the sequence from *Richard II* to *Henry V* (67-70), and argues that these plays give contrary perspectives on historical truth. She also examines *Richard II* as a Janus-like play that eulogizes medievalism even as it anticipates a disquieting Elizabethan present (117-37), and links this duality to Shakespeare's dramatic practice, which she sees as manipulating audience perspective in order to interrogate the act of history itself. For Rackin, the *Henry IV* plays and *Henry V* contain a "proliferation of subplots" that, instead of implying a stable teleology, suggest an unstable connection by analogy, parody, contrast, and juxtaposition (137); and she sees this phenomenon undermining the project of depicting a glorious past on a modern stage (137-42). She regards Henry V as the Shakespearean king who most resembles Elizabeth, but whose manhood and authority ironically depend upon French women—i.e., his inheritance of France through the female line and his "conquest" of Katherine (164-68).

84. Sprague, Arthur Colby. *Shakespeare's Histories: Plays for the Stage.* London: The Society for Theatre Research, 1964. Repr., in part, in Quinn (no. 261).

Sprague treats all ten of Shakespeare's English histories as acting pieces, but is also concerned with integrating "opinions held by literary critics and the practice of the stage" (ix). Hence each of his four separate chapters on individual plays of the second tetralogy (29-110) provides eclectic references to numerous productions from the eighteenth to the twentieth century as well as the responses of literary critics from the same period. The book cannot be said to argue a consistent "line" on the second tetralogy; rather it is a highly selective but nonetheless informative compendium of details relating to performance history, punctuated by Sprague's own critical responses to selected episodes.

See also nos. 28, 30, 37, 59, 68, 89.

E. Collections of Essays.

85. Holderness, Graham, ed. *Shakespeare's History Plays: "Richard II" to "Henry V."* London: Macmillan, 1992.

This volume reprints criticism on the second tetralogy by Robert Ornstein (no. 65), Leonard Tennenhouse (no. 34), Linda Bamber (no. 43), Coppélia Kahn (no. 61), Robert S. Knapp, Catherine Belsey (no. 26), James L. Calderwood (no. 37), Derek Cohen (no. 180), Graham Holderness (no. 30), Annabel Patterson (no. 214), and Jonathan Dollimore and Alan Sinfield (no. 235). In his introduction (1–34), Holderness traces criticism on the histories from Tillyard (no. 35) up to 1992, with an eye to how various ideological approaches to the plays have developed. The introduction is an extremely useful and detailed short history of twentieth-century perspectives on the histories, with particular attention to the criticism excerpted in the book, but by no means confined to it.

86. Waith, Eugene M, ed. *Shakespeare: The Histories. A Collection of Critical Essays.* Englewood Cliffs, N.J.: Prentice Hall, 1965.

In his introduction (1–12), Waith places Shakespeare's histories in the context of the Elizabethan chronicle play, and provides a brief summary of important twentieth-century scholarship on the plays. The volume reprints excerpts from scholarship on all ten of Shakespeare's English histories, including excerpts from the following on the plays of the second tetralogy: Campbell (no. 27); Tillyard (no. 35); Reese (no. 32); Traversi (no. 74); Dorius (no. 50); Wilson (no. 195); and Walter (no. 212).

F. Bibliographies.

87. Burden, Dennis H. "Shakespeare's History Plays: 1952–1983." *Shakespeare Survey* 38 (1985): 1–18.

This essay continues the summary of critical trends begun by Harold Jenkins (no. 90). Burden concludes that the scholarly problems in the ensuing thirty years are in many respects the same as those treated by Jenkins. Like Jenkins, Burden discusses no single play in detail, but alludes frequently to the second tetralogy in discussing recent critical developments.

88. Champion, Larry S., comp. *The Essential Shakespeare: An Annotated Bibliography of Major Modern Studies.* Second edition. New York: G. K. Hall, 1993.

This bibliography attempts to provide "a convenient and annotated checklist of the most important criticism on Shakespeare in the twentieth century" (xiii). It includes 32 items in a general section on "The English History Plays" (143–53); 52 items on *1* and *2 Henry IV* (153–68); 26 items on *Henry V* (168–75); and 36 items on *Richard II* (197–208). The items on the individual plays are subdivided under the following categories: Reference Works; Editions; Textual Studies; Criticism. This edition deletes some useful items found in the first, 1986, edition.

89. Dutton, Richard. "The Second Tetralogy." In *Shakespeare: A Bibliographical Guide*, new edition, ed. Stanley Wells, 337-80. Oxford: The Clarendon Press, 1990.

This section of Wells's guide contains Dutton's brief introduction to each of the plays of the second tetralogy. Dutton traces critical trends and attitudes, including stage and film productions, from roughly the mid-twentieth century forward. Selected bibliographies of important studies on the plays are also provided (365-80).

90. Jenkins, Harold. "Shakespeare's History Plays: 1900-1951." *Shakespeare Survey* 6 (1953): 1-15.

Although examining no play in detail, this essay provides a useful summary of critical trends and developments in the study of Shakespeare's histories in the first half of the twentieth century. There are frequent allusions to the plays of the second tetralogy as they form a part of this development. The essay is extended by Dennis H. Burden (no. 87).

91. Sajdak, Bruce T., comp. *Shakespeare Index: An Annotated Bibliography of Critical Articles on the Plays 1959-1983*. 2 vols. Millwood, N.Y.: Kraus International Publications, 1992.

Volume 1 of this work, *Citations and Author Index*, contains 12 sections covering general topics about the plays, a section on the Apocrypha (covering *Sir Thomas More*, *Edward III*, and *The Two Noble Kinsmen*), and 35 sections on individual plays (the *Henry VI* plays being treated as one). *1 Henry IV* is covered in 1.345-65 (items V 1-178); *2 Henry IV* in 1.367-73 (items W 1-56); *Henry V* in 1.375-85 (items X 1-93); and *Richard II* in 1.623-37 (items NN 1-136). Volume 1 concludes with an "Author Index" (1.771-801). Volume 2, *Character, Scene, and Subject Indexes*, includes a highly detailed "Character Index" (2.803-1033) with ample subdivisions for aspects of character and a variety of other matters relating to character; a "Scene Index" (2.1035-1197) that goes through each play scene-by-scene and lists detailed aspects about each episode; and a massive "Subject Index" (2.1199-1765) that lists a vast array of topics about the plays. Only articles are included in Sajdak's bibliography; chapters in books are included only if they were also published separately as articles. The work ably fulfills Sajdak's purpose—i.e., to make it easier for readers to locate information "*on specific ideas, characters, or scenes*" (1.xi) amid thousands of possible sources.

III. RICHARD II

A. Editions.

92. Black, Matthew W., ed. *The Life and Death of King Richard the Second.* A New Variorum Edition of Shakespeare. Philadelphia: J. B. Lippincott Co., 1955.

This is the most comprehensive edition of the play, containing a diplomatic reprint of the F1 text of *Richard II*, fully collated against all textually important editions to 1954, and supplying detailed collation and commentary notes at the foot of each page that record all significant scholarship on textual and interpretive aspects of the play from the earliest times to the 1950s. The apparatus also includes full appendices on "The Text"; "The Date of Composition"; "The Authenticity of the Text"; "Dramatic Time"; "The Sources"; "Criticisms"; "Stage History"; and "Elizabeth, Essex, and *Richard II*." The sections on sources and criticisms are particularly useful, providing generous excerpts from major scholarly works in both categories. Black's variorum edition is an indispensable starting place for consideration of all textual, historical, and interpretive scholarship on the play up to 1954. A bibliographical supplement to this edition was published in 1977 (no. 145).

93. Gurr, Andrew, ed. *King Richard II.* The New Cambridge Shakespeare. Cambridge: Cambridge Univ. Press, 1984.

Gurr bases his text on Q1 (1597), with heavy reliance on the First Folio's alternative readings and stage directions. In his introduction (1–50), he fixes the date of composition as 1595, seeing the play as the deliberate launching of Shakespeare's second tetralogy; he further examines its relationship to Essex's political ambitions, considering particularly the publication in 1599 of Sir John Hayward's prose *Henry IV*, an apparently subversive history of Richard II that seemed to favor the Essex party. Gurr identifies Holinshed's *Chronicles*, the anonymous play *Woodstock*, Berners's translation of Froissart, and Daniel's *Civil Wars* as sources for the play, and is generally much more accepting of multiple influences on *Richard II* than is Ure (no. 95). He sees, again in contrast to Ure, the essence of the play's structure as "balance," locating this principle in its imagery, language, and action, and centering this balance in the two opposing characters of Richard and Bolingbroke. The original staging and dramaturgy of the play are treated extensively as a way of interpreting important scenes and gestures, and Gurr notes how the play's lack of movement, its ceremonial formality, and its emphasis on the throne as a stage property deepen and enrich its meanings. The introduction concludes with a brief but evidential stage history; appendices treat Shakespeare's use of Holinshed, and print extracts from Daniel, *The Homily Against Disobedience*, and *England's Parnassus*. Textual, glossarial, and critical notes appear at the foot of each page of text.

94. Muir, Kenneth, ed. *The Tragedy of King Richard the Second*. The Signet Classic Shakespeare. New York: Penguin, 1988.

This volume is essentially a reprint of Muir's 1963 Signet edition of *Richard II*, with the addition of new dramatic criticism and an updated bibliography, and begins with "Prefatory Remarks" on Shakespeare's life, career, and theatre by Sylvan Barnet (vii–xxi). Muir's introduction (xxiii–xxxvii) dates the composition of *Richard II* in 1595, situating it during the period of the composition of the Sonnets and emphasizing its heavy emphasis upon rhyme. Muir briefly surveys diverse opinions regarding the character of Richard, as well as the predominant religious tone of the play, linking the latter to Richard's development as a character and the concept of divine right. He sees Bolingbroke as a calculating politician, who contrasts with the witty and frivolous Richard, and also defends Shakespeare's drawing of minor characters, particularly York, Aumerle, and Mowbray, each of whom is briefly discussed as integral to the play. Three appendices to the text include a short "Textual Note," which discusses the early quarto and folio printings; a section on "The Sources of *Richard II*," which briefly treats backgrounds to the play and reprints a lengthy excerpt from Holinshed; and a section on "Commentaries," which includes excerpts from criticism on *Richard II* by Walter Pater (no. 66), Richard D. Altick (no. 106), Derek Traversi (no. 74), and Samuel Schoenbaum, as well as an original essay by Muir, "*Richard II* on Stage and Screen," which provides a thumbnail sketch of performances of the play from 1595 to 1986. A select bibliography of "Suggested References" completes the volume. Glossarial and explanatory notes appear at the foot of each page of text.

95. Ure, Peter, ed. *King Richard II*. The Arden Shakespeare. London: Methuen, 1956. Introduction, repr., in part, in Cubeta (no. 143).

Ure bases his text on Q1 (1597), with the First Folio supplying the deposition scene (4.1). In his monograph-length introduction (xiii–lxxxiii) he gives a thorough overview of problems relating to the text, and assigns a probable 1595 date for the composition of the play. He regards Holinshed's *Chronicles* as the primary source for *Richard II* and Daniel's *Civil Wars* as a probable influence; he is less sure of Shakespeare's supposed indebtedness to the anonymous play *Woodstock*, Berners's translation of Froissart, *The Mirror for Magistrates*, Créton's *Histoire*, and the anonymous *Traïson*, but does not completely dismiss their possible influence. Ure's critical remarks treat the metaphorical and emblematic significance of the garden scene (3.4) as well as the play's possible relation to Elizabeth's problems with Essex and the publication in 1599 of Sir John Hayward's *Henry IV*, a political treatise widely interpreted as favoring rebellion. Ure sees the design of the play as emphasizing Richard's tragedy rather than the struggle between two mighty opposites and affirms that the king's fall has nothing to do with his so-called "poetic" nature but rather with his failures as a ruler; Bolingbroke's taciturnity and hidden motives define him as a temperamental but not moral opposite to Richard. Printed as appendices are excerpts from Holinshed, Daniel, John Eliot's *Ortho-Epia Gallica,* and Joshua Sylvester's translation of Du Bartas. Textual, glossarial, and critical notes appear at the foot of each page of text.

B. Dating and Textual Studies.

96. Bergeron, David M. "The Deposition Scene in *Richard II.*" In *Renaissance Papers 1974,* ed. Dennis G. Donovan and A. Leigh DeNeef, 31–37. Durham, N.C.: The Southern Renaissance Conference, 1975.

Countering the opinion that part of the deposition scene (4.1.154–318) was censored from the 1597 and 1598 quartos of *Richard II* for political reasons, Bergeron conjectures that this segment of the scene was not written until sometime after 1601. He bases his conjecture not on textual evidence but on the belief that the scene in the earlier quartos makes perfect dramatic sense and that those supporting the unsuccessful Essex rebellion in 1601 would very likely have found the shorter version of the scene more suitable to their purposes than the expanded one.

See also nos. 92, 93, 94, 95.

C. Influences; Sources; Historical and Intellectual Backgrounds; Topicality.

97. Black, Matthew W. "The Sources of Shakespeare's *Richard II.*" In *Joseph Quincy Adams Memorial Studies,* ed. James G. McManaway, Giles E. Dawson, and Edwin E. Willoughby, 199–216. Washington, D.C.: The Folger Shakespeare Library, 1948.

Black's intention is to debunk the theory put forth by J. D. Wilson in his edition of *Richard II* (Cambridge: Cambridge Univ. Press, 1939) that Shakespeare's primary source for the play was a now lost drama on the reign of Richard. Black affirms that Shakespeare consulted a number of sources for *Richard II* (Holinshed, Hall, Froissart, Daniel, Créton, *Thomas of Woodstock,* and two versions of the *Chronique de la Traïson et Mort de Richart Deux Roy Dengle-terre*), and that he could easily have assimilated these sources—without having to rely on some earlier play—in preparing to write *Richard II.*

98. Gilman, Ernest B. "*Richard II* and the Perspectives of History." In *The Curious Perspective: Literary and Pictorial Wit in the Seventeenth Century,* 88–128. New Haven: Yale Univ. Press, 1978.

This study seeks to illustrate how displays of metaphysical wit in literature are similar to displays of visual wit in pictures or devices in Renaissance art that "manipulate the conventions of linear perspective to achieve ingenious effects"

(1). Gilman interprets the "seventeenth century" liberally to include such Shakespearean works as *Twelfth Night* and *A Midsummer Night's Dream* as well as *Richard II*. In his discussion of *Richard II*, Gilman treats the idea of "curious perspective" (i.e., optical trickery or paradox) as an important feature of Shakespeare's art; he emphasizes the way in which this technique can suggest simultaneous visual paradoxes (as in Hans Holbein's anamorphic painting *The Ambassadors*), and argues further that *Richard II* may be regarded "as a wedged contrariety that contains two opposed points of view" (97), neither certain, but both necessary to its full understanding. Gilman sees opposition and contrariety everywhere in the play, from the complex visual structure of the tournament scenes (1.1 and 1.3)—ironically paralleled later in the deposition scene (4.1) and in the Yorks' begging scene (5.3)—to the last three scenes (5.4, 5.5, and 5.6), which suggest darkly the repetition of the sin of Cain *and* the merciful redemption of England. For Gilman these two perspectives "comprise the play's two bodies, a spiritual and physical nature paradoxically incorporate in one dramatic form" (126).

99. Hexter, J. H. "Property, Monopoly, and Shakespeare's *Richard II*." In *Culture and Politics from Puritanism to the Enlightenment*, ed. Perez Zagorin, 1-24. Berkeley: Univ. of California Press, 1980.

Noting that Shakespeare found in Holinshed abundant examples of Richard II's unfitness and Bolingbroke's capability to rule, Hexter examines why the dramatist would de-emphasize these and focus instead upon "the legal forms of entry of a rightful heir into an estate held by military tenure" (8), as outlined in York's speech (2.1.201-4), to justify Bolingbroke's rebellion. He cites a 1603 law case (Allen v. Darcy) in which the legal prerogative of the monarch was determined *not* to extend to a subject's inheritance or inherited rights, among which was included the right to make a living. Hexter further suggests that a typical audience at the Globe would have been extremely sensitive to this issue because of perceived monopolistic threats to their livelihoods and hence to their inheritances; thus in providing Bolingbroke with a motive for deposing Richard, Shakespeare played adroitly upon the topical concerns of London playgoers.

100. Kantorowicz, Ernst H. "Shakespeare: King Richard II." In *The King's Two Bodies: A Study in Mediaeval Political Theology*, 24-41. Princeton: Princeton Univ. Press, 1957. Repr. in Brooke (no. 141) and in Newlin (no. 144).

This book is an extended study of the legal fiction of "the King's Two Bodies" (i.e., the simultaneous presence in the royal person of a semi-divine Body Politic and a natural Body Personal), which examines in detail the philosophical, religious, and cultural background to this prevailing idea from the middle ages through the Renaissance. Regarding the concept of "the King's Two Bodies" as basic to an understanding of *Richard II*, Kantorowicz examines three major scenes: (3.2) on the Welsh coast; (3.3) at Flint Castle; and (4.1) at Westminster. He sees the first as one in which Richard begins as a godlike embodiment of the Body Politic but gradually becomes a figure of common manhood and mortality; the same movement occurs at Flint Castle, but in this case with more intensity since here Shakespeare depicts Richard as a stereotypical Fool, thus reducing him to a wretchedness beneath even that of mere man. For Kantorowicz, the episode at Westminster signals a new low in Richard's fortunes, for now he comes to realize that he has been (unlike Christ) a traitor to himself, a realization poignantly evoked in the mirror episode (4.1.275ff.), where the shattered glass represents the breaking apart of any possible duality of being. Kantorowicz's short chapter is of seminal importance to many later interpretations of *Richard II*.

101. Liebler, Naomi Conn. "The Mockery King of Snow: *Richard II* and the Sacrifice of Ritual." In *True Rites and Maimed Rites: Ritual and Anti-Ritual in Shakespeare and His Age*, ed. Linda Woodbridge and Edward [I.] Berry, 220–39. Urbana: Univ. of Illinois Press, 1992.

Liebler examines the tournament scenes (1.1 and 1.3) in light of changing attitudes in Richard II's time toward ritual combat, and sees these episodes reflecting a civilization whose rituals and ceremonies are in the process of moving from meaningful events into less meaningful outward shows. She sees this "crisis of ritual" (225) as characteristic of the play generally, and cites Richard's ceremonial "decoronation" in the presence of his supporters (3.3.147–53) and later before Bolingbroke (4.1.203–15), as well as York's description of Bolingbroke's entry into London and Richard's disgrace (5.2.23–36), as "instances of rituals aborted, inverted, and finally rejected in favor of a new order, which in turn, proved more disordered than Richard's" (226). Throughout, Liebler regards Richard as the last real defender of an ancient system of ritual and values being debased by Bolingbroke and his followers.

102. MacKenzie, Clayton G. "Paradise and Paradise Lost in *Richard II*." *Shakespeare Quarterly* 37 (1986): 318–39.

Drawing upon the commonplace notion in the moral and religious writings of the Renaissance of new life springing from death, MacKenzie explores how Shakespeare situates the related notion of England as a second paradise (and its "anti-mythology," the fallen paradise) in a distinctly earthly context. He argues that the term "paradise" in *Richard II* refers to an enclosure of some sort—in this case an enclosure surrounded by the sea, as personified by Neptune, a figure depicted in the play as both protecting and assaulting the island. For MacKenzie the postlapsarian world of *Richard II* is one in which physical and spiritual life are no longer complementary, and this condition is apparent in Shakespeare's use of an "anti-mythology" of paradise lost to counter the pervading English model; the most "arresting figure" in this context is that of Death, personified by Richard himself as an "antic jester" who "confirms an Hebraic scheme of the fallen world" (333, 338). The essay is highly allusive, referring throughout to the iconographical, moral, theological, and historical backgrounds to *Richard II*.

103. Nuttall, A. D. "Ovid's Narcissus and Shakespeare's Richard II: The Reflected Self." In *Ovid Renewed: Ovidian Influences on Literature and Art from* *the Middle Ages to the Twentieth Century*, ed. Charles Martindale, 137–50. Cambridge: Cambridge Univ. Press, 1988.

In exploring the relationship between Ovid's story of Narcissus (in Book III of the *Metamorphoses*) and *Richard II*, Nuttall focuses upon the way in which both Narcissus and Richard objectify the self in order to become fully conscious of it and to acquire self-knowledge—Narcissus by gazing on his image in the pool, and Richard by viewing his reflection in the mirror (4.1.276–91). In each case, Nuttall argues, the objectification of the self frustrates the "elaborate gestures of self-love and self-glorification" (149) indulged in by each figure: for Narcissus the image in the pool expresses the impossibility of neutral introspection; for Richard the image in the mirror provokes a brief and unendurable moment of painful self-knowledge.

104. Schell, Edgar. "*Richard II* and Some Forms of Theatrical Time." *Comparative Drama* 24 (1990): 255–69.

Schell examines the scene in which Richard seizes Bolingbroke's lands (2.1) in an attempt to counter the view that Bolingbroke is duplicitous—an idea he claims is erroneously based on the assumption that the duke is depicted here as already returning to England *before* he learns of his confiscated patrimony. In Schell's view, 2.1 is strongly indebted to medieval plays like the Fleury *Slaughter of the Innocents* and *The Castle of Perseverance*, where the future and the past are "*laid over*" the present (256); in *Richard II* Shakespeare uses a similar temporal "layering" (257) to represent Bolingbroke not as deceptive, but rather (in a departure from his source in Holinshed) as a figure slowly lured—in part by Richard himself—into claiming the crown.

105. Thompson, Karl F. "Richard II, Martyr." *Shakespeare Quarterly* 8 (1957): 159–66.

Thompson sees the "martyrdom" of Richard as different from the orthodox martyrdom of the believer who testifies to his faith and then dies assured of salvation; rather, Richard's "martyrdom" is analogous to those found in Foxe's *Book of Martyrs*, where the faithful die nobly while their persecutors feel God's retributive justice in the here and now. In Thompson's view, this sense of God's justice manifesting itself in earthly time and space provides an important moral context for the later plays of the tetralogy.

See also nos. 92, 93, 94, 95, 96, 108, 111, 115, 117, 118, 120, 121, 124, 126, 129, 131, 143.

D. Language and Linguistics.

106. Altick, Richard D. "Symphonic Imagery in *Richard II*." *PMLA* 62 (1947): 339–65. Repr. in Muir (no. 94), in Brooke (no. 141), in Newlin (no. 144), and, in part, in Cubeta (no. 143).

This essay examines in detail the complex interaction of repetitive words and imagery in *Richard II*, comparing this iteration to leitmotivs in music that evoke powerful imaginative and emotional responses. Altick discusses the thematic and structural significance of the following patterns of allusion: 1) earth, land, and ground; 2) gardens; 3) blood; 4) sun and blushing; 5) weeping; 6) speech; 7) snakes and venom; 8) illness and bodily injury; 9) blots and stains; 10) sourness and sweetness; 11) generation and inheritance; and 12) jewels and the crown. Throughout, Altick treats these strands of imagery both independently and in relation to each other, stressing the sense of structural and harmonic design they impart to the play. The essay is a seminal study of the artistic unity of *Richard II*.

107. Baxter, John. *Shakespeare's Poetic Styles: Verse Into Drama.* London: Routledge & Kegan Paul, 1980.

Drawing upon Yvor Winters's notion that the "plain style" was central to the formation of the English Renaissance lyric, Baxter seeks to apply Winters's ideas (and the refinements worked upon them by J. V. Cunningham) to English Renaissance drama. In addition to an opening chapter on the process of turning verse into drama, a second chapter on Fulke Greville's *Mustapha* examined in light of Sidney's *Defence of Poetry*, and a final chapter on *Macbeth*, seven of Baxter's ten chapters (chaps. 3-9, pp. 46-195) are devoted to *Richard II*. In his extended discussion of the play, Baxter describes a wide range of poetic styles in *Richard II*, most notably the plain style (which tends to focus upon moral perception) and the golden or Petrarchan style (which tends to focus upon the presentation of feeling); the latter is by far the more subtly expressive of the two, but unless joined to the moral weight of the plain style can easily degenerate into "the libertine golden style" (120), irresponsibly detached from reality, that Richard assumes for much of the play. Baxter maintains that out of the plain and golden styles develop two additional styles (a "metaphysical" and a "Shakespearean"), the latter being a golden enhancement of the former, just as the golden is an enhancement of the plain; to each of these enhancements of the plain style, however, the plain style is fundamental. Applying these various stylistic permutations to the play, Baxter finds the poetic styles of Richard, Bolingbroke, and York to be either evasive or limited: Richard uses rhetorical libertinism to deflect reality; Bolingbroke's reductive style of golden speech is blunt and pleasant but lacking in moral sincerity; and York's plain moralisms are insufficient to confront a complex moral world. In Baxter's view, only Gaunt possesses a style which, by virtue of its connection with the moral values that "give order to human lives" (104), is able to express a genuine sense of the tragic. Throughout his highly detailed study, Baxter is at great pains to distinguish among the various types of rhetorical styles used by a single character—sometimes in a single passage—and the various modes of perception or the moral complexities these styles suggest. The book is the most detailed analysis available of the rhetorical styles of *Richard II*.

108. Friedman, Donald M. "John of Gaunt and the Rhetoric of Frustration." *ELH* 43 (1976): 279-99.

Friedman challenges the notion that *Richard II* supports orthodox Tudor doctrine, and argues his case with detailed attention to the rhetoric of Gaunt's dying speech (2.1). He sees Gaunt's speech as embodying the sense of frustration in the play generally over the dissolving connection between sign or word and the object signified, and notes further that the rhetorical figure of auxesis (the succession of examples leading to a climactic point) fails to come when expected, but instead gives way to Gaunt's frustrated outburst over the leasing out of England. In Friedman's view, Gaunt's anger and frustration derive largely from his feudal belief that the nobility own the land—a view Bolingbroke also shares; the play thus becomes a highly problematic text that constantly reminds us of the gap between the sign and the thing signified, and that further expresses frustration over the "dissolution of the bonds between value and that which is valued" (296). The argument also alludes to possible sources for Gaunt's speech, most notably Du Bartas's *Creation du Monde* as it appears in English translations by John Eliot and Joshua Sylvester.

109. Harris, Kathryn Montgomery. "Sun and Water Imagery in *Richard II*: Its Dramatic Function." *Shakespeare Quarterly* 21 (1970): 157–65.

The argument here is that images of the sun (including fire) and water (including sea, river, rain, etc.) serve as opposing metaphors for 1) the conflict in the play between Richard and Bolingbroke, and 2) Richard's ensuing loss and discovery of self. Harris demonstrates that during the early sequences Richard is associated with the sun and Bolingbroke with water, while the pattern reverses itself as the play proceeds, the key transitional moment being Richard's weeping during the deposition scene (4.1).

110. Heninger, S. K., Jr. "The Sun-King Analogy in *Richard II*." *Shakespeare Quarterly* 11 (1960): 319–27.

Heninger contends that the essential dramatic tension of *Richard II* inheres in its juxtaposition of an ideal order with the inability of man to fulfill the terms of that order, and further that this tension is tellingly underscored by Shakespeare's use of cosmological imagery, particularly that of the sun-king. He sees this metaphor functioning in three important ways: 1) as a symbol of royal prerogative passing from Richard to Bolingbroke; 2) as a mirror revealing the deficiencies of the old and the new king; and 3) as a rhetorical device signaling Richard's transition from villain to sympathetic victim.

111. Maveety, Stanley R. "A Second Fall of Cursed Man: The Bold Metaphor in *Richard II*." *Journal of English and Germanic Philology* 72 (1973): 175–93.

Maveety sees the overriding "bold metaphor" of *Richard II* as that of the Fall, and proceeds to examine the play in light of the Genesis narratives of the fall of Adam and the murder of Abel by Cain. Linking this overriding metaphor with a series of "image clusters" including blood, exile, speech, the serpent, plant-life, gardening, the earth, fertility, birth, and inheritance, Maveety argues that the effect of this tissue of allusion is to underscore the flawed characters of *both* Richard and Bolingbroke, and further to suggest the disastrous consequences of their actions: "a curse visited upon a land and a race of men" (191). He sees the crux of the play not in the conflict between the personalities of Richard and Bolingbroke, but rather in the dire consequences of the "Cain-like" murder of a king who is himself guilty of the "Cain-like" murder of the Duke of Gloucester.

112. Potter, Lois. "The Antic Disposition of Richard II." *Shakespeare Survey* 27 (1974): 33-41.

Potter takes issue with conventionally sympathetic readings of Richard, arguing that he is a rhetorician of considerable strength rather than weakness, and "rather less virtuous than has often been thought, and, just for that reason, a 'better' dramatic character" (33). She sees him as exhibiting irony and duplicity throughout the play, most notably in his enigmatic and arbitrary responses to Mowbray and Bolingbroke at the tournament (1.3), but also later during the deposition scene (4.1), where he uses highly ambiguous language to avoid complying with Bolingbroke's demands; indeed at the end of the scene he actually opens the way for a conspiracy against Bolingbroke by making it clear to all present that he is really *not* willing to resign the crown. Potter sees Richard's language and rhetoric functioning in the play to reveal him as not merely a victimized king of sorrows, but also a "sharp-tongued, self-mocking, and quite unresigned" (40) manipulator of others.

113. Suzman, Arthur. "Imagery and Symbolism in *Richard II*." *Shakespeare Quarterly* 7 (1956): 355-70.

This essay examines how the action of *Richard II* and its iterative imagery of rise and fall coalesce to suggest symbolic meaning. Suzman traces this pattern of imagery throughout the play, but focuses particularly on the tournament scenes (1.1 and 1.3), the episode at Flint Castle (3.3), and the deposition scene (4.1). He contends that after 4.1 the imagery of rise and fall no longer indicates Richard's demise, but reflects the "spiritual transformation in the two central characters in the play" (365) as Richard rises in our esteem and Bolingbroke declines. Suzman's essay is more of a catalogue of every conceivable allusion to the rise and fall pattern than a critical elaboration upon it, but is nonetheless useful as a starting place for any consideration of this important feature of the play.

See also nos. 93, 94, 102, 114, 117, 122, 133, 134, 135, 136.

E. Criticism.

114. Berger, Harry, Jr. "Psychoanalyzing the Shakespeare Text: The First Three Scenes of the *Henriad*." In *Shakespeare and the Question of Theory*, ed. Patricia Parker and Geoffrey Hartman, 210-29. New York: Methuen, 1985. Repr. in Bloom (no. 140).

This essay seeks to correlate psychoanalytic criticism with political and metatheatrical criticism by focusing upon the father/son conflicts raised in 1.1,

1.2, and 1.3. Berger sees his critical project as "doggedly textual in orientation" and thus "*anti*theatrical" (213), and further regards the text as "performing a critique of mimesis ... in the very act of producing a mimesis" (214). His method is to provide exhaustive close readings of the three opening scenes of *Richard II*, stressing how their rhetoric hides, mystifies, or justifies motives other than those expressed; he thus reads Bolingbroke's speech (1.1.104-8, 187-95) and the Duchess of Gloucester's remarks (1.2.25-36, 44-57) as implying that Gaunt has been displaced (even "deposed") by Bolingbroke, and Gaunt's speech during the tournament (1.3.237-46) as revealing the fear and guilt of a bad father who has betrayed his son. Berger also sees Bolingbroke's accusation of Mowbray as a means of psychological displacement by which he manages both to accuse Richard and to rebuke his father, and further maintains that "the most fundamental process" of *Richard II* is this very transformation of conflict from subterranean hiddenness to the "safety" of "ritualized combat and behavior" (227). Although Berger does admit that the repressed power of the play may be felt in performance, he believes that its real "fury, splendor, frustration, and politics can only be understood and evaluated by the excavation that psychoanalyzes the text" (229).

115. Black, James. "The Interlude of the Beggar and the King in *Richard II*." In *Pageantry in the Shakespearean Theater*, ed. David Bergeron, 104-13. Athens, Ga.: Univ. of Georgia Press, 1985.

Black disputes Zitner's contention (no. 132) that the Aumerle episodes (5.2 and 5.3) mock the seriousness of *Richard II*; rather he sees these two scenes—particularly the moment in which Bolingbroke refers to York's entreaties as a scene from "The Beggar and the King" (5.3.79-80)—as heightening the seriousness of the rest of the play by contrast. Examining the action of *Richard II* against the background of the medieval cycle plays as well as the Elizabethan masque, Black stresses how 5.3 causes us to reconsider the "ceremonials of kingship and grief that precede it" (112), especially since it rhetorically echoes the deposition scene (4.1), where questions of kingship and begging also figure prominently.

116. Bogard, Travis. "Shakespeare's Second Richard." *PMLA* 70 (1955): 192-209.

Operating on the premise that the "imperfect" earlier pieces of a writer help to illuminate both his mature work and his process of composition, Bogard examines *Richard II* as a play in which Shakespeare "first became himself" (192). He compares the technique of *Richard II* with that of *Richard III*, seeing the earlier play as an example of "explicit" drama—that is, a play that sets forth its meanings by explanatory statements rather than by "implicitly" embedding those meanings into its overall dramatic patterns. Bogard sees Shakespeare in *Richard II* moving uncertainly from "explicit" to "implicit" modes of representation, even claiming that Richard's shattering of the mirror (4.1.288) marks the place where both character and dramatist abandon the old "external manner of lamenting" for the deeper and unseen expression of true grief (208).

117. Brockbank, Philip. "*Richard II* and the Music of Men's Lives." *Leeds Studies in English*, n.s., 14 (1983): 57-73.

Brockbank is concerned with the development of action in *Richard II*, particularly its relationship to theatrical ceremony and "verbal music" (61). Citing Jean Bodin's *Six Books of a Commonweale* (trans. 1606) as a possible influence on the play, he focuses on 1.1, 1.3, 4.1, and 5.1, arguing that certain ceremonies of government that begin the play in decorous fashion (like the tournament [1.3]) become impotent and farcical at the end (like the Duke and Duchess of York's pleading with Bolingbroke [5.3]). He sees this evolution as a "dissolving false order" (67) that intensifies with the awareness that the king's authority is merely a show; but he also contends that the politically empty ceremonials of the play can retain a powerful degree of emotional solace for those who engage in them, most notably Richard himself. At dramatic moments like the scene of Richard's death (5.5), Brockbank argues, Shakespeare's imaginative art "puts political disorder into a satisfying verbal order" (72); out of an historical episode of bad government the playwright fashions a good play, making history (however provisionally) yield to dramatic form.

118. Elliott, John R., Jr. "History and Tragedy in *Richard II.*" *SEL: Studies in English Literature 1500-1900* 8 (1968): 253-71.

This essay uses *Richard II* to explore the history play as a dramatic genre. Elliott notes that Shakespeare's sources offered him conflicting perspectives on events, and that he seems to have preferred Holinshed's view to Hall's, thus giving a more balanced—and more political—slant to the action, particularly as regards the prerogatives of kingship and the right of rebellion. Arguing for an explicitly political dimension to *Richard II*, Elliott sees this quality reflected in the ongoing conflict between Richard and Bolingbroke—a conflict that also informs the structure of the play by focusing on the successive stages by which Bolingbroke threatens, captures, and retains the crown. In this scheme York and Gaunt are key figures, since their reactions to Richard mark important stages in the play's structure, which, instead of containing the finality of pure tragedy, contains the open, episodic, and contingent rhythms of history.

119. Folland, Harold F. "King Richard's Pallid Victory." *Shakespeare Quarterly* 24 (1973): 390-99.

The primary focus here is on how Richard, despite the readiness with which he delivers the crown to Bolingbroke, achieves a sort of moral victory in the deposition scene (4.1) by shrewdly passing on to his successor a diminished sense of royal power. Folland demonstrates how Richard, first at Flint Castle (3.3) and later more trenchantly in the deposition scene (4.1), makes it clear to Bolingbroke that a usurper cannot be both a king and legitimately king. Throughout, Folland emphasizes Richard's rhetorical and theatrical ability to make himself seem the victim of ruthless power; even in his death he leaves the new king with "an appalled realization" (399) of guilt that plagues him throughout his career.

120. French, A. L. "Who Deposed Richard the Second?" *Essays in Criticism* 17 (1967): 411-33.

French's contention is that the widespread assumption on the part of critics that Richard is deposed is "not wholly borne out by the text of the play" (413); his sympathetic reading of the character of Bolingbroke focuses upon 3.2, 3.3, and 4.1 as crucial scenes indicating that Richard brings his fall upon himself. French attributes ambiguities regarding Bolingbroke's motives to Shakespeare's careless artistry rather than to any disingenuousness on the part of the character, even going so far as to suggest that Shakespeare started to write a play about a king who abdicates, then changed his mind and introduced a series of confusing references to "deposition" that essentially express Richard's view of events but not those of the play. Underlying the whole argument is a challenge to Tillyard's providential reading of *Richard II* (no. 35), particularly the idea that the two tetralogies demonstrate God's punishment for the sin of deposing a lawful king. In "The Critical Forum" section of *Essays in Criticism* 18 (1968): 225-33, Peter Ure disputes the argument and French replies.

121. Gaudet, Paul. "The 'Parasitical' Counselors in Shakespeare's *Richard II*: A Problem in Dramatic Interpretation." *Shakespeare Quarterly* 33 (1982): 142-54.

Noting the almost universal depiction of Bushy, Bagot, and Green in the chronicles and in the anonymous play *Woodstock* as parasitical, Gaudet affirms that such a view need not be Shakespeare's or that of his audience for *Richard II*. He argues, rather, that the three characters are faithful if passive servants to the king, seen as evil only by Richard's enemies; they thus become "dramatic reflectors" through which Shakespeare manipulates audience response to the main contending forces in the play while reinforcing its "ambivalent mode of experience" (154).

122. Halvorson, John. "The Lamentable Comedy of Richard II." *English Literary Renaissance* 24 (1994): 343-69.

The argument here is that *Richard II* cannot be generically contained by the traditional genres of tragedy or history; rather it is a comedy on the order of the theatre of the absurd that mocks its own rhetoric (particularly Richard's), trivializes ceremony, and presents treason as farcical. Halvorson takes up virtually every important scene in the play in arguing that Richard exposes his own ridiculousness through an absurd use of language (especially from the third act on), and also denies that the king goes through any process of growth or self-knowledge. For Halvorson, the play undermines not only Richard himself but also the principle of divine right that he represents; thus it becomes a highly subversive dramatic text.

123. Hapgood, Robert. "Three Eras in *Richard II*." *Shakespeare Quarterly* 14 (1963): 281-83.

In disputing Peter G. Phialas's claim that *Richard II* contrasts the reign of Richard with that of Edward III (no. 128), Hapgood argues that the play looks backward to the past *and* forward to the future. He posits "three eras" in

Richard II, each represented by a single royal figure: Edward, Richard, and Henry IV. Hapgood argues that in Edward's time ceremony and other traditional values functioned as part of an integral social harmony, while in Richard's time this harmony devolves into mere appearances devoid of meaning; in Henry's time ceremony disguises action, for during his reign the status of the king depends upon adroit manipulation of popular opinion.

124. Mack, Maynard, Jr. "This Royal Throne Unkinged." In *Killing the King: Three Studies in Shakespeare's Tragic Structure*, 15-74. New Haven: Yale Univ. Press, 1973. Repr., in part, in Bloom (no. 140).

This study consists of three extended essays on *Richard II*, *Hamlet*, and *Macbeth*, treating regicide in its political, religious, social, personal, and metaphysical contexts. In his chapter on *Richard II*, Mack suggests that the play places Gaunt's nostalgic view of kingship as vigorous Christian service in opposition to Bolingbroke's new model of "expedient realism" (34); Richard's behavior is consistently ineffective and conforms fully to neither view, but as the play proceeds the king grows into a figure of sympathy and complexity—especially in the deposition scene (4.1), where he emerges as "*both* king and rebel, both traitor and betrayed" (61). Mack sees Richard's imaginative role-playing at Pomfret Castle (5.5.31-41) as an attempt to assess the spiritual, political, and psychological aspects of man, each of which he finds wanting; the king's death signals the defeat of Gaunt's nostalgic vision of kingship, which ironically lives on as a deeply rooted ideal that Bolingbroke, and even his more successful son Henry V, cannot fully embody.

125. McMillin, Scott. "Shakespeare's *Richard II*: Eyes of Sorrow, Eyes of Desire." *Shakespeare Quarterly* 35 (1984): 40-52.

Using Bushy's speech to the queen (2.2.14-27) and York's description of Richard at the end of the play (5.2.12-20) as a frame for his essay, McMillin explores the problem of seeing and identity in *Richard II*. He is particularly concerned with the ways in which Shakespeare tries to make the "normally hidden" (e.g., hollowness, absence, or loss) "a matter of perception in the theatre" (43), and considers Richard's smashing of the mirror (4.1.288) and his prison soliloquy (5.5.1-66) as dramatic heightenings of the issue of a king who longs to remain unseen. McMillin regards Richard's parting from his queen as a futile attempt to seek a literary form to manifest inward grief, unlike York's (and the citizens') viewing of Bolingbroke (5.2), which acknowledges the forward movement of history away from the lost and unseen.

126. Moore, Jeanie Grant. "Queen of Sorrow, King of Grief: Reflections and Perspectives in *Richard II*." In *In Another Country: Feminist Perspectives on Renaissance Drama*, ed. Dorothea Kehler and Susan Baker, 19-35. Metuchen, N.J.: The Scarecrow Press, 1991.

This essay focuses upon Queen Isabel, seeing her "as a mirror and as a perspective glass through which we may view the drama," and connecting this "perspective metaphor ... to a feminist view disclosing a subtext of political ambiguity beneath the formal pageantry of the play" (20). Moore examines how the mirror and perspective glass both reflect and distort reality, and relates this phenomenon to the status of Renaissance women generally, and Isabel particularly, as oblique and subversive reflections of men. She sees the Queen—in her repeated weeping, in her infrequency of appearance, and even in her childlessness, which ironically brings forth Bolingbroke as metaphorical heir to the kingdom—as an oblique yet palpable reflection of Richard's "nothingness"; thus Isabel, who at first appears to be "nothing," gradually becomes "something" by her perspectivist reflection of Richard's tragedy (32).

127. Nevo, Ruth. "*Richard II.*" In *Tragic Form in Shakespeare*, 59–95. Princeton: Princeton Univ. Press, 1972. Repr. in Bloom (no. 140).

This study examines *Romeo and Juliet, Julius Caesar, Hamlet, Othello, Macbeth, King Lear, Antony and Cleopatra,* and *Coriolanus* in addition to *Richard II*, and focuses on the structure of tragedy, particularly the progress of the tragic hero through the following stages of development: "challenge, temptation or dilemma, disintegration, and despair to the final recognition in which all that was hidden is revealed, and self and destiny fully and finally confronted" (30). Nevo traces the action of *Richard II* through these successive stages, emphasizing (in highly detailed and evidential discussions of individual passages) how Richard's demise produces an acute and poignant self-awareness—but not, as many critics contend, a self-awareness associated with weakness, since his tragic progress leads to the prison scene at Pomfret (5.5), where we see him bearing witness to "his own personal self-definition, to some distinctive form of human integrity, some inalienable individual perception of value of which his life is the gauge" (89). Even in his moment of utmost dispossession, Nevo argues, Richard finds within himself a willed defiance finally redemptive of folly and vanity.

128. Phialas, Peter G. "The Medieval in *Richard II.*" *Shakespeare Quarterly* 12 (1961): 305–10.

Phialas disagrees with the view of Tillyard (no. 35) that the world of *Richard II* is one in which means are more important than ends. He argues further that the play looks to the past with a sense of longing, particularly the past as represented by the storied reign of Edward III, a stark contrast to the devitalized England of Richard's time; the Duchess of Gloucester, York, and Gaunt all evoke this happier past, thus highlighting the contrast between the Black Prince and his ineffective son. The argument is in part disputed by Robert Hapgood (no. 123).

129. Sanders, Wilbur. "Shakespeare's Political Agnosticism: *Richard II.*" In *The Dramatist and the Received Idea: Studies in the Plays of Marlowe and Shakespeare*, 158–93. Cambridge: Cambridge Univ. Press, 1968.

Sanders's critical agenda here is to question the docile historicism that simplifies the complex relationship of art to culture by insisting upon neat orthodoxies or stable "world pictures"; he probes the relationship of the artist to the "received ideas" of his culture in extended essays on *Richard III, Macbeth,* and *Richard II*, as well as on Marlowe's *The Massacre at Paris*, *The Jew of Malta*, *Edward II*, and *Doctor Faustus*. In his chapter on *Richard II*, Sanders argues that a climate of moral obscurity pervades the play, and that no character seems able to preserve his integrity amidst the threatening realities of political life; Bolingbroke is a sort of moral cipher, betraying no sense of commitment beyond that of public resourcefulness, while Richard is a creature of severe emotional and political deficiencies who attempts to stage-manage a reality he does not wish to understand. For Sanders the proper word for the prevailing climate of the play is "agnosticism"—a view of life that reveals the old order in its death throes, its moral and religious certainties giving way to the idea of "Necessity" as represented in new men like Bolingbroke and Northumberland (193).

130. Stirling, Brents. "Bolingbroke's 'Decision.'" *Shakespeare Quarterly* 2 (1951): 27–34. Repr. in Newlin (no. 144).

Stirling emphasizes the structural and thematic importance of the episode at Flint Castle (3.3), where Richard advocates his own deposition and Bolingbroke agrees to it. For Stirling this is the first of three pivotal moments in *Richard II* where Bolingbroke makes "a decisive step" (34), the other two occurring at the end of the deposition scene (4.1), where he sends Richard to the Tower, and in the Exton episode at the end of the play (5.6), where he disowns Exton's murder of the king; in each of these episodes Bolingbroke openly reveals his duplicity—"taciturnity marked by sudden revelations of shifting purpose" (33).

131. Ure, Peter. "The Looking-Glass of *Richard II*." *Philological Quarterly* 34 (1955): 219–24.

Noting that the mirror was traditionally associated with both truth-telling *and* flattery, Ure argues that when Richard sees his image in the glass during the deposition scene (4.1.265–67) the glass both deceives and instructs him, for his "recognition of the mirror's falsity" paradoxically enables him "to perceive the truth about himself" (223). For Ure, Richard's smashing of the mirror, although symbolizing his repudiation of *Vanitas*, is ultimately a desperate act of self-annulment—the tragic action of a man who finally recognizes no middle ground between kingship and non-being.

132. Zitner, Sheldon P. "Aumerle's Conspiracy." *SEL: Studies in English Literature 1500–1900* 14 (1974): 239–57.

Noting the tendency of directors to cut the "Aumerle" scenes (5.2 and 5.3) from *Richard II*, and of literary critics to see them as inferior, Zitner attempts to reassess their thematic and tonal importance: they are "fully intended farce, sometimes roaring, sometimes savage, but farce with such salt and savor as to distress the taste for pageant, pathos, and elevated death the play otherwise appeals to and satisfies" (243–44). Zitner emphasizes the "harsh geriatric slapstick" (248) of 5.2, particularly what he regards as the cruel humor of the aged York trying to put on his riding boots while his angry wife shouts at him and then insultingly follows him to court; this same sense of the comic and the pathetic continues in 5.3, where the blend of doggerel and comic absurdity recalls the Pyramus and Thisbe episode from *A Midsummer Night's Dream* (5.1). Zitner sees in the abrupt tonal changes produced by 5.2 and 5.3 a growing disaffection on Shakespeare's part with historical tragedy, especially its capacity for truth: "In the Aumerle scenes, in short, are the origins of Falstaff" (256).

F. Stage History; Performance Criticism.

133. Berger, Harry, Jr. *Imaginary Audition: Shakespeare on Stage and Page.* Berkeley: Univ. of California Press, 1989.

Part one of Berger's study, "Against New Histrionicism" (3–42), attacks the sort of performance-based criticism of Shakespeare that advocates the immediate, trustworthy, and supposedly unbiased reactions of an audience in the theatre over the considered opinions of literary critics who formulate their interpretive responses by *reading* rather than *viewing* plays. In Berger's scheme, Richard Levin's critique of "slit-eyed analysis" (*New Readings vs. Old Plays: Recent Trends in the Reinterpretation of English Renaissance Drama* [Chicago: Univ. of Chicago Press, 1979]) and Gary Taylor's defense of "wide-eyed play-going" (*Moment by Moment by Shakespeare* [London: Macmillan, 1985]) serve to advance the "New Histrionicism" that disparages "armchair" interpretation of drama (xiv). In opposition to critics like Levin and Taylor, Berger argues for a sort of critical *via media* that reaffirms the legitimacy of "text-centered reading" but seeks to incorporate into it the "interlocutory politics and theatrical features of performed drama" (xiv). Part two, "Imaginary Audition in *Richard II*" (45–137), is Berger's attempt to follow this critical agenda, with specific reference to two episodes from the play: the deposition scene (4.1) and the scene of Richard's return to England (3.2). As regards 4.1, Berger draws upon speech-act theory to insist that here Richard's resourceful speech acts allow him to affirm his power over Bolingbroke even as he claims to be losing it, for he so manages the scene as to make Bolingbroke "the double, the shadow, the spiritual son and scapegoat who carries off [his] guilt and self-affright" (73). As regards 3.2, Berger attempts to counter the notion that Richard's overt theatricality here is that of a mere *poseur*; rather he is a master of "interlocutory" politics whose rhetorical panache "demands a finely-tuned but flexible deployment of the auditory imagination" (75). For Berger this "complexity of audition" (75) lies at the heart of our appreciation of Richard; indeed the character's "self-auscultation" (76) accounts for the success and power of the play. Throughout the discussion Berger emphasizes how Richard's rhetorical acts are essentially *performative* in nature and powerful in their real effect on himself and on others. The book concludes with an "Epilogue" (139–56) in which Berger reiterates that his stage-centered reading of the play derives not from "unmediated performance" but from "the graphic inscription of texts" (143). The argument is crammed with evidential and illuminating close readings of various lines from 4.1 and 3.2, and amounts to a complete rethinking of the purported "weakness" of Richard's theatrical character.

134. Brown, John Russell. "Narrative and Focus: *Richard II.*" In *Shakespeare's*

Plays in Performance, 115–30. London: Edward Arnold, 1966. Repr. in Brooke (no. 141) and in Newlin (no. 144).

In addition to the essay on *Richard II*, this study includes extensive essays on *Hamlet, Romeo and Juliet,* and *Twelfth Night* as well as ten additional essays on various aspects of Shakespearean production. Brown sees *Richard II* as a play that shifts artfully from scenes of wide focus to scenes of more intimate focus, thus providing a "stage-picture ... at once comprehensive and subtle" (119). He examines repeatedly the ways in which Shakespeare manipulates figures on stage to direct the audience's focus or visual perspective, at times highlighting either Bolingbroke or Richard to make a thematic point *dramatically* by the use of gesture, stage position, speech, silence, and the like. The essay examines virtually every major episode in *Richard II*, emphasizing the play as a subtly interwoven theatrical whole. For Brown, the "visual and formal language" of the play can affect an audience unconsciously, and "suggest vast implications" that "awaken a response without limiting it by definition, declaration or propaganda" (130). Brown's essay is an early and influential study of the dramatic artistry of the play.

135. Gielgud, John. "*King Richard the Second.*" In *Stage Directions*, 28–35. London: Heinemann, 1963. Repr. in Brooke (no. 141) and in Newlin (no. 144).

Gielgud approaches the play (and specifically the character of Richard) from the perspective of an actor who has played the role; he sees the play as essentially ceremonial, and Richard as a callous but highly sensitive figure who becomes more sympathetic as the action proceeds. He further discusses the actor's problem of portraying these outward qualities of Richard while also attending to the subtlety of Shakespeare's language and the "infinite shades of colour and tempo" it imparts to the "intricate nature" of the character (30). Gielgud touches briefly upon the roles of many of the characters in *Richard II*, noting that in performance the play must be "finely orchestrated, melodious, youthful, headlong, violent and vivid" (34); the greatest difficulty that the play presents in performance is the quality of the verse, which each actor must try to render in its full musicality while still remaining faithful to the individual character. The essay first appeared as the introduction to the Folio Society edition of the play (London: The Folio Society, 1958).

136. McGuire, Philip C. "Choreography and Language in *Richard II.*" In *Shakespeare: The Theatrical Dimension*, ed. Philip C. McGuire and David A. Samuelson, 61–84. New York: AMS Press, 1979.

The emphasis here is on how the rhetoric of *Richard II* and its "choreographic patterns" (61) of movement and stage gesture combine to create meaning in performance. McGuire examines such repetitive actions as exiting and entering, departing and returning, waiting, exchanging gages, kneeling and rising, and even the "action" of remembering as it appears in the behavior of Richard (5.1.40–45) and of the Gardener (3.4.104–7). Throughout, McGuire emphasizes how seemingly disparate episodes are subtly connected by shared verbal and gestural allusion, except, that is, for the death of Woodstock, which stands apart from this integrative pattern, and by so doing ironically heightens the verbal and gestural unity of the play as a whole.

137. Page, Malcolm. *"Richard II": Text and Performance.* Houndmills: Macmillan Education; Atlantic Highlands, N.J.: Humanities Press International, 1987.

This volume is divided into two parts: "Part One: Text" (13–47) and "Part Two: Performance" (48–82). In part one, Page briefly outlines the basic contours of the play in a mixture of criticism and plot outline, then moves on to very brief comments on Richard's theatricality, Bolingbroke's bluff and hearty competence, and York's vacillation, concluding with a discussion of *Richard II* as a history play and the drama's relevance for modern readers and audiences. In part two, Page begins with a brief survey of twentieth-century performances of the role of Richard on stage and television, then proceeds to examine four stage productions of *Richard II* in some detail: 1) the 1973–74 production by the Royal Shakespeare Company directed by John Barton, in which Richard Pasco and Ian Richardson alternated in the roles of Richard and Bolingbroke; 2) the 1979 production by the Stratford Festival in Ontario, Canada, directed by Zoe Caldwell, in which Richard Russell, Nicholas Pennell, and Frank Maradan alternated in the role of Richard, playing opposite to Craig Dudley, Rod Beattie, and Jim McQueen respectively in the role of Bolingbroke; 3) the 1980–81 production by the Royal Shakespeare Company, directed by Terry Hands, with Alan Howard as Richard and David Suchet as Bolingbroke; and 4) the 1982–84 Théâtre du Soleil production, directed by Ariane Mnouchkine, which was strongly indebted to kabuki drama. Throughout both sections of the book, Page punctuates his remarks with frequent passing references to the stage business of several modern productions as well as the observations of numerous modern literary and dramatic critics. The book also includes a plot synopsis and list of sources for *Richard II* (11).

138. Rackin, Phyllis. "The Role of the Audience in *Richard II*." *Shakespeare Quarterly* 36 (1985): 262–81.

This essay examines the reactions of an audience at a performance of *Richard II*, affirming that we begin as detached contemplators of a distant action, then gradually become participants in that action by virtue of our complicity with Bolingbroke's rebellion, and finally experience a release from the play *and* from our feelings of guilt. Rackin sees the audience as actually playing a "role" in *Richard II*, identifying the stages of this role as "entrapment" (263), "recognition and remorse" (267), and finally "purgation and release" (273). In Rackin's scheme, our release from guilt comes through the character of York, who in his development from a respected elder statesman to an object of ridicule becomes, for the audience, a sort of psychological scapegoat: "When York becomes ridiculous, we repudiate him, and with him our own part in Richard's deposition" (280).

139. Shewring, Margaret. *Shakespeare in Performance: "King Richard II."*

Manchester: Manchester Univ. Press, 1996.

Shewring's book is divided into three sections. Part one (2–45) takes up the structure and context of the play, analyzes the twin issues of deposition and regicide, and provides a brief but pithy stage history of the play from the mid-seventeenth to the mid-nineteenth century, with particular attention to questions of politics and aesthetics. Part two (48–151) examines productions of the play on stage and television from 1857 to 1987, and discusses in particular the Victorian production of the play by Charles Kean; Barry Kyle's 1986 Royal Shakespeare Company production (with Jeremy Irons as Richard); Frank Benson's 1896 production; John Gielgud's performances as Richard in 1929 and 1937; Ian McKellen's performance as Richard in 1968; Anthony Quayle's 1951 staging of the second tetralogy at Stratford-upon-Avon; the 1964 Royal Shakespeare Company's *Wars of the Roses*; the 1987 English Shakespeare Company's *Wars of the Roses*; John Barton's 1973–74 production of *Richard II*; the 1954 NBC television broadcast of the play with Maurice Evans as Richard; and the 1975 BBC television broadcast of the play with Derek Jacobi as Richard. Part three (154–79) treats the politics and aesthetics of *Richard II* on the European stage, with particular attention to productions by Jean Vilar (1947–48), Giorgio Strehler (1948), and Ariane Mnouchkine (1981). An afterword (180–84) briefly traces performances of the play in the 1990s. Appendices print the Lambarde Document of 1601, which includes Elizabeth's celebrated identification of herself with Richard; the Entry into London from Charles Kean's acting version (1857); and cast lists and staff lists for productions discussed in the volume. Throughout her study, Shewring cites literary criticism and theatrical criticism side-by-side in order to illuminate the play and its ideas, and she is especially alert to the play in its various cultural settings. The book is a treasure trove of information, not only on the productions Shewring chooses to discuss in detail, but on critical and theatrical reception of the play from the seventeenth century to the present.

See also nos. 92, 93, 94, 99, 114, 132, 141, 144.

G. Pedagogy and Collections of Essays.

140. Bloom, Harold, ed. *William Shakespeare's "Richard II."* New York: Chelsea House, 1988.

This volume reprints criticism on *Richard II* by Ruth Nevo (no. 127), Maynard Mack, Jr. (no. 124), Stephen Booth, James L. Calderwood (no. 37), Harry Berger, Jr. (no. 114), Susan Wells, and Northrop Frye. In his brief introduction (1–5), Bloom discusses Richard as a narcissistic and self-indulgent figure who nonetheless embodies "an extraordinary aesthetic dignity" (3), and in whom we see analogies to Marlowe's Edward II and even to Marlowe himself.

141. Brooke, Nicholas, ed. *"Richard II": A Casebook.* London: Macmillan, 1973.

Brooke reprints selections from literary and theatrical criticism on *Richard II* by the following: John Dryden, Nahum Tate, Samuel Johnson, Samuel Taylor Coleridge, William Hazlitt, Edward Dowden, Walter Pater (no. 66), C. E. Montague, William Butler Yeats (no. 78), Algernon Charles Swinburne, John Gielgud (no. 135), John Russell Brown (no. 134), Richard D. Altick (no. 106), E. M. W. Tillyard (no. 35), M. C. Bradbrook, Brents Stirling, Ernst H. Kantorowicz (no. 100), J. A. Bryant, Jr., M. M. Mahood, A. P. Rossiter (no. 72), and Nicholas Brooke. In his brief introduction (11–16), Brooke traces the fluctuating critical fortunes of the play from the sixteenth to the twentieth century.

142. Cookson, Linda, and Bryan Loughrey, eds. *Critical Essays on "Richard II."* Harlow: Longman, 1989.

This volume is designed for students and contains ten original essays on *Richard II* by Andrew Gibson, Nicholas Potter, John E. Cunningham, Stephen Hazell, Graham Holderness, Diana Devlin, Ronald Draper, Charles Moseley, Raman Selden, and Cedric Watts. Each essay is followed by discussion questions. "A Practical Guide to Essay Writing" serves as an appendix.

143. Cubeta, Paul M., ed. *Twentieth Century Interpretations of "Richard II": A Collection of Critical Essays.* Englewood Cliffs, N.J.: Prentice Hall, 1971.

This volume reprints excerpts from criticism on *Richard II* by Irving Ribner, E. M. W. Tillyard (no. 35), Derek Traversi, Leonard F. Dean (no. 49), Richard D. Altick (no. 106), Peter Ure (no. 95), Brents Stirling, Jan Kott, and Alvin B. Kernan (no. 62). In his introduction (1–12), Cubeta touches upon the historical, intellectual, and literary backgrounds to the play, then provides a brief but evidential discussion of its elegiac tone and deep sense of frustration and loss; he sees the drama as anticipating Shakespeare's tragedies, particularly *Hamlet* and *King Lear*, in its concern with the struggle to define the self in a hostile world.

144. Newlin, Jeanne T., ed. *"Richard II": Critical Essays.* New York: Garland Publishing, 1984.

Newlin's collection of critical and dramaturgical assessments of *Richard II* includes twenty responses to the play, ranging from Queen Elizabeth's purported comment "I am Richard II, know ye not that?" (3), to twentieth-century literary interpretations. Selections appear from the following authors: J. Dover Wilson, E. M. W. Tillyard (no. 35), Robert Ornstein (no. 65), Ernst H. Kantorowicz (no. 100), Irving Ribner, C. E. Montague, W. B. Yeats (no. 78), T. C. Worsley, Harley Granville-Barker, John Gielgud (no. 135), John Russell Brown (no. 134), Stanley Wells, Samuel Taylor Coleridge, Walter Pater (no. 66), E. K. Chambers, Brents Stirling (no. 130), Alessandro Manzoni, Algernon Charles Swinburne, and Richard D. Altick (no. 106). In her brief introduction (xi–xvii), Newlin contextualizes the essays in her collection by discussing critical and dramaturgical reassessments of the play in the twentieth century.

H. Bibliographies.

145. Black, Matthew W., and G. Harold Metz, comps. *"The Life and Death of King Richard II": A Bibliography to Supplement the New Variorum Edition of 1955.* New York: The Modern Language Association of America, 1977.

This bibliography supplements Black's variorum edition of *Richard II* (no. 92); it includes 702 new bibliographic entries under the following headings: Editions; Text; Commentary; Criticism; Sources; Music; Staging and Stage History. The items are largely unannotated, although a brief phrase of description is provided for selected entries.

146. Roberts, Josephine A., comp. *"Richard II": An Annotated Bibliography*, 2 vols. New York: Garland Publishing, 1988.

This is the most comprehensive annotated bibliography of *Richard II*, containing over 2,600 entries covering chiefly the period from 1940 to 1988 but including several items before 1940 as well. Roberts arranges her work under the following headings: I. Criticism; II. Sources and Historical Background; III. Dating; IV. Textual Studies; V. Individual Editions; VI. Complete and Collected Editions; VII. Influence, Adaptations, and Altered Versions; VIII. Staging and Stage History; IX. Criticism of Films and Other Media; Screenplays, Scripts, and Music; Films and Film Strips; Phonograph Records and Audio Cassettes; X. Translations; XI. Bibliographies. In her introduction (xi–xxxviii) Roberts traces in broad outline important interpretive, scholarly, and performance-based responses to the play. The work is an indispensable source of scholarly information on *Richard II*.

IV. 1 AND 2 HENRY IV

A. Editions.

1 Henry IV

147. Bevington, David, ed. *Henry IV, Part 1.* The Oxford Shakespeare. Oxford: Clarendon Press, 1987.

Bevington bases his text on the two quartos of 1598 (Q0 and Q1), the former containing only four leaves. In his introduction (1–110), he briefly traces the reception, reputation, and date of composition (which he fixes between August 1596 and March 1597), with particular attention to the latter's relationship to the Oldcastle controversy. He notes that Shakespeare uses "a remarkable variety of sources" (10) for the play, but emphasizes (and examines in detail) the dramatist's reliance upon Holinshed's *Chronicles,* Daniel's *Civil Wars,* and either the anonymous *Famous Victories of Henry the Fifth* or a play (or plays) very much like it. He also devotes full attention to the literary and cultural genesis of Falstaff, and sees the character as deriving from sources as diverse as the Vice figure, the *miles gloriosus,* the picaresque hero, the stage clown, the Bible, emblem books, Elizabethan soldiers and highwaymen, the historical Oldcastle, and the Lord of Misrule. He relates this "rich ambivalence" (34) in Falstaff's character to the sense of ambivalence in the play as a whole (locating the central conflict in a tension between Divine Providence and Renaissance skepticism), and also to the play's "pattern of oppositions" (41)—i.e., Hotspur and Falstaff, Chivalry and Pragmatism, Fathers and Sons (and the related issue of role-playing and identity). For Bevington, Falstaff's mendacity is linked not only to his playfully theatrical character, but also to Shakespeare's habit in *1 Henry IV* "of using illusion to depict historical life" (59); and Hal's "reformation" is seen favorably as a young man's struggle to find himself that results in "a revelation of his true identity" (62). The introduction concludes with extensive and detailed sections on performance history (66–85) and textual problems (85–110). A single appendix on "Shakespeare's Chronicle Sources" (287–97) gives "a point-by-point comparison of Shakespeare's text with pertinent excerpts from Holinshed, Daniel, Stow, and others, arranged scene by scene and line by line" (287). Textual, glossarial, and critical notes appear at the foot of each page of text.

148. Evans, G. Blakemore, ed. *Supplement to "Henry IV, Part 1."* A New Variorum Edition of Shakespeare. *Shakespeare Quarterly* 7, 3 (Summer 1956): ii + 121.

This is a supplement to Hemingway's variorum edition of *1 Henry IV* (no.

149) that "brings together with some degree of completeness all (mere nonsense aside) that has been written relating to the play from 1935 to July of 1955" (i). A section on "Textual and Critical Notes" (1-45) provides supplementary readings and emendations geared to the text of Hemingway's edition, and is followed by short excerpts of scholarship and criticism arranged under the following headings: The Text; Date of Composition; Sources; General Criticism; Characters; Style, Imagery, and Language; Stage History; List of Books and Articles. An index is also included, as well as a list of passages referred to in the *Supplement*. The volume is an indispensable source of information on the play. A bibliographical supplement to Evans's *Supplement* was published in 1977 (no. 207).

149. Hemingway, Samuel Burdett, ed. *Henry the Fourth Part I*. A New Variorum Edition of Shakespeare. Philadelphia: J. B. Lippincott Co., 1936.

This comprehensive edition of the play contains a diplomatic reprint of the Q1 (1598) text of *1 Henry IV*, fully collated against all textually important editions to 1891, with consultation of selected editions to 1919 (the textual notes on each page thus reflect textual history to 1919). The commentary notes at the bottom of each page, as well as all other apparatus in the book except the textual notes, take account of scholarship to 1935. The apparatus includes full appendices on "The Text"; "Date of Composition"; "Sources of the Plot"; "General Criticism"; "Characters"; "Stage History"; and "Stage Versions." Hemingway's edition is an indispensable starting place for consideration of all historical and interpretive scholarship on the play to 1935, and is especially useful for stage history. Two important supplements to this edition have been published (nos. 148 and 207).

150. Hodgdon, Barbara, ed. *The First Part of King Henry the Fourth*. Texts and Contexts. Boston: Bedford Books, 1997.

Part one of this volume (17-118) consists of a reprint of Bevington's edition of *1 Henry IV* from *The Complete Works of Shakespeare* (see no. 1). Part two (119-391) reprints excerpts from 25 different contemporary texts in the hope that readers will see the play "not just as a literary work of art ... but as a document marked by the specific historical and cultural conditions prevailing at the time it was written" (ix); this is an approach, Hodgdon affirms, that "refuses to make simple distinctions between literature and history, text and context" (ix). Hodgdon's introduction (1-16) emphasizes the status of *1 Henry IV* as a play situated both in the early fifteenth century and in Shakespeare's own time—a text that not only interrogates the history it describes, but also explores such problematic issues as class relations, gender roles, authority and its subversion, homoeroticism, and Falstaff as an interruptive representation of popular rather than elitist culture. Part two is divided into six sections, each preceded by a short introduction that treats the cultural importance and significance for the play of the documents excerpted within it. Section one, "Historiography and the Uses of History," reprints excerpts from Hall's *Union*, Holinshed's *Chronicles*, and Daniel's *Civil Wars*; section two, "Civic Order and

Rebellion," reprints excerpts from the *Homily Against Disobedience* and John Ponet's *A Short Treatise of Political Power*; section three, "Cultural Territories," reprints excerpts from Harrison's *Description of England* and Stow's *Survey of London*, the full text of a 1592 letter from the Lord Mayor of London to John Whitgift, Archbishop of Canterbury, and excerpts from Gosson's *School of Abuse*, Heywood's *Apology for Actors*, Dekker's *Of Lantern and Candlelight*, John Dod and Robert Cleaver's *A Godly Form of Household Government*, Joseph Swetnam's *The Arraignment of Lewd, Idle, Froward, and Unconstant Women*, Holinshed's *Chronicles*, and prompt copy of the Welsh passages from 3.1 of *1 Henry IV*; section four, "The 'Education' of a Prince," reprints excerpts from Ascham's *Schoolmaster*, the anonymous *Famous Victories of Henry the Fifth*, Machiavelli's *Prince*, the *Brut*, and John Speed's *History of Great Britain*; section five, "Honor and Arms: Elizabethan Neochivalric Culture and the Military Trades," reprints excerpts from Sir William Segar's *Honor Military and Civil*, Matthew Sutcliffe's *The Right Practice, Proceedings, and Laws of Arms*, Barnaby Rich's *A Pathway to Military Practice*, and George Silver's *The Paradoxes of Defense*; section six, "The Oldcastle Controversy: 'What's in a Name?,'" reprints excerpts from Foxe's *Acts and Monuments*, Holinshed's *Chronicles*, and Drayton, Hathaway, Munday, and Wilson's *Sir John Oldcastle*.

151. Humphreys, A. R., ed. *The First Part of King Henry IV*. The Arden Shakespeare. London: Methuen, 1960.

Humphreys bases his text on the two quartos of 1598 (Q0 and Q1), the former containing only four leaves. In his introduction (xi–lxxxii), he dates the composition of the original version of the play in 1596, and the revised and extant version (with Falstaff replacing Oldcastle) in 1597. After detailing the various changes Shakespeare made in revising his original, Humphreys treats the sources of *1 Henry IV*, noting their range and complexity, but placing particular emphasis upon Holinshed's *Chronicles*, Daniel's *Civil Wars*, various "Wild Prince Hal" stories, Stow's *Chronicles* and *Annals*, *The Famous Victories of Henry the Fifth*, other purported Prince Hal plays, the anonymous *Woodstock*, *The Mirror for Magistrates*, popular ballads on Percy and Douglas, and Kyd's *Soliman and Perseda*. Each of these is given detailed attention. He also analyzes the backgrounds to the character of Falstaff, with reference to the Lollard martyr Sir John Oldcastle, the Vice figure of the moralities, the Elizabethan Fool, the *miles gloriosus*, and the parasite of both classical and English comedy, and concludes that Falstaff represents no single figure but is the embodiment of "the large comedy of humanity" (xlv). He defends the unity of the play, arguing that the two separate plot lines are "branches belonging to a single trunk" (xlvi), and proceeds to detail a complex web of parallels and contrasts that unite the worlds of Tavern and Court. Humphreys sees the play as reflecting an Erastian world where religious values become secularized and are, at best, "perfunctory" (li); but he also, like Barber (no. 158), sees the shifting in the play between comedy and seriousness as saturnalian rather than satiric, then goes on to affirm the inclusiveness of Shakespeare's vision of history and praise the imaginative and linguistic texture of the play as rich and various. Eight appendices treat matters of text and date, and also reproduce source material from Holinshed, Daniel, and *The Famous Victories*, as well as excerpts from a variety of other doubtful or conjectural sources. Textual, glossarial, and critical notes appear at the foot of each page of text.

2 Henry IV

152. Humphreys, A. R., ed. *The Second Part of King Henry IV.* The Arden Shakespeare. London: Methuen, 1966.

Humphreys bases his text on the quarto of 1600 (Qa), but also consults the second issue (Qb) and the 1623 First Folio to supply readings in several instances. In his extensive introduction (xi–xci), Humphreys (repeating much of the argument from his edition of *1 Henry IV* [no. 151]), fixes the date of composition as 1597, and details the revisions made in the play and their likely connection to the Oldcastle controversy. Citing Jenkins (no. 188), he endorses the idea of part one and part two as complementary but independent plays—"both one play and two" (xxv)—and thinks that they were planned from the outset as separate works, not, as Jenkins asserts, a single play expanded into two. As in his introduction to part one, Humphreys discusses Holinshed, Daniel, Stow, *The Mirror for Magistrates*, "Wild Prince Hal" stories, *The Famous Victories*, and other purported Prince Hal plays, along with Elyot's *Governor*, as sources for the play, and gives each of these detailed attention. He finds the play to be the equal of part one in imaginative vitality, "unified by the powerful treatment of a nexus of themes" (xliv), and proceeds to discuss these under the headings of Richard and Henry; Henry and Necessity; Statecraft and Morality; Miscalculation; Anarchy; Age and Disease; and Life in Place and Time. He sees the Falstaff of part two as less masterful than in part one, a figure whose behavior disqualifies him from royal favor, and his rejection as anticipated by much of the earlier action of the play; the rejection itself (5.5) is justified despite whatever emotional reservations we may have about its tenor and tone. For Humphreys, the play demonstrates a structural complexity and maturity of style that is "cogent and picturesque, perpetually enlivened by physical realization" (lxiv); and he quotes generously from Knights (no. 189) in supporting this claim. Eight appendices follow the text; seven of these reprint extracts from certain, probable, and possible historical sources and assess their likely influence upon Shakespeare; the other treats "The Continuity of Scenes in Act IV, i–ii, and iv–v." Textual, glossarial, and critical notes appear at the foot of each page of text.

153. Melchiori, Giorgio, ed. *The Second Part of King Henry IV.* The New Cambridge Shakespeare. Cambridge: Cambridge Univ. Press, 1989.

Melchiori bases his text for the play on the 1600 quarto. In his introduction (1–52), he notes that the play acquires certain metadramatic qualities as a sequel, then proceeds to date its composition as late 1597 to early 1598. After discussing the omissions and inconsistencies of Q, he mentions the sources for the play, and argues that the lost original of the anonymous *Famous Victories of Henry the Fifth* (1598), not the surviving version of it, likely influenced Shakespeare. He argues for an earlier (not extant) one-part version of the *Henry IV* plays (an ur-*Henry IV*) as a Shakespearean "remake" (9) of the first part of *The Famous Victories*, and reconstructs how Shakespeare might have fashioned the *Henry IV* plays from this beginning, with particular attention to the creation of Falstaff from the character of Oldcastle. He concludes that *2 Henry IV* was not planned in advance as a separate play, but "thought of at most as an open option" (14). Melchiori takes the morality structure of *2 Henry IV* very seriously, seeing the play as a wider, more secular, and more political version of the simpler morality pattern of part one; he also examines its complex use of Jonsonian humors comedy, its expansion of "city comedy" into a sort of "country comedy" that undercuts pastoral (21), its varied and subtle linguistic texture, its elaboration of the father-son theme carried over from part one, and its pervading images of time and disease. As regards performance, Melchiori discusses the doubling of parts, the physical characteristics of the Curtain theatre (where the play was first staged), and a brief but pithy history of performances and adaptations from Shakespeare's time to the present. A "Textual Analysis," and appendices on "Shakespeare's Use of Holinshed," "Some Historical and Literary Sources," extracts from *The Famous Victories* relevant to *2 Henry IV*, and an item from Richard Tarlton's *Tarlton's Jests* (1638) relevant to the role of the Lord Chief Justice are printed following the text. A select "Reading List" completes the volume. Textual, glossarial, and critical notes appear at the foot of each page of text.

154. Shaaber, Matthias A., ed. *The Second Part of Henry the Fourth.* A New Variorum Edition of Shakespeare. Philadelphia: J. P. Lippincott Co., 1940.

This comprehensive edition contains a diplomatic reprint of the F1 (1623) version of the play, reproduced "with scrupulous accuracy" from a copy in the Furness Memorial Library at the University of Pennsylvania; "except in a few places where the interpolation of a passage from Q has dislocated the line division of F, the text follows the original line for line" (xi). The textual notes at the bottom of each page reflect collation of all textually important editions to 1923, with consultation (on disputed passages) of selected editions to 1936. The commentary notes, printed beneath the textual notes, as well as all other apparatus in the book, take account of scholarship to 1939. The apparatus includes full appendices on "The Text"; "The Date of Composition"; "The Authenticity of the Text"; "The Sources"; "Criticisms"; "The Dering MS" (a seventeenth-century fusion of *1* and *2 Henry IV* into a single five-act play); "Acting Versions"; and "Stage History." Shaaber's edition is an indispensable starting place for consideration of all historical and interpretive scholarship on the play to 1939, and is especially useful for matters of text and criticism. Shaaber published a bibliographical supplement to this edition in 1977 (no. 208).

B. Dating and Textual Studies.

155. Goldberg, Jonathan. "The Commodity of Names: 'Falstaff' and 'Oldcastle' in *1 Henry IV*." In *Reconfiguring the Renaissance: Essays in Critical Materialism*, ed. Jonathan Crewe, 76–88. Special Issue of the *Bucknell Review* 35, 2 (1992). Lewisburg, Pa.: Bucknell Univ. Press; London: Associated Univ. Presses, 1992.

Although Goldberg argues against Gary Taylor's substitution of "Oldcastle" for "Falstaff" in *1 Henry IV* (no. 157), he nevertheless supports Taylor's larger idea—i.e., that Shakespearean texts are unstable and cannot be permanently fixed with any sense of certainty. Goldberg affirms that the play called *Sir John Oldcastle* was *not* identical to *1 Henry IV* (as Taylor supposes), and defends his position with both internal and external evidence. He further argues that since *1 Henry IV* is a text revised to exclude the censored "Oldcastle," to restore "Oldcastle" would be to tie Shakespeare "to a singular historical referent, and a singular meaning" (83), thus limiting the multiplicity and contingency of history, and furthering censorship rather than restoration of the text.

156. Pendleton, Thomas A. "'This is not the man': On Calling Falstaff Falstaff." *Analytical & Enumerative Bibliography*, n.s., 4 (1990): 59–71.

Pendleton argues against the decision of Taylor (no. 157) to change the name of "Falstaff" to "Oldcastle" in *1 Henry IV*; he is particularly skeptical of the metrical or linguistic evidence usually cited to defend the substitution, including the pun on Oldcastle's name (1.2.41–42), which he does not see as an unrevised remnant of an earlier version, but rather as an allusion that "entered the play only after 'Oldcastle' had left" (64). Pendleton amasses considerable topical evidence to suggest that the change in the character's name was motivated less by Sir William Brooke's objections than "by the displeasure of a significant part of Shakespeare's audience at his treatment of a hero of their religion" (69); this he considers ample justification for the change in names and reason enough for editors to respect Shakespeare's decision.

157. Taylor, Gary. "The Fortunes of Oldcastle." *Shakespeare Survey* 38 (1985): 85–100.

Noting that Falstaff was originally called "Oldcastle," and that the name was changed in order to placate Sir William Brooke, Lord Cobham, and his family, Taylor argues for restoring the name "Oldcastle" in modern edited texts of *1 Henry IV* (since that play was affected directly by the censors), but for keeping "Falstaff" in *2 Henry IV*, *The Merry Wives of Windsor*, and *Henry V* (since these plays were written after Shakespeare was forced to change his notion of the character). He takes modern editors to task for treating Shakespeare's texts as if they were "Holy Writ" (89), and cites their reluctance to change "Falstaff" to "Oldcastle" as an example of an unwarranted editorial timidity that "succumbs to the weight of tradition" (93). Taylor amasses much textual and historical evidence in attempting to show that a failure to change Falstaff's name "fictionalizes, depoliticizes, secularizes, and in the process trivializes the play's most memorable character" (95).

See also nos. 147, 148, 149, 151, 152, 153, 154, 164, 170, 171.

C. Influences; Sources; Historical and Intellectual Backgrounds; Topicality.

158. Barber, C. L. "Rule and Misrule in *Henry IV*." In *Shakespeare's Festive Comedy: A Study of Dramatic Form and its Relation to Social Custom*, 192–221. Princeton: Princeton Univ. Press, 1959. Repr., in part, in Bevington (no. 202), in Bloom (no. 203), in Bloom (no. 204), and in Hunter (no. 205).

Barber is concerned with "the Saturnalian pattern" of Shakespearean comedy, which "appears in many variations, all of which involve inversion, statement and counterstatement, and a basic movement which can be summarized in the formula, through release to clarification" (4). He explores the way in which the social form of Elizabethan holidays (the May Game; Lord of Misrule; aristocratic entertainments; and a wide variety of sports, games, shows, and pageants) contributes to the form of "festive comedy," with particular attention to Nashe's *Summer's Last Will and Testament* and Shakespeare's *Love's Labor's Lost, A Midsummer Night's Dream, The Merchant of Venice, As You Like It, Twelfth Night*, and *1* and *2 Henry IV*. Barber sees the *Henry IV* plays as fusing the two saturnalian traditions of stage clowning and holiday folly and mixing these masterfully with history. In this context Hal emerges as a figure who can balance the holiday and the serious, and Falstaff as a figure of saturnalian reversal who radically challenges received ideas but is finally sacrificed in the manner of the scapegoat of saturnalian ritual. Throughout, Barber maintains that "the dynamic relation of comedy and serious action is saturnalian rather than satiric, that the misrule works, through the whole dynamic rhythm, to consolidate rule" (205). Barber's book is one of the most influential treatments of comic elements in Shakespeare's plays.

159. Dessen, Alan C. *Shakespeare and the Late Moral Plays*. Lincoln: Univ. of Nebraska Press, 1986.

By "late moral plays" Dessen means a neglected and "highly heterogeneous group of plays written, published, and performed during the first half of Queen Elizabeth's reign" (2). He urges us to examine the influence of these plays based, not on modern assumptions about the history of drama, but on the actual Elizabethan evidence, which he sees as providing fresh paradigms with which to approach Shakespearean texts. In addition to chapters on *Richard III* and *All's Well That End's Well*, and four chapters on general problems relating to the moral play, the book contains chapters on "Dual Protagonists in *1 Henry IV*" (55–90) and "The Two Phased Structure of *2 Henry IV*" (91–112). In the former, Dessen notes in plays such as W. Wager's *Enough is as Good as a Feast* (1560) and *The Trial of Treasure* (1567, possibly by Wager) an emphasis on dual protagonists representing two opposed attitudes rather than a focus on a single, dominant character. He finds the "entire dramatic strategy" (64) of plays such as these analogous to Shakespeare's in *1 Henry IV*, particularly as regards the relationship between Hal and Hotspur, and probes this relationship by examining such techniques as alternating scenes, symbolic companions, and visually analogous moments that contrast the two characters in the manner of the moral play. The essay on *2 Henry IV* argues for its structural coherence based upon a model derived from the two-phased moral play; this model emphasizes the idea of a public Vice (Falstaff), as well as the contrast between two distinct political phases: the "sick" kingdom under Henry IV and the "new" kingdom under Henry V. In this context the rejection of Falstaff (5.5) acquires a dramatic and political logic, is fully justified, and even is expected. Both essays rely on highly detailed readings of individual scenes and frequent allusion to the conventions of the late moral play.

160. **Hawkins, Sherman H.** "Virtue and Kingship in Shakespeare's *Henry IV*." *English Literary Renaissance* 5 (1975): 313–43.

Hawkins examines the literary and philosophical backgrounds (particularly Cicero, Plato, and Aristotle as the three authorities who most influenced Renaissance thinkers) to two competing claims for kingship in the *Henry IV* plays: primogeniture and virtue (the latter as embodied in the four cardinal virtues of prudence, justice, fortitude, and temperance). He undertakes a thorough examination of the *Henry IV* plays, demonstrating how they incorporate these four cardinal virtues into their rhythms and ideas (temperance and fortitude in part one; prudence and justice in part two), focusing on Prince Hal as the embodiment of these virtues. Hawkins argues that Hal/Henry V unites the twin claims of primogeniture and virtue in himself, and that the *Henry IV* plays are carefully unified. The argument is learned and allusive.

161. **McAlindon, Tom.** "Pilgrims of Grace: *Henry IV* Historicized." *Shakespeare Survey* 48 (1995): 69–84.

In seeking to reevaluate the historical context of the *Henry IV* plays, McAlindon finds certain "old" historicists like Tillyard (no. 35) inattentive to material realities and many "new" historicists like Greenblatt (no. 29) not attentive enough to the "high politics of Tudor England"; instead he tries to reformulate another "old" historicist, Lily B. Campbell (no. 27), by relating the *Henry IV* plays to the "religio-political and cultural experiences of sixteenth-century England," particularly the idea of grace (70). His method is to link the rebellions in the *Henry IV* plays with the Northern Rebellion of 1569–70 and, more importantly, with an earlier northern rebellion (1536) known as the Pilgrimage of Grace—a peaceful anti-Reformation movement that was treacherously suppressed by Henry VIII. McAlindon emphasizes spiritual "grace" as a divine gift and secular "grace" as courtly propriety and *sprezzatura*, and sees the theme of grace as deeply embedded in *1* and *2 Henry IV*, where it occurs in a variety of social, religious, or aesthetic contexts. He traces this complex network of allusion in a tripartite structure under the headings Grace, Rebuke, and Pardon, stressing both its moral dimension and its detailed connection with virtually every major character in the plays.

162. Melchiori, Giorgio. *Shakespeare's Garter Plays: "Edward III" to "Merry Wives of Windsor."* Newark: Univ. of Delaware Press; London: Associated Univ. Presses, 1994.

At the heart of Melchiori's study is the contention that six plays (the "Shakespearean" *Edward III*, the four plays of the second tetralogy, and *The Merry Wives of Windsor*) may be seen as "ideologically, a single dramatic structure, whose five acts [are] each a separate history play, with the addition of the Falstaff comedy [*The Merry Wives of Windsor*] in the spirit of the final jig that was the customary conclusion of all shows on the public stage" (12). Melchiori sees these plays as united by a series of open or covert allusions to the Order of the Garter—a pattern of reference that is linked to Falstaff as antihero, as well as to a concern with the principles of Policy and Honor. His method of investigation is to consider the genesis of the six plays in light of Elizabethan stage conditions, particularly such matters as censorship, the day-to-day work of actor and playwright, and the popularity of sequels. The book is divided into two parts. Part one (chaps. 1-3, pp. 21-73), argues that the second tetralogy was originally conceived as a trilogy of remakes of old plays centering around the concept of Policy, and that censorship caused the writing of *1 Henry IV* and commercial reasons the addition of *2 Henry IV*. Melchiori attempts to reconstruct the original one-play version of *Henry IV* (containing Oldcastle rather than Falstaff) as well as account for Shakespeare's final authorial decisions as the character evolved into Falstaff. He sees this new Falstaff, a figure in whom is located the problematic interrelationship of Honor, Policy, and Power, as calling into question the values of Elizabethan chivalry. Part two (chaps. 4-6, pp. 77-132) focuses on Falstaff's "five Shakespearean reincarnations: Sir John Fastolf disgartered by Lord Talbot in *1 Henry VI*, Sir John Oldcastle in the one-play version of *Henry IV*, the 'abominable misleader of youth' in *1 Henry IV*, the old man rejected by Prince Hal in *2 Henry IV*, and finally the philandering Knight of the Garter Inn in *The Merry Wives of Windsor*" (14). This section takes up the origins of Falstaff as a dramatic character; it traces these origins to Anthony Munday's *Two Italian Gentlemen* (1585) as well as to a court entertainment presumably given on the Garter feast of 23 April 1597, and reconsiders the sequence of composition of all the Falstaff plays. Melchiori concludes by linking Shakespeare's Garter plays to *Edward III*, seeing it not only as a Garter play, but also as a "moral history based on the interplay of sexuality and power" (15). Melchiori's study, highly detailed and allusive, amounts to a complete reevaluation of the origins of the second tetralogy (particularly *1* and *2 Henry IV*) as well as these plays' relationship to their surrounding culture.

163. Palmer, D. J. "Casting Off the Old Man: History and St. Paul in *1 Henry IV*." *Critical Quarterly* 12 (1970): 267-83. Repr. in Bevington (no. 202).

Palmer sees the Pauline allusion in Hal's "redeeming time" in *1 Henry IV* (1.2.217) as basic to the dramatic structure of the *Henry IV* plays. He cites several allusions to *The Epistle to the Ephesians* in both plays, arguing that they help invest *1* and *2 Henry IV* with a structural unity and a thematic coherence. Modifying the views of Jorgensen (no. 168), Palmer cites numerous passages from *1 Henry IV*, suggesting that the concept of "redeeming time" is closely linked to settling debts (a usage he traces back to marginal glosses in the Geneva Bible), and also to the related idea of recovering one's lost reputation, as well as to the concept that a person must strive to be worthy of his calling—i.e., his "vocation" and his "name." Palmer sees Hal as a figure who, having attained his true name and vocation in part one, moves on to a new name and vocation as king in part two; here "redeeming time" becomes associated with Hal's duty to the nation—a duty that involves casting off the old man (symbolically evoked by Falstaff and his father) and claiming his rightful place as royal leader.

164. Poole, Kristen. "Saints Alive! Falstaff, Martin Marprelate, and the Staging of Puritanism." *Shakespeare Quarterly* 46 (1995): 47–75.

The contention here is that Shakespeare's depiction of Sir John Oldcastle (in the person of Falstaff) "is perfectly in keeping with the tenor of anti-puritan literature of the late sixteenth century, especially the anti-Marprelate tracts and the burlesque stage performances of the Marprelate controversy (1588-90), which frequently depicted puritans as grotesque individuals living in carnival-esque communities" (54). Drawing heavily on writers on both sides of the Marprelate controversy, Poole strives to create a different notion of Elizabethan puritans than that of "dry, dour, Casaubon-like figures" (63); rather she emphasizes the importance of a competing representation of puritanism, "the grotesque puritan" (64), embodied in such figures as Zeal-of-the-Land Busy in Jonson's *Bartholomew Fair*, who serve as models of the type that Shakespeare exploited in his depiction of Oldcastle/Falstaff. In Poole's scheme, Falstaff does not merely satirize puritans, he is himself satirized as a grotesque representation of the Lollard martyr Oldcastle; as such, he assumes a voice similar to that of Martin Marprelate, who also, like Falstaff/Oldcastle, "challenges the hierarchies that constitute the very structure of church and state" (74). Poole also argues against Taylor's decision (no. 157) to change Falstaff's name to Oldcastle; this change she sees as a rewriting of history that denies the text's "socio-political setting" (52 note).

165. Somerset, J. A. B. "Falstaff, the Prince, and the Pattern of *2 Henry IV*." *Shakespeare Survey* 30 (1977): 35-45.

Somerset is skeptical of the *humanum genus* morality play pattern often imposed upon the *Henry IV* plays by Wilson (no. 195) and others, noting that plays of this type died out around 1550. Instead he argues for the indebtedness of *2 Henry IV* to a later group of morality plays from the period 1565-1580 (*Like Will to Like, All for Money, The Tide Tarrieth No Man, Enough is as Good as a Feast, The Trial of Treasure*, etc.) whose themes are social and moral and whose plots replace the single Mankind hero "with a varied array of social type figures" (39). Somerset locates many of the features of these plays in *2 Henry IV* (e.g., the lack of a single hero, a sense of the decline of law and justice, the separateness of the moral from the immoral figures), and sees Falstaff and his confederates as evoking characteristics of the "vice-group of the late morality variety shows" (41). For Somerset, Hal is no *humanum genus* figure; rather he is a man mysteriously aloof from Falstaff as well as from the court, who embraces neither "disorder or excessive rigour" (44), and whose rejection of Falstaff (*2 Henry IV*, 5.5) both follows the pattern of the later moralities and "leaves us to ponder its disturbing implications" (45).

166. Womersley, David. "Why is Falstaff Fat?" *Review of English Studies*, n.s., 47 (1996): 1–22.

Taking Barbara Everett's essay on Falstaff (no. 183) as his critical locus, Womersley examines Falstaff's fatness in the context of the historical forces that shaped the character. He notes the existence of a 1566 Catholic tract by Nicholas Harpsfield, *Dialogi Sex*, to which John Foxe responded by disparaging Harpsfield's depiction of Oldcastle as "some grandpaunch Epicure," suggesting that "a fat Oldcastle was first imagined, not in the *Henry IV* plays, but in a work of religious and historical controversy" (4). The bulk of the essay, however, is not devoted to Falstaff; rather it attempts to argue that in the histories Shakespeare adopted a "Protestant philosophy of history" (4), running from Tyndale to Foxe (and far more obvious in Holinshed than in Hall), that imagined Henry V as an oppressor of true religion and a dupe of the pope. This attitude Womersley examines in some detail in 4.1 of *Henry V*, the scene with Bates, Court, and Williams on the eve of Agincourt, where he sees Henry "forsaking Catholicism" and adopting "the solifidianism central to reformed religion" (20). He concludes that the fatness of Falstaff was not attributable to any Catholic sympathies on Shakespeare's part, but rather to his determination to "unify political and spiritual authority in the person of Henry" (21).

See also nos. 147, 148, 149, 150, 151, 152,
153, 154, 155, 156, 157, 167, 168, 169,
177, 180, 182, 183, 186, 187, 191, 193, 195, 196, 200, 201.

D. Language and Linguistics.

167. Davis, Norman. "Falstaff's Name." *Shakespeare Quarterly* 28 (1977): 513–15.

Davis questions the contention of George Walton Williams (no. 170) and Robert F. Willson, Jr. (no. 172), that Falstaff's name signifies aspects of the character. He calls attention to a contemporary document relating to Sir John Fastolf's will—Fastolf Paper 85(2), dated 1463—which refers to "Fastolf" as "Falstalf," and from this evidence argues that the name "Falstaff" was not invented by Shakespeare.

168. Jorgensen, Paul A. *Redeeming Shakespeare's Words*. Berkeley: Univ. of California Press, 1962. The essay on "Redeeming Time" is repr. in Hunter (no. 205).

Jorgensen's book is "devoted to the fullest possible explication of words that are either thematic or significant in certain plays" (vii), including *Othello, Much Ado About Nothing, Coriolanus, Hamlet*, and the plays of the second tetralogy. The book contains a brief discussion of Pistol's name (70-74), noting that the weapon after which he was named was noisy and inaccurate. As regards "Hotspur's 'bright Honour' " (43-51), Jorgensen traces the use of the word "honor" to the hortatory and gratulatory tracts dating from 1589 to 1597 which attempted to restore a vocabulary of chivalry in an age increasingly given over to the realistic language of battle. In an essay on " 'Redeeming Time' in *Henry IV*" (52-69), he notes the importance of time as a concept in the *Henry IV* plays, and emphasizes the idea of its redemption as expressed in Hal's opening soliloquy (1.2.195-217). He denies that the words "redeeming time" (1.2.217) mean "making up for lost time" as many commentators assert; rather he affirms (adducing the Homilies, the Bible, contemporary religious writings, and early plays like *Lusty Juventus*) that for Elizabethans the phrase "would be clearly understood as meaning to take full advantage of the time that man is given here on earth for salvation" (59). In this context, Hal's use of the word "idleness" in the soliloquy (1.2.196) becomes very significant, since for Elizabethans the word carried the clear religious implication of sinfulness to be avoided. Jorgensen maintains that, although Hal undergoes no radical spiritual transformation, he does grow as a result of his experiences, "redeeming time" in his own way, "sociably, actively, and interestingly" (69).

169. **Knowles, Richard.** "Unquiet and the Double Plot of *2 Henry IV.*" *Shakespeare Studies* 2 (1966): 133-40.

Noting that the word *rumor* (and hence by analogy the character Rumor who opens *2 Henry IV*) still retained in Elizabethan times some of its original meaning of "noise," Knowles associates this figure with the motif of "unquiet" and noise that pervades the play—a motif developed by a series of implicit contrasts and analogies in which the "unquiet" of a scene from the upper plot is "exactly parodied in the comic scene that immediately follows it" (135). Knowles examines the language of virtually every key scene in the play from this perspective (pairing upper plot scenes with their lower plot counterparts), arguing that the repeated emphasis on sound and noise helps invest *2 Henry IV* with a dramatic and poetic unity.

170. **Williams, George Walton.** "Fastolf or Falstaff." *English Literary Renaissance* 5 (1975): 308-12.

In upholding the name "Fastolf" for the cowardly knight in *1 Henry VI*, Williams argues that the name was changed to "Falstaff" (as it appears in the First Folio) only well after the performance of the play, perhaps to capitalize on the popularity of the later "Falstaff" of the *Henry IV* plays and *The Merry Wives of Windsor*. He notes that the puns on the name "Falstaff" apply to the character in the *Henry IV* plays, but not to the "Fastolfe" of *1 Henry VI*, and speculates that when Shakespeare had to change the name of "Oldcastle" to accommodate the Cobham family he inserted "Falstaff"—a name that suggests "on the one hand the flamboyant mendacity of the fat knight and on the other the gradual extinction of his prowess military and erotic" (312).

171. Williams, George Walton. "Second Thoughts on Falstaff's Name." *Shakespeare Quarterly* 30 (1979): 82–84.

In responding to Davis (no. 167), Williams refers to the first of the 1598 quartos of *1 Henry IV* (Q0), which contains two erroneous prefixes for Falstaff printed "*Fast.*" Williams conjectures that in substituting Falstaff (spelled "Falstalffe") for "Oldcastle" in *1 Henry IV* the dramatist may inadvertently have let slip the name "Fastolfe" on these two occasions, and reaffirms his original contention that Shakespeare created the name (contra Davis) without reference to any manuscript material, probably wanting it to "be suggestive of falling and falsity" (83).

172. Willson, Robert F., Jr. "Falstaff in *1 Henry IV*: What's in a Name?" *Shakespeare Quarterly* 27 (1976): 199–200.

Willson explores the possible literary reasons why Shakespeare would change the historical name "Fastolfe" to "Falstaff" for *1 Henry IV*. He posits three senses in which the name "Falstaff" functions symbolically in the play: 1) as a fallen staff or pole used as a weapon; 2) as the "staff of life," ironically highlighting the character's gluttony and love of drink; and 3) as a sexual pun on the wilted phallus, suggesting the effects of drunkenness on desire.

See also nos. 148, 155, 156, 157, 163, 177, 193, 194.

E. Criticism.

173. Abrams, Richard. "Rumor's Reign in *2 Henry IV*: The Scope of a Personification." *English Literary Renaissance* 16 (1986): 467–95.

Abrams sees Rumor as a sort of usurping tyrant representing "England's emblazoned sinfulness—a nightmare apparition drawn from the king's and people's guilty consciences, symptomatic of present malaise" (468); moreover, this notion of Rumor as a usurper is restated in *2 Henry IV* through a series of personifications that supplant actual characters (the most notable of these personifications being Time). Quoting extensively from the *Henry IV* plays, Abrams shows how Rumor serves as a type for virtually every central character, particularly Hal, Falstaff, Henry, and Hotspur; he also argues that Henry and the rebels in part two are ironically united by both their mutual association with Rumor and their victimization by it. Abrams sees Rumor's reign declining at the moment when Henry accepts Hal's explanation of the stolen crown (4.5), thus renewing his bond with Hal "in an extraverbal realm where Rumor cannot intrude" (488). In Abrams's scheme, Hal purges Rumor through the rejection of Falstaff (5.5), who serves as Rumor's substitute; in this manner the new king re-forms Rumor into fame, making it a viable force in his new regime.

174. Auden, W. H. "The Prince's Dog." In *The Dyer's Hand and Other Essays*, 182-208. New York: Random House, 1962. Repr. often. The essay is repr. in Bevington (no. 202) and in Hunter (no. 205).

This essay is one of four essays on Shakespeare that, with three other related essays, constitute section four, "The Shakespearian City," of this collection of Auden's prose. It was first published in *Encounter* 13 (November 1959): 21-31. In his essay on Falstaff, Auden stresses that the character's natural milieu is an eternal present rather than "the historical world of suffering and death" (191), and likens him to such figures from opera as Tristan, Isolde, and Don Giovanni. He sees Falstaff's situation as essentially tragic: the old man loves and admires Hal as a sort of surrogate son, but Hal cares no more for him than he does for "the King's jester" (191). For Auden, Falstaff is a character devoted to the impulse of the moment rather than any notion of obligation or responsibility; but, rather than functioning as a mere Lord of Misrule, he is "a comic symbol for the supernatural order of Charity as contrasted with the temporal order of Justice symbolized by Henry of Monmouth" (198). Auden reformulates Falstaff's dishonesty, seeing it as "parabolically, a sign for a lack of pride, humility which acknowledges its unimportance and dependence upon others" (203), and regards the character's idleness, drinking, surrender to immediacy, and refusal to accept reality as signs of the "Unworldly Man" (204); Falstaff is a figure whose devotion to laughter "becomes a comic image for a love which is absolutely self-giving" (206), even to the point that such love invites comparison with that of "the Christian God" (207). The essay is the most stunning defense of Falstaff's character since Morgann's (no. 191).

175. Barish, Jonas A. "The Turning Away of Prince Hal." *Shakespeare Studies* 1 (1965): 9-17. Repr. in Bevington (no. 202).

In upholding Bradley's view of the rejection of Falstaff in *2 Henry IV* (5.5. [no. 179]), Barish contends that the episode jars us abruptly from the world of comedy to that of history, and further that Hal's turning away of Falstaff is in some respects a turning away of himself—a "*self*-rejection" (10) that produces a restriction of character and narrowing of options. For Barish, Hal's much touted reformation is actually a dehumanization which forces him to abandon part of his human vitality in order to be a political success.

176. Bergeron, David M. "Shakespeare Makes History: *2 Henry IV*." *SEL: Studies in English Literature 1500-1900* 31 (1991): 231-45.

Bergeron argues that *2 Henry IV* reflects a self-consciousness about history not apparent in the earlier English history plays, and that the many versions of history in the play "culminate in Falstaff, the special artifice of Shakespeare's construction of history, the one who brings narrative history and narrative fiction face to face" (231). He sees the play as concerned with the "making" of history, a process that both underscores its fictional quality and suggests the impossibility of any single notion of historical truth, and traces this process in three separate historical strands: "ahistory" (in Falstaff), "national" history (in Hal and the royal party), and "literary" history (within the text of the play).

Bergeron sees these various narratives meeting in Falstaff, whose rejection (5.5) becomes the overthrow of "Rumour" or false history, so that a "correct" history "can be inscribed in national life": thus the dramatist "dismembers history in order to *re*-member it" (233).

177. Berry, Edward I. "The Rejection Scene in *2 Henry IV.*" *SEL: Studies in English Literature 1500–1900* 17 (1977): 201–18.

In exploring the "psychology" of Hal's rejection of Falstaff (5.5), Berry suggests that Hal's harshness toward the fat knight indicates that "there is a part of Falstaff in himself that he must suppress" (204–5). Berry rejects both the "rhetoric of resentment" and the "rhetoric of approbation" so often taken by critics who disagree on Hal's behavior toward Falstaff (206). Instead he emphasizes the new king's capacity to "perform," stressing that the various roles Hal/Henry V assumes are "extensions of the self" (207), and locating this principle of constructive and artistic role-playing in such works as Elyot's *Governor* and Castiglione's *Courtier*. Berry also places great emphasis on the theme of time in the *Henry IV* plays, noting that Hal/Henry V, while himself an adept manipulator of time, nonetheless does not defeat it. He sees this situation as analogous to the sense of unease we often feel over the rejection scene, where "the triumphs permitted by history are always equivocal and too perplexing for joy" (218). The essay is detailed and allusive.

178. Black, James. "Henry IV's Pilgrimage." *Shakespeare Quarterly* 34 (1983): 18–26.

Black examines Henry IV's obsession with a voyage to the Holy Land, calling it "a pilgrimage not just of remorse or of politics, but of the heart" (19). He traces each reference to travel by Henry from *Richard II* through *2 Henry IV*, noting that Henry tends habitually to think in terms of expiatory pilgrimages involving weary travel, hard marching, and compelled wandering. For Black, these references are too deeply entrenched in Henry's imagination to be dismissed as expressions of mere Machiavellian policy; rather the king's obsession with the Holy Land creates a verbal and psychological context in which his death in the Jerusalem chamber can be seen as expressing, instead of ironic futility, a king and a kingdom finally at peace.

179. Bradley, A. C. "The Rejection of Falstaff." In *Oxford Lectures on Poetry*, 247–75. London: Macmillan, 1909. Repr. often. The essay is repr. in Bevington (no. 202), in Hunter (no. 205), and, in part, in Berman (no. 259).

This book consists of Bradley's Oxford lectures on aesthetics, Romantic poetry, Shakespeare's life and sensibility, his theatre and audience, *Antony and Cleopatra*, as well as the essay on Falstaff. Bradley regards the rejection of Falstaff (*2 Henry IV*, 5.5) as thematically necessary but emotionally deflating, and uses it as the basis for his understanding of both Hal/Henry V and Falstaff; the former is a chilly mixture of decency and policy, who acts in character in rejecting Falstaff, and the latter is a sublime comic creation whom Shakespeare could not make us condemn, even in the rejection scene, where the logic of the play demands it. For Bradley, Falstaff is a "humorist of genius" rather than a mere object of humor, a figure whose behavior—mendacious and objectively venal as it may be—is nonetheless "contagious and prevents our sympathy with it from being disturbed" (261-62); moreover, this condition persists despite the best intentions of Shakespeare, who has created in Falstaff a comic figure he cannot fully control. Bradley's highly sympathetic reading of Falstaff, heavily indebted to that of Morgann (no. 191), is a seminal essay on the character.

180. Cohen, Derek. "The Rite of Violence in *1 Henry IV.*" *Shakespeare Survey* 38 (1985): 77-84. Repr. in Holderness (no. 85).

Cohen focuses upon Hotspur as a figure who, in the carefully prepared ritual of his death (5.4.77-86), becomes "hero, god, and sacrificial creature of society" (77). For Cohen, Hotspur is the ritual object of Hal's quest—a quest that is founded upon the prince's sacred vow to his father (3.2.129-59) and evocative of ancient rites of purification; moreover, we are complicit in this sacrificial rite by virtue of our silent witness to its "good violence" (79). Cohen sees Hal's vow to his father as a moment of transformation, for here Hal (in a manner common in ritualized oathtaking) undergoes a major change, in this case from protagonist to hero. In Cohen's view, the play thus gives us two "heroes," Hotspur and Hal, each representative of opposed ideologies, and in this context Falstaff's abuse of Hotspur's corpse (5.4) becomes a crime against the ethos of heroism as well as a negation of blood sacrifice. Cohen's essay is a deft analysis of the subtle tensions (especially the tension between antipathy and identification) implicit in the violence of ritual.

181. Crewe, Jonathan. "Reforming Prince Hal: The Sovereign Inheritor in *2 Henry IV.*" *Renaissance Drama* 21 (1990 [pub. 1991]): 225-42.

Crewe challenges readers like Greenblatt (no. 29) who argue that Hal undergoes no substantive reform, by noting that "their priviliged text is *1*, not *2, Henry IV*" (225); he suggests that the elements of Hal's reform in part one (including his staged appearance of change) are no longer effectual in part two, for here Hal becomes "an 'inward' protagonist oppressed and divided by a troublesome demand" actually to reform (229). Crewe sees this transition as not simply a shift from the political to the psychological, but a merging of the two that creates "a psychologized politics or a politicized psychology" (229). His essay is a detailed examination of the psychological process by which Hal transfers his reputed wildness and criminality to his father (the original usurper), thus allowing the son to become a legitimate (and reformed) heir.

182. Empson, William. "Falstaff and Mr. Dover Wilson." *The Kenyon Review* 15 (1953): 213-62. Repr., in part, in Hunter (no. 205).

Empson begins by questioning Wilson's notion that Shakespeare originally intended Falstaff to appear in *Henry V* but changed his mind (no. 195); he then claims that "the whole Falstaff series needs to be looked at in terms of Dramatic Ambiguity ... and that if this is done the various problems about Falstaff and Prince Hal, so long discussed, are in essence solved" (222-23). Basically, Empson argues that, as regards the relationship between Hal and Falstaff, Wilson falls into the critical trap of taking sides between two opposing viewpoints instead of "letting both be real" (223). Empson takes up many aspects of Wilson's argument point by point, arguing that Shakespeare depicts both Hal and Falstaff in a more uncertain and ambiguous light than Wilson allows, particularly as regards what Wilson sees as the high-minded goodness of the prince and the venality of Falstaff. For Empson, Falstaff is a complex embodiment of sharp moral tensions and complexities (nationalism, Machiavellianism, the class system), and Hal's contact with him refines the prince's sensibility to these subjects—a point evident in *Henry V* where the new king succeeds in bringing about national unity. The essay, which often exhibits a wry annoyance over Wilson's perceived royalist sympathies, is an important modern contribution to Falstaff criticism.

183. Everett, Barbara. "The Fatness of Falstaff: Shakespeare and Character." *Proceedings of the British Academy* 76 (1990 [pub. 1991]): 109-28.

In defining character in Shakespeare as "an insight embodied into brilliant forms of the real," Everett cites Launce's dog in *The Two Gentlemen of Verona*, Richard III, Bottom, Shylock, and Falstaff (particularly in his fatness) as examples of the dramatist's ability to create characters who are "recognizably opaque," "essentially thingy," and possessed of a compelling "physicality" (114-15). She further suggests that Falstaff's original name (Oldcastle) reinforces this sense of the bodily; the name associates the figure with the ruined castles and "fading mansions" of Shakespeare's time, and also with mankind itself, since "the fading *man*sion is *man*hood, the ruinous castle where men live all their lives" (118). Everett sees such realized physicality as an important feature of the *Henry IV* plays, and even finds analogies between their structural form and Falstaff's body; from the moment in *1 Henry IV* when Falstaff stabs Hotspur's dead body (5.4.127-29) and throughout *2 Henry IV* "his fatness loses its airy poise, its grace of imagination, and begins to solidify, greasily, into unnerving realisms of social class and gender," thus mirroring the "centrifugal loss of energy" (126) that characterizes the transition from part one to part two.

184. Gottschalk, Paul A. "Hal and the 'Play Extempore' in *1 Henry IV*." *Texas Studies in Literature and Language* 15 (1974): 605-14. Repr. in Bevington (no. 202).

Gottschalk takes issue with the contention of Richard L. McGuire (*Shakespeare Quarterly* 18 [1967]: 47-52), who regards the "play extempore" in the tavern scene (2.4) as a moment of crisis in which Hal discovers his true self through pretense. Instead Gottschalk claims that "Hal has already made his crucial commitment to regality in Act I," and that Shakespeare hides the "fulfillment of Hal's character from Hal's contemporaries while revealing it to us" (607). For Gottschalk, this phenomenon occurs most clearly in the play extempore, where two types of role-playing confct with each other: Falstaff's fictionalizing, which translates the serious into unreal play, and Hal's realistic role-playing, which anticipates his future as king. The episode thus dramatizes a major shift in the action of the play, since it shows Falstaff losing his power over Hal and coming "under the aspect of royalty" (614).

185. Hawkins, Sherman H. "*Henry IV*: The Structural Problem Revisited." *Shakespeare Quarterly* 33 (1982): 278-301.

Noting Harold Jenkins's contention that *1* and *2 Henry IV* are both one play and two, complementary *and* incompatible (no. 188), Hawkins challenges Jenkins's basic theory that part two was an "unpremeditated addition" (279). Hawkins conducts a meticulous, point-by-point refutation of Jenkins's essay, claiming that it "involves mistaken arithmetic, a dubious assumption, and some very questionable evidence" (283). Instead, he presents a fabric of symmetries, balances, and apparently intentional parallels and contrasts between the two plays as evidence of a conscious design on Shakespeare's part. Hawkins also is concerned to defend Shakespeare's artistic mastery over his material (a point questioned by Jenkins) by pointing out that in *Henry IV* the dramatist fashions a two-part play in diptych form that mirrors the diptych structure of the two great tetralogies—i.e., an eight-play historical sequence with two separate four-play elements. The argument, highly detailed and massively evidential, is an important counter to an influential reading of the *Henry IV* plays.

186. Hunter, G. K. "*Henry IV* and the Elizabethan Two-Part Play." *Review of English Studies*, n.s., 5 (1954): 236-48.

In treating the unity of the *Henry IV* plays, Hunter maintains that they do not possess "unity" in the sense of continuity or development (as do long novels); rather their unity is one of theme: they resemble "a diptych, in which repetition of shape and design focuses attention on what is common in the two parts" (237). He examines other two-part plays of the period (Chapman's *Conspiracy and Tragedy of Charles Duke of Byron*, Marlowe's *Tamburlaine*, and Marston's *Antonio and Mellida*) to show that the structure of these plays depends upon "a parallel setting out of the incidents rather than on any picking-up of all the threads of Part One" (243), and relates this method to Shakespeare's. For Hunter, the central aspect of the unity of *1* and *2 Henry IV* is their focus on the conflict between Rebellion and Order—a conflict that relates not only to the career of Hal, but also to that of Falstaff, who, like Chapman's Byron, proceeds "directly and blindly through a repetition of the acts of Part One to a purgation by death or dismissal at the end of Part Two" (247).

187. Hunter, Robert G. "Shakespeare's Comic Sense As It Strikes Us Today: Falstaff and the Protestant Ethic." In *Shakespeare: Pattern of Excelling Nature*, ed. David Bevington and Jay L. Halio, 125-32. Newark: Univ. of Delaware Press; London: Associated Univ. Presses, 1978. Repr. in Bevington (no. 202).

Hunter maintains that the *Henry IV* plays dramatize, in the rejection of Falstaff (*2 Henry IV*, 5.5), "the victory of the Protestant ethic, presenting that social triumph as a psychological event, the decision of Henry the Fifth to labor in his vocation, to do his duty in that royal station to which it pleased God to call him" (125). For Hunter, Falstaff is the "antiembodiment" of the Protestant Ethic, a system of belief opposed (via Luther and Calvin) to "sensuous culture of all kinds" (126), which stresses duty and success in worldly affairs as evidence of moral rightness. Hunter conducts a detailed analysis of Falstaff as a character (his appetites, sense of circular time, methods of play, contradictions of conventional notions of success, love of carnival, etc.) to demonstrate that he defines the Protestant ethic not only "by being what it isn't, but also by being a different variety of what it is: a means of coping with the fears engendered by the realities of the human condition" (132).

188. Jenkins, Harold. *The Structural Problem in Shakespeare's "Henry the Fourth."* London: Methuen, 1956. Repr., in part, in Hunter (no. 205).

This is the printed text of a lecture delivered at Westfield College, University of London, on 19 May 1955. Jenkins addresses the question of whether the *Henry IV* sequence is one play or two by examining the structural continuities within *1 Henry IV*; he finds the play to be a symmetrical whole as regards the thematic and structural contrast between Hal and Hotspur, but incomplete (i.e., anticipatory of actions unfulfilled) in its references to Hal's eventual kingship and the rejection of Falstaff. He contends that "after the middle of Part I *Henry IV* changes its shape" (19), and attributes this shift to a change of mind on Shakespeare's part as he was writing the play. According to Jenkins, Shakespeare originally intended to have Hal ascend the throne and reject Falstaff at the end of *1 Henry IV*, but abandoned this idea as he was writing the fourth act, deferring this crucial sequence to 5.5 of *2 Henry IV*, a play that "sometimes depends on what has happened in Part I" and sometimes, in its disregard for the action of the earlier play, "denies that Part I exists" (26). Jenkins concludes that *Henry IV* is both one play *and* two; the two parts are "complementary" but also "independent and even incompatible" (26). See no. 185.

189. Knights, L. C. "Time's Subjects: The Sonnets and *King Henry IV, Part II.*" In *Some Shakespearean Themes*, 45–64. London: Chatto & Windus, 1959. Repr. in Bloom (no. 204) and in Hunter (no. 205).

In addition to "Time's Subjects," this book contains specific discussions of *Troilus and Cressida*, *King Lear*, *Macbeth*, *Antony and Cleopatra*, and *Coriolanus*, as well as essays on Shakespearean criticism and Shakespeare's "Public World." Knights sees the Sonnets and *2 Henry IV* as centrally concerned with time and change, and the latter as "a tragi-comedy of human frailty" focusing upon "age, disappointment and decay" (52)—a motif apparent in the deep and continual sense of frustration that pervades the play, and particularly in the failed expectations of Falstaff, Northumberland, and Henry IV. For Knights, this sense of somberness invests even characters like Falstaff, Doll, Shallow, and Silence with a touching pathos; but the play also implies, ironically, that men are time's subjects because of their pursuit of "policy" (62), a value existing in, and bounded by, time.

190. Kris, Ernst. "Prince Hal's Conflict." In *Psychoanalytic Explorations in Art*,

273-88. New York: International Universities Press, 1952; New York: Schocken Books, 1964.

Kris's wide-ranging study employs the techniques of psychoanalysis to shed light on creative art. His lone chapter on Shakespeare approaches the *Henry IV* plays from a Freudian perspective and focuses on the theme of father-son relationships, with particular attention to Hal's "conflict" with Henry IV. Kris sees Hal as a figure not unlike Hamlet, i.e., a young man who grapples with regicidal thoughts even as he seeks after moral justification. For Kris, Hal's strong moral aversion to the regicide committed by his father (which even permits Hal to idealize Richard II), forces the prince to retreat into the tavern world in order to "avoid contamination with regicide" (282)—a situation complicated by the fact that his own impulse to regicide (and hence parricide) "is alive in his unconscious" (282). In this psychological context Falstaff serves as the father-substitute, a figure against whom Hal/Henry V unleashes his latent filial hostilities in the cruelty of the rejection scene (*2 Henry IV*, 5.5).

191. Morgann, Maurice. *An Essay on the Dramatic Character of Sir John Falstaff.* In *Maurice Morgann: Shakespearian Criticism*, ed. Daniel A. Fineman, 143-215. Oxford: Clarendon Press, 1972. Repr., in part, in Bevington (no. 202) and in Hunter (no. 205).

Morgann's 1777 essay seeks to prove that Falstaff is not a coward but instead a man of courage. Morgann sees Falstaff's feigning death at Shrewsbury in *1 Henry IV* (5.4) as a reasonable stratagem, finds the common opinion about him in the *Henry IV* plays to support the view that he is an able soldier, and affirms that since he derives from a noble family he is the inheritor of "personal strength and natural courage" (162)—a point evidenced by his service as a youth to Thomas Mowbray as well as by his "attendants, title, and honourable pension" (173). Morgann sees no evidence at all of the *miles gloriosus* in Falstaff, dismisses John of Lancaster's rebuke to him in *2 Henry IV* (4.3.26-29) as politically motivated, and cites Coleville's surrender to Falstaff in *2 Henry IV* (4.3.1-23) as evidence against Lancaster's censure. Quoting copiously from the *Henry IV* plays, Morgann turns almost every action of Falstaff, or statement by or about him, to the character's advantage, and sees even his fleeing from the robbery at Gadshill in *1 Henry IV* (2.2) as circumspect. Morgann does not deny the obvious faults of Falstaff (lying, drunkenness, lasciviousness, gluttony, insolence, etc.), but denies that they produce either "disgust" or "pernicious effect" (204); rather Falstaff is a great figure of comic incongruity, whom we admire, love, and enjoy. The essay is the starting place for all criticism on Falstaff. A section on "The Longer Revisions of *An Essay on Falstaff*" follows the text of the essay (219-88), as does Morgann's "Commentary on *The Tempest*" (291-47) and brief "Miscellaneous Comments" (351-52). Fineman's "Biographical Introduction" (3-36), "Critical Introduction" (37-126), and "Textual Introduction" (127-40) round out the volume.

192. Nuttall, A. D. "*Henry IV*: Prince Hal and Falstaff." In *A New Mimesis: Shakespeare and the Representation of Reality*, 143-61. London: Methuen, 1983.

Repr. in Bloom (no. 203).

In attacking structuralist approaches to literature as overly concerned with the mechanisms of art and artistic technique, Nuttall reaffirms the connection between literature and reality by arguing for the restoration of mimesis as a fundamental principle of literary criticism. His study concentrates on *Julius Caesar*, *Coriolanus*, *The Merchant of Venice*, *Othello*, and the *Henry IV* plays. As regards *1* and *2 Henry IV*, he argues that Shakespeare sets up the stereotype of the wild young man in conflict with an authoritarian father (Henry IV) only to undermine it by introducing Falstaff as an aged reprobate (and alternate father) whose irresponsibility contrasts with the adult seriousness of the young prince; even in the Hal-Bolingbroke relationship "the old man ... is the outlaw and the son is the possible agent of control" (153). Nuttall closely examines Hal's opening soliloquy in *1 Henry IV* (1.2.195–217), finding it "an essentially mimetic statement about the *character*" of Prince Hal that depicts him as a "White Machiavel" (147)—a quality also evident in *2 Henry IV* when he defends his premature taking of his father's crown (4.5). In episodes such as these, Nuttall argues, Shakespearean mimesis has a "glaringly obvious, single, clarifying source in reality itself" (158). The argument is wide-ranging, detailed, and allusive.

193. Rumrich, John P. "Shakespeare's Walking Plays: Image and Form in *1* and *2 Henry IV*." In *Shakespeare's English Histories: A Quest for Form and Genre*, ed. John W. Velz, 111–41. Binghamton, N.Y.: Medieval & Renaissance Texts & Studies, 1996.

This essay examines the act of walking and images of walking in the *Henry IV* plays as essential elements of the plays' meaning and form. Rumrich adduces virtually every mention of feet and walking in the plays and relates them to the Elizabethan custom of "processioning" (119)—that is, the act of traversing by foot along the boundaries of a parish by its inhabitants to ensure that no outsiders had encroached on community property or attempted to enclose it. He sees this practice of clarifying legal boundaries by walking over land as central to *1* and *2 Henry IV*, and probes in detail its significance regarding such matters as self-interest, identity, and possession. In Rumrich's scheme, Hal emerges as a worthy prince and ruler, whose comparison to the fleet-footed Mercury in *1 Henry IV* (4.1.104–10) is fully in keeping with "the imagery that underwrites the dramatic design" of the *Henry IV* plays (141). The essay is meticulously and evidentially argued.

194. Traub, Valerie. "Prince Hal's Falstaff: Positioning Psychoanalysis and the Female Reproductive Body." In *Desire and Anxiety: Circulations of Sexuality in Shakespearean Drama*, 50–70. London: Routledge, 1992.

Traub's book "is structured as an investigation of one problematic: the relation between erotic desire and its corollary, anxiety, and their role in the construction of male and female subjects in Shakespearean drama" (3); it contains extensive treatments of *Hamlet*, *Othello*, *The Winter's Tale*, *Troilus and Cressida*, *As You Like It*, and *Twelfth Night*, in addition to the essay on the *Henriad*. In the latter she maintains that Shakespearean drama and psychoanalytic theory both regard the female reproductive body as a Bakhtinian "grotesque body" (51), and that they repress this figure in their separate narratives of psychic development; thus the *Henriad* exhibits the "kinds of repressions a phallocentric culture requires to maintain and reproduce itself" (53). In this scheme Falstaff becomes a pre-Oedipal maternal figure against whom Hal must differentiate himself, and Katherine (in *Henry V*), a materially and linguistically subjugated figure who shows how much male sexuality—specifically male heterosexuality—depends upon the repression and control of a female other. The argument, strongly indebted to Freud and Lacan, is detailed and allusive.

195. Wilson, J. Dover. *The Fortunes of Falstaff.* Cambridge: Cambridge Univ. Press; New York: Macmillan, 1944. Repr. often. The essay is repr., in part, in Waith (no. 86), in Bevington (no. 202), in Hunter (no. 205), and in Berman (no. 259).

This volume consists of an introduction, followed by printed versions of five Clark lectures delivered at Cambridge in May 1943, each comprising a single chapter. Wilson is concerned to debunk "romantic" readings of Falstaff's character such as those of Morgann (no. 191) and Bradley (no. 179). Aligning himself in his introduction (1–14) with Samuel Johnson, he argues that criticism of a play should proceed in serial fashion; he maintains in addition that *1* and *2 Henry IV* comprise a unified and continuous dramatic action. In chap. 2 (15–35), Wilson takes the biblical and morality play origins of the *Henry IV* plays very seriously, and sees Shakespeare, in reworking these materials, creating his own didactic myth of the Prodigal Prince (Hal) and Riot (Falstaff); he argues further that Falstaff's association with feasting and joyous community give us "appetizing images" about him (31), and that his pattern of "*mock*-repentance" in the *Henry IV* plays (32) also connects him with the biblical story of the prodigal son. In chap. 3 (36–59), Wilson claims that from the outset of *1 Henry IV* we see Falstaff as an "impossible companion" (39) for Hal, and the latter as superior to Falstaff in intellect, judgment, and responsibility; Falstaff is "a butt and a coward" (46), but one who elicits from us "affectionate mirth" (48). As regards the Gad's Hill robbery (2.2.81–111), however, Wilson expresses some skepticism about Falstaff's cowardice, and argues that, in recounting the episode (2.4), the fat knight reveals to alert members of the audience that he actually did recognize Hal and Poins from the beginning. Chapter 4 (60–81) treats the maturation of Hal, and argues (contra Bradley) that the prince is both chivalric and honorable, one who values deeds over personal reputation; in comparison both Hotspur (as rebel) and Falstaff (as opportunist) debase the honor that Hal represents. Wilson also sees Hal's seizing of his father's crown and his subsequent defense of the act (*2 Henry IV*, 4.5) as reflecting positively on his character. Chapter 5 (81–113) notes the literary origins of Falstaff in the *miles gloriosus* of classical comedy, but claims that unlike this figure Falstaff is no sham soldier; rather he is an "Old Soldier on the make" (84), a man of no military reputation who turns war to his advantage. Wilson sees Falstaff transformed in *2 Henry IV* into a figure of real (albeit undeserved) reputation, more ludicrous and pretentious than before, and less capable of inspiring our affection; he also stresses the importance of the Lord Chief Justice in *2 Henry IV* as both a foil and a nemesis to Falstaff, a figure of law and sobriety who undermines "our pleasure in Falstaff's company" (99). Chapter 6 (114-28) argues that the alternation of scenes in *2 Henry IV* "drive[s] home the inevitability, the justice, of the choice Hal is about to make" in rejecting Falstaff (114), and defends the rejection (5.5) as illustrating Shakespeare's ability to "balance" the two principles of Order and Liberty (127-28). Wilson also argues that Shakespeare originally intended to include Falstaff in *Henry V*, but abandoned the idea, probably because Will Kemp, the actor who played Falstaff, left the acting company. The study contains many detailed and provocative readings of virtually all the key scenes in the *Henry IV* plays, and is one of the most important justifications of Hal (and his behavior toward Falstaff) in the critical tradition.

F. Stage History; Performance Criticism.

196. Hodgdon, Barbara. *Shakespeare in Performance: "Henry IV, Part Two."* Manchester: Manchester Univ. Press, 1993.

This book consists of an introduction, followed by individual chapters on each of the following productions of *2 Henry IV*: 1) the 1951 Shakespeare Memorial Theatre production, directed by Michael Redgrave, with Harry Andrews as Henry, Richard Burton as Hal, and Anthony Quayle as Falstaff; 2) the 1979 BBC television production, directed by David Giles, with Jon Finch as Henry, David Gwillim as Hal, and Anthony Quayle as Falstaff; 3) the 1975 Royal Shakespeare Theatre production, directed by Terry Hands, with Emrys James as Henry, Alan Howard as Hal, and Brewster Mason as Falstaff; 4) the 1982 Royal Shakespeare Company production, directed by Trevor Nunn, with Patrick Stewart as Henry, Gerard Murphy as Hal, and Joss Ackland as Falstaff; and 5) the 1986-89 English Shakespeare Company production, directed by Michael Bogdanov, with Patrick O'Connell, John Castle, and Michael Cronin as Henry, Michael Pennington and John Dougall as Hal, and John Woodvine and Barry Stanton as Falstaff. The introduction (1-17) takes up such questions as the cultural significance of Rumor, Falstaff, the Boar's Head Tavern for Elizabethan and modern spectators, as well as the play's ideological emphasis on the creation of an historical past. It also includes a brief stage history of the play from its origins to the present, with particular attention to the productions represented in the book. Throughout, Hodgdon is alert to the ways in which literary criticism and theatrical practice interact. The discussions of individual productions are an illuminating blend of literary analysis and theatrical criticism, and take up virtually every important scene in the play. An appendix (146-47) gives complete cast lists for all the productions discussed, as well as for Orson Welles's 1966 film *Chimes at Midnight*. A bibliography (149-52) completes the volume.

197. McMillin, Scott. *Shakespeare in Performance: "Henry IV, Part One."* Manchester: Manchester Univ. Press, 1991.

This book consists of an introduction, followed by individual chapters on each of the following productions of *1 Henry IV*: 1) the 1945 Old Vic production, directed by John Burrell, with Nicholas Hannen as Henry, Michael Warre as Hal, Ralph Richardson as Falstaff, and Laurence Olivier as Hotspur; 2) the 1951 Shakespeare Memorial Theatre production, directed by Anthony Quayle, with Harry Andrews as Henry, Richard Burton as Hal, Anthony Quayle as Falstaff, and Michael Redgrave as Hotspur; 3) the 1964 Royal Shakespeare Company production, directed by Peter Hall, with Eric Porter as Henry, Ian Holm as Hal, Hugh Griffith as Falstaff, and Roy Dotrice as Hotspur; 4) the 1975 Royal Shakespeare Company production, directed by Terry Hands, with Emrys James as Henry, Alan Howard as Hal, Brewster Mason as Falstaff, and Stuart Wilson as Hotspur; 5) Orson Welles's 1966 film *Chimes at Midnight*, with John Gielgud as Henry, Keith Baxter as Hal, Orson Welles as Falstaff, and Norman Rodway as Hotspur, and the 1979 BBC television production, directed by David Giles, with Jon Finch as Henry, David Gwillim as Hal, Anthony Quayle as Falstaff, and Tim Pigott-Smith as Hotspur; and 6) the 1986 English Shakespeare Company production, directed by Michael Bogdanov, with Patrick O'Connell as Henry, Michael Pennington as Hal, John Woodvine as Falstaff, and John Price as Hotspur. The introduction (1–14) notes the changes in the conception of *1 Henry IV* from pre-twentieth-century emphases on Falstaff and/or Hotspur to twentieth-century emphases on politics and the character of Hal, traces the play's performance history from 1596 to the present and its place in the larger cycle of history plays, and contextualizes the chapters to follow. The book is a highly allusive, detailed, and judicious survey of the performance history of the play that engages virtually every important scene in *1 Henry IV* from a critical as well as dramaturgical point of view. A bibliography (123–25) and an appendix (126–28) listing significant twentieth-century productions and adaptations, as well as major actors in the productions described, round out the volume.

198. Pechter, Edward. "Falsifying Men's Hopes: The Ending of *1 Henry IV*." *Modern Language Quarterly* 41 (1980): 211–30.

Pechter claims that *1 Henry IV* involves the audience "in a sequence of problematic expectations about the ways in which the play can or should end, making us increasingly conscious of the nature of our desires for order and disorder, and of the different needs these desires seek to satisfy in both dramatic and actual experience" (212). He sees the histories (and *1 Henry IV* specifically) as dramatizing the tension betweeen two basic human impulses, the rage for order and the rage for chaos, and also suggests that the play is not only about civil war, "but furnishes an experience of civil war for its audience" (216). This sense of self-division he links to the play's multiple styles, accents, roles, and voices, all of which offer a pleasurable sense of variety for the audience but no single dramatic hero or clear center of authority. Pechter sees the play's many conflicts as dramatic strengths, since they allow the audience to enter into a responsive sympathy with all the roles, and its ending (neither comic nor tragic) as resisting "all endeavors to make it conform to a normative, coherent structure" (229); in its "irresolute resolution" (230) the ending contains all of the various meanings its audience has experienced.

199. Sider, John W. "Falstaff's Broken Voice." *Shakespeare Survey* 37 (1984): 85–88.

Sider argues (on the basis of evidence from *1* and *2 Henry IV* as well as other Shakespearean plays) that Falstaff's voice should sound aged and high-pitched, not strong and robust as actors from the eighteenth century onward have depicted it. The contention here is that seeing Falstaff as a less robust figure than he has traditionally been represented in stage and critical tradition would greatly enrich the ironic dimensions of his character, particularly as he interacts throughout the plays with old and young alike.

200. Wharton, T. F. *"Henry the Fourth" Parts 1 and 2: Text and Performance.* London: Macmillan, 1983. Repr., in part, in Bevington (no. 202).

This volume is divided into two parts: "Part One: Text" (9–43) and "Part Two: Performance" (44–80). In part one, Wharton argues for the histories (and *1* and *2 Henry IV* in particular) as a national epic united around the themes of the interpretation of history; sickness and disease; the uses and abuses of time; and Hal's relationship to Falstaff and his father. Each of these themes is given detailed treatment, with frequent allusion to the text. In part two Wharton examines these "key themes" (44) as they combine with character and staging in four modern productions of the *Henry IV* plays: 1) the 1964 Royal Shakespeare Company production, directed by Peter Hall, John Barton, and Clifford Williams, with Eric Porter as Henry, Ian Holm as Hal, Roy Dotrice as Hotspur, and Hugh Griffith as Falstaff; 2) the 1975 Royal Shakespeare Company production, directed by Terry Hands, with Emrys James as Henry, Alan Howard as Hal, Stuart Wilson as Hotspur, and Brewster Mason as Falstaff; 3) the 1982 Royal Shakespeare Company production, directed by Trevor Nunn, with Patrick Stewart as Henry, Gerard Murphy as Hal, Timothy Dalton as Hotspur, and Joss Ackland as Falstaff; and 4) the 1979 BBC television production, directed by David Giles, with Jon Finch as Henry, David Gwillim as Hal, Tim Pigott-Smith as Hotspur, and Anthony Quayle as Falstaff. Throughout, Wharton compares and contrasts these productions' handling of the plays' major themes. The book also includes a plot synopsis and list of sources for *1* and *2 Henry IV* (8).

201. Wiles, David. "Falstaff." In *Shakespeare's Clown: Actor and Text in the Elizabethan Playhouse*, 116–35. Cambridge: Cambridge Univ. Press, 1987.

Wiles is interested in the relationship between the actor and playwright generally and Will Kemp and Shakespeare particularly. His book not only traces the history of the role of the Elizabethan clown (from the Vice of the moralities, through Richard Tarlton, to Kemp and Robert Armin), it also claims that specific lines were written by Shakespeare for the individual clowns who acted in his plays—i.e., first Kemp and later Armin. In the chapter on Falstaff, Wiles argues that the role of Falstaff is that of the clown, that Kemp played the role, and that the part was written with him in mind. Wiles cites Kemp's special qualities as an actor (his size, reputation as a solo entertainer, pace as an actor, etc.) in order to link him with the character of Falstaff, and also points out that with "Kemp/Falstaff's dismissal by Hal [in *2 Henry IV*], and his reappearance in the jig, the conventional structure of comedy is restored" (129). He also maintains that Falstaff's/Kemp's modes of speech establish a "communality with the audience" that Hal and his father never achieve (132), thus investing the character with a status radically different from that of others on the Elizabethan stage. The discussion is taut, allusive, and evidential.

See also nos. 79, 81, 147, 148, 149, 153, 154, 162, 195, 202.

G. Collections of Essays.

202. Bevington, David, ed. *"Henry the Fourth Parts I and II": Critical Essays.* New York: Garland Publishing, 1986.

This book reprints literary criticism and performance criticism on the *Henry IV* plays from the eighteenth century to 1983, and includes the work of Corbyn Morris, Samuel Johnson, Elizabeth Montagu, Maurice Morgann (no. 191), Henry Mackenzie, Richard Cumberland, Samuel Taylor Coleridge, William Hazlitt, Edward Dowden, George Bernard Shaw, A. C. Bradley (no. 179), Mark Van Doren (no. 75), John Dover Wilson (no. 195), E. M. W. Tillyard (no. 35), W. H. Auden (no. 174), Northrop Frye, Arthur Colby Sprague, Robert Langbaum, Bernard Spivack, C. L. Barber (no. 158), G. K. Hunter, R. J. Dorius (no. 50), Jonas A. Barish (no. 175), Sigurd Burckhardt (no. 45), D. J. Palmer (no. 163), Paul A. Gottschalk (no. 184), Robert G. Hunter (no. 187), Ronald R. Macdonald (no. 40), Robert N. Watson, R. L. Smallwood, and T. F. Wharton (no. 200). In his introduction (xi-xxii), Bevington briefly traces critical attitudes toward the *Henry IV* plays from the eighteenth century to the mid 1980s, illustrating critical trends by alluding both to the works included in his volume and to other important studies. The book provides a useful introduction to the major contours of criticism on the *Henry IV* plays over the past three centuries.

203. Bloom, Harold, ed. *William Shakespeare's "Henry IV, Part 1."* New York: Chelsea House, 1987.

This volume reprints criticism on *1 Henry IV* by Harold C. Goddard (no. 55), Wyndham Lewis, C. L. Barber (no. 158), Ricardo J. Quinones (no. 69), Michael McCanles, Eliot Krieger, David Sundelson, A. D. Nuttall (no. 192), and E. Talbot Donaldson. In his introduction (1-7), Bloom focuses exclusively on Falstaff, whom he sees as a character more suited to the world of comedy than that of history—a figure who, except for his misplaced "love" for Hal, "is freedom itself, because he seems free of the superego" (3). For Bloom, the fat knight is one of the supreme creations in all of literature, "the essence of invention," a "super-mimesis" who allows us to see a reality that we could not otherwise comprehend (7).

204. **Bloom, Harold,** ed. *William Shakespeare's "Henry IV, Part 2."* New York: Chelsea House, 1987.

This volume reprints criticism on *2 Henry IV* by Harold C. Goddard (no. 55), C. L. Barber (no. 158), L. C. Knights (no. 189), Zvi Jagendorf, Moody E. Prior, M. C. Bradbrook, John W. Blanpied (no. 44), Harry Berger, Jr., and Stephen Greenblatt (no. 29). The introduction reprints Bloom's introduction to his volume of essays on *1 Henry IV* (no. 203).

205. **Hunter, G. K.,** ed. *"Henry IV Parts I and II": A Casebook.* London: Macmillan, 1970.

This volume reprints criticism on *1* and *2 Henry IV* by Samuel Johnson, Maurice Morgann (no. 191), A. C. Bradley (no. 179), H. B. Charlton, J. Dover Wilson (no. 195), E. M. W. Tillyard (no. 35), J. I. M. Stewart (no. 73), William Empson (no. 182), Harold Jenkins (no. 188), L. C. Knights (no. 189), W. H. Auden (no. 174), C. L. Barber (no. 158), and Paul A. Jorgensen (no. 168). In his introduction (9-20), Hunter notes the varied nature of Shakespeare's histories and their resistance to neat generic categorization, and provides a brief summary of critical responses to the plays from the eighteenth century onward. He stresses the ethical and political complexity of *1* and *2 Henry IV*, cautions against seeing the plays as abstract moral treatises, and points out the structural problems they create as two separate but obviously related dramas. He also notes the importance of Falstaff as the embodiment of wit, energy, and comic complexity. According to Hunter, Falstaff's relationship with Hal is one of simultaneous opposition and connection throughout part one—a state of "equipoise"—but all this changes in part two when, after the rejection of Falstaff (*2 Henry IV*, 5.5), Hal becomes an unsatisfactory "free-standing figure," a leader whose patriotism sounds "strident" without a "base note" to oppose it (20).

H. Bibliographies.

206. **Gira, Catherine, and Adele Seeff,** comps. *"Henry IV" Parts 1 and 2: An Annotated Bibliography.* New York: Garland Publishing, 1994.

This annotated bibliography contains over 1,500 entries on *1* and *2 Henry IV*, covering chiefly the period from 1940 to 1985 but including selected items before 1940 as well. The work is arranged under the following headings: I. Criticism; II. Sources and Background; III. Textual Studies, Bibliographies, and Dating; IV. Editions; V. Stage History, Performances, and Film; and VI. Adaptations, Influence, and Synopses. In their introduction (vii-xxxvii) Gira and Seeff trace in broad outline important interpretive, scholarly, and performance-based responses to the play. The work, though at times unevenly annotated, is nonetheless a useful source of scholarly information on the two plays.

207. **Kiernan, Michael,** comp. *"Henry the Fourth, Part One": A Bibliography to Supplement the New Variorum Edition of 1936 and the Supplement of 1956.* New York: The Modern Language Association of America, 1977.

This bibliography supplements Hemingway's variorum edition of *1 Henry IV* (no. 149) and Evans's *Supplement* to that edition (no. 148). It includes 280 new bibliographic entries under the following headings: Editions; Text; Criticism; Sources; Commentary; Music; Staging and Stage History. The items are largely unannotated, although a brief phrase of description is provided for selected entries.

208. Shaaber, M[atthias] A., comp. *"Henry the Fourth, Part Two": A Bibliography to Supplement the New Variorum Edition of 1940.* New York: The Modern Language Association of America, 1977.

This bibliography supplements Shaaber's 1940 variorum edition (no. 154). It includes 398 new bibliographic entries under the following headings: Editions; Text; Date; Criticism; Sources; Commentary; Music; Staging and Stage History. The items are largely unannotated, although a brief phrase of description is provided for selected entries.

See also no. 148.

V. HENRY V

A. Editions.

209. Craik, T. W., ed. *King Henry V.* The Arden Shakespeare. London: Routledge, 1995.

In his monograph-length introduction (1-111) Craik argues for a 1599 date of composition for *Henry V*, and for Holinshed and the anonymous *Famous Victories of Henry the Fifth* as the chief sources for the play. He summarizes the differences between the 1600 Quarto and 1623 Folio versions (his text is based on F but respectful of Q as illustrative of changes made for performance), and provides a thorough discussion of the editorial problems resulting from "bad" quartos, "foul papers," and performance-based texts as they relate to *Henry V*. Craik summarizes the action, regarding the play as epic and celebratory, downplaying its (perceived) deflationary ironies, and suggesting how it might take shape in performance. In reviewing major critical opinions on the play from Hazlitt to the present, he notes how *Henry V* lends itself to the purposes of politics, but warns that making it "a problematic play full of ambiguities and ironies" does not make it a better one (75). Craik also provides a brief performance history (including film and television versions) that focuses on the play as a piece for *acting*, and cautions against "fashionable innovations which may interpose between a director and the script" (95). His introduction concludes with a detailed description of the textual characteristics and provenance of the early Quartos and F. Appendices provide a reduced photographic facsimile of the full text of Q1 (1600); a map of France and the south of England at the time of the play; a map of the route of Henry V's army from 13 August to 17 November 1415; a genealogical table of the English and French royal houses; and a doubling chart showing how a single actor might play various roles. Craik's edition is extremely alert to performance. Textual, glossarial, and critical notes appear at the foot of each page of text.

210. Gurr, Andrew, ed. *King Henry V.* The New Cambridge Shakespeare. Cambridge: Cambridge Univ. Press, 1992.

In his introduction (1-55) Gurr dates the composition of *Henry V* in the early summer of 1599, situating the play in a period of patriotic militarism and political uncertainty. He discusses the importance of the Chorus at some length, seeing it as "coercive" (6) in its consistent misrepresentation of the action it purports to introduce, and probes the nature of this misrepresentation in the body of the play, specifically in the recurring references to "the Jerusalem theme" (13), to the "dogs of war" (14), and finally, in the use of *syllepsis* and *antanaclasis* in the speeches of both the Chorus and Henry. As regards each of these repetitive patterns, Gurr uncovers deflationary aspects of the play and its protagonist expressed ironically through the Chorus. He goes on to trace Shakespeare's debt to Holinshed and Hall (the latter chiefly through his influence on *The Famous Victories of Henry V*), but pays special attention to two "potent issues" of the day (28): the succession question, as reflected in John Stubbes's *Gaping Gulf* (1579) and the collaborative *Sir John Oldcastle* (c. 1599); and the proper conduct of war, as treated in Alberico Gentili's *De Jure Belli* (1579), where Henry's decision to kill the French prisoners is disparaged, and Richard Crompton's *Mansion of Magnanimitie* (1599), where it is weakly defended. Gurr also examines the related themes of "brotherhood" and "differentiation in social status" (33), again seeing both of these as having an ironic edge. In surveying staging and stage history, he notes that patriotic renderings of the play dominated the stage until the 1960s and 1970s, when anti-war productions began to appear, and further provides a brief performance history (including film and television versions) from the seventeenth century to the present. He explains in a "Note on the Text" appended to the introduction, that the "target text for this edition is what we might loosely call the playscript" (56), and argues for the superiority of F to Q on the grounds that, despite its many inconsistencies, F "is a printed copy of the manuscript submitted to the company before the play went into rehearsal" (57) and hence more likely to represent the playscript than Q, which was derived from a transcript of the performed play "adjusted from memory by some of the original players" (57). The textual characteristics and provenance of F and Q are treated in a "Textual Analysis" appended to the text (in which Gurr agrees with Taylor [no. 211] that Q's Bourbon should replace F's Dauphin in 3.7, 4.2, and 4.5); three other appendices follow, treating, in order, the relationship of *The Famous Victories*, Holinshed, and *The Mansion of Magnanimitie* to *Henry V*. A select "Reading List" completes the volume. Textual, glossarial, and critical notes appear at the foot of each page of text.

211. Taylor, Gary, ed. *Henry V*. The Oxford Shakespeare. Oxford: Clarendon Press, 1982.

Taylor's monograph-length introduction (1–74) begins by noting the sharp division of critical opinion elicited by the play and its protagonist, then proceeds to date its composition as no later than May or early June of 1599, amid the swirl of patriotic interest over Essex's campaign in Ireland. Taylor thoroughly describes the textual characteristics of F and Q; and, although he follows traditional editorial practice by basing his edition on F, he is nonetheless respectful of Q, noting with temerity that "In accepting Q's version of Agincourt [substituting Bourbon for the Dauphin in 3.7, 4.2, and 4.5], this edition departs from the practice of all editors since 1623" (25). He believes that Shakespeare "indisputably" consulted both Holinshed and Hall (29), and assigns them preeminent status as sources. Citing Anne Barton with approval (no. 217), he takes a skeptical view of so-called "romance" elements in the play, and sees Henry as a figure of indomitable will disturbingly estranged from others.

He also regards as "indisputable" (54) Shakespeare's reliance upon Chapman's *Seven Books of the Iliads of Homer* (1598) for roughly the first hundred lines of act 4, yet refuses to see the "epic" elements of the play as undermining its "dramatic" quality (55), and defends even the speeches of the Chorus as theatrically effective. In discussing the characters of *Henry V*, Taylor asks us to reconsider the importance of virtually each of the so-called "minor roles" (58), particularly their often vivid significance as revealed through performance. The entire introduction is marbled with detailed references to stage productions from the earliest times to the present, often relying upon these to illustrate critical points. A brief section on "Editorial Procedures" (75-86) follows the introduction; and seven appendices—"The Two Versions of 4.5"; "Four Textual Cruces" (Chorus, 2.41-42, 2.3.16, 4.1.290-93, and Chorus, 5.39-40 [Taylor's lineation, not *Riverside's*]); "Alterations to Lineation"; "Paraphrased Passages from Holinshed"; "Pre-Restoration Allusions to *Henry V*"; "Passages Not in Q"; and "Profanities in Q"—complete the volume. Textual, glossarial, and critical notes appear at the foot of each page of text.

212. **Walter, J. H.**, ed. *King Henry V*. The Arden Shakespeare. London, Methuen, 1954. Introduction repr., in part, in Waith (no. 86) and in Quinn (no. 261).

Walter's text is based upon that of the Cambridge Shakespeare, edited by W. Aldis Wright (9 vols, London: Macmillan, 1891), but departs from it in some details, including the handling of Shakespeare's French; the general intent is "to bring the text nearer to that of the Folio" (vii). In his introduction (xi-xlvii), Walter accepts the view that the copy for F was in the main Shakespeare's foul papers, although parts of it "may have been a playhouse transcript" (xl). He also argues that Shakespeare originally planned the play to include Falstaff as a character, but altered this purpose because the Brooke family (Oldcastle's descendants) had raised objections to the continued identification of their ancestor with Falstaff. Walter dates the composition of *Henry V* in the spring or summer of 1599 and describes the early quarto editions, then goes on briefly to survey the diversity of critical opinions on the play from Samuel Johnson through the twentieth century. He sees the play as a dramatic epic on the ideal Christian prince as propounded in the writings of such figures as Erasmus, Elyot, Chelidonius, and Hooker, and takes the notion of Prince Hal's "conversion" very seriously, relating it to Renaissance religious and theological traditions. Throughout, Walter defends the character and behavior of Henry, seeing the king as a figure of great "spiritual strength" and "moral courage" who inspires others (xxxiv). In his discussion of sources and influences, Walter concludes that Shakespeare used both Hall and Holinshed, the *Henrici Quinti Angliae Regis Gesta*, Pseudo-Elmham's *Vita et Gesta Henrici Quinti*, the *Brut*, the chronicles of Fabyan and Le Fèvre, and a lost volume that served as the source for *The Famous Victories of Henry V*. Appendices reprint extracts from Holinshed; an extract from the *Chronicle of John Strecche for the Reign of Henry V, 1414-1422* (for the tennis balls episode [1.2]); and extracts from the wooing scene of *The Famous Victories*. Textual, glossarial, and critical notes appear at the foot of each page of text.

B. Dating and Textual Studies.

213. Jones, G. P. "*Henry V*: The Chorus and the Audience." *Shakespeare Survey* 31 (1978): 93-104.

In noting the implied contradiction between the epic confidence of the Chorus and its defensiveness about the unsuitability of the stage for the subject of *Henry V*, Jones challenges the traditional view of the Chorus as epic unifier of the play's many episodes—i.e., "the very voice of the public playhouse" (95). He argues instead that the Chorus is incompatible with the public theatre, and makes better sense when seen as a device for adapting the play to a performance at court; thus the Folio text (with Chorus) is the court version of the play, while the 1600 quarto (without Chorus) is the public playhouse version. Jones defends a likely court performance on internal grounds (likening the Chorus's promptings for imaginative collaboration by the audience to the physical participation of the audience at a court masque), and further suggests a 1605 date as probable for topical reasons, speculating that the play may have been performed the night following Jonson's *Masque of Blackness*; it would thus have been performed on 7 January 1605. He also suggests a later and unrecorded performance at the Royal Cockpit sometime prior to 2 February 1605.

214. Patterson, Annabel. "The Two Versions of *Henry V*." In *Shakespeare and the Popular Voice*, 71-92. Oxford: Basil Blackwell, 1989. Repr., in part, in Holderness (no. 85).

Patterson's critical agenda is to reassess Shakespeare's social assumptions, particularly his attitudes toward "ordinary working people inside and outside his plays" (1); her study alludes to many Shakespearean works, but *Hamlet, A Midsummer Night's Dream, King Lear*, and *The Tempest*, in addition to *Henry V*, receive detailed attention. She argues that for *Henry V* "the story of the text is inseparable from the political history that is both its content and its context, as also from the thematics of the popular, here defined as not protest or festival but as the relationship of the many to the charismatic leader" (72), and further contends that the Folio and Q1 (1600) versions of the play give substantially different perspectives on events, with Q allowing for a much more positive interpretation of the action than F. Patterson seeks to reevaluate these two texts in terms of their relationship to actual people and events, particularly John Hayward's *History of Henry IV* (1599), and the struggle for power between Elizabeth and Essex that surrounded its publication. She sees the F text (which includes the choruses absent in Q) as "thematizing the *popular*" (85) as regards the Essex rebellion, and embodying a "representational instability ... by allowing the analogy between Essex and Henry to confuse the more 'natural' analogy between Henry and Elizabeth" (86). Patterson also entertains the possibility that Michael Williams (the common soldier often referred to in F's speech headings as "Will.") could represent Shakespeare's *private* association (since speech-headings are never spoken) with the reproachful voice of the common man, at once applicable to Elizabeth and Essex.

215. Wells, Stanley, and Gary Taylor. *Modernizing Shakespeare's Spelling: With Three Studies of the Text of "Henry V."* Oxford: Clarendon Press, 1979.

This is a pilot study to the since-published Oxford edition of Shakespeare (Oxford: Clarendon Press, 1986) under the general editorship of Wells and Taylor. Wells's essay, "Modernizing Shakespeare's Spelling" (3-36) attempts to rationalize the principles of modernizing orthography and punctuation adopted in the Oxford edition. Taylor contributes three essays on the text of *Henry V* that explore the relationship between Q1 (1600) and F1 (1623). In "Quarto Copy for the Folio Text: A Refutation" (41-71), he opposes the theory of A. S. Cairncross ("Quarto Copy for Folio *Henry V*," *Studies in Bibliography* 8 (1956): 67-93) that F was printed from an annotated copy of a reprint of Q, and concludes that no transmission from an annotated printed copy of Q occurred. In "We Happy Few: The 1600 Abridgement" (72-123) he attempts to prove that Q is based upon an abridgement of the play designed for performance in the provinces by a cast of eleven, and provides cast charts in defense of his contention. In "Corruption and Authority in the Bad Quarto" (124-62) he discusses how far Q may be trusted in verbal detail, and attempts to locate Q readings that could be corrections of authorial revisions of those found in F; here he tries to formulate principles that are also applicable to other surviving memorially reported texts. In a "Postscript: Implications" (163-64), he describes four classes of variant that could represent authorial revision: 1) verbal substitutions; 2) verbal additions; 3) adaptations not "the result of mechanical imperatives," e.g., "Clarence" for "Bedford"; and 4) adaptations that "run counter to mechanical imperatives," e.g., "Bourbon" for "Dauphin" (164).

See also nos. 209, 210, 211, 212, 239.

C. Influences; Sources; Historical and Intellectual Backgrounds; Topicality.

216. Altman, Joel B. "'Vile Participation': The Amplification of Violence in the Theater of *Henry V*." *Shakespeare Quarterly* 42 (1991): 1-32.

Altman seeks to "develop a model of *Henry V*" sensitive to both formalism and New Historicism, but one that enriches these approaches "by explaining the play's power in terms of its crafted interaction with the needs of its players and its first audiences" (3). He is especially interested in the historical context of the play (e.g., the Irish invasion), and the specific problem of presenting the king/subject relationship to an audience in a time of war and national emergency; this he sees Shakespeare doing by relating the sense of "contrariety" found in *Henry V* to contemporary ambivalence over involvement in Ireland (8). For Altman, Henry's "participation" in *Henry V* (i.e., his sense of presence and psychic interaction with others) serves as a complex locus of thought and action, where the historical past and the historical present, royal person and common playgoer, join sacramentally, poetically, and politically. The term Altman uses for Shakespeare's "guiding of [the] mental and emotional energies" of the audience so that they can (in an inseparable thought) ease their anxiety about the king and accept the disturbing violence of the play is "amplification" (17), a practice that calls for the dramatist both to "divide" his subject into parts in order to dissect it, and also to "presence" it by casting it into language that imprints it on the mind of the audience. The essay is densely and meticulously argued, and refers to virtually every major episode in *Henry V*.

217. Barton, Anne. "The King Disguised: Shakespeare's *Henry V* and the Comical History." In *The Triple Bond: Plays, Mainly Shakespearean, in Performance*, ed. Joseph G. Price, 92-117. University Park: Pennsylvania State Univ. Press, 1975. Repr. in Bloom (no. 260).

Barton traces the motif of the disguised king who converses with his subjects, with reference to Elizabethan history plays (1587-1600) and popular ballads of the day, noting that in each of these instances the king is just and tolerant, and the meetings result in harmony and understanding, the premise being that the king is a man like all men and sensitive to the problems of others. She sees Henry's meeting with his soldiers in *Henry V* (4.1) as evoking this naive notion only to reject it as falsely romantic; rather, the episode demonstrates the wide gap that divides monarch from subject as well as the high price Henry pays for subordinating his individuality to his role as king. For Barton, this variation on the theme of "the king's two bodies" even appears in the wooing of Katherine (5.2), where we see the dilemma of a man whose "personal relations" become severely inhibited by his "corporate self" (107)—a condition that contributes to "tragic" rather than "comical" history. The essay concludes with a discussion of the influence of *Henry V* on the collaborative *Sir John Oldcastle* (1599-1600), a play that, in hearkening back to the folk romance of the earlier history plays and popular ballads, abandons Shakespeare's "tragical history" for the "comical" histories of his contemporaries (117).

218. Cubeta, Paul M. "Falstaff and the Art of Dying." *SEL: Studies in English Literature 1500-1900* 27 (1987): 197-211.

The emphasis here is on Falstaff as the comic embodiment of a long-standing tradition relating to the art of dying. In his death as described by the Hostess in *Henry V* (2.3), Falstaff seems to be "attempting a meditation in the Renaissance manner of *ars moriendi*, perhaps as broken and as incomplete as the narrated account of it" (202). Cubeta associates Falstaff with ancient myths and rituals, and further maintains that throughout the *Henry* plays he makes a travesty of traditional penitential norms that require prayerful meditation in anticipation of death. For Cubeta, Falstaff's death is a bittersweet, mysterious, and allusive event, evocatively combining the morbid admonitions of the *ars moriendi* tradition with the character's "vital comic spirit" (208).

219. Dean, Paul. "Chronicle and Romance Modes in *Henry V*." *Shakespeare*

Quarterly 32 (1981): 18-27.

In extending points made by Anne Barton (no. 217), and in taking issue with the arguments of Richard Levin on the structure of *Henry V* (*The Multiple Plot in English Renaissance Drama* [Chicago: Univ. of Chicago Press], 1971, 116-19), Dean relates *Henry V* to the conventions of romance and to such plays as Lyly's *Campaspe*, Greene's *Friar Bacon and Friar Bungay* and *James IV*, the anonymous *Edward III*, and Heywood's *Edward IV*. He compares elements of the main plot and comic subplot of *Henry V*, "which imply an equivalence, and not a contrast, between them, and accumulate to qualify radically our approval of the King" (24), and concludes that *Henry V* contains an equilibrium that renders irrelevant the distinction between chronicle and romance history, since it includes both kinds within itself. Moreover, he sees Shakespeare's handling of these conventions as hinting at his unhappiness with their representations of reality; thus *Henry V* presents a world where the juxtaposition of "chronicle" and "romance" modes (the former encouraging a sober realization of power, and the latter a light-hearted realization of its privileges) "stretches the history-play genre to its limits" (27).

220. Eggert, Katherine. "Nostalgia and the Not Yet Late Queen: Refusing Female Rule in *Henry V*." *ELH* 61 (1994): 523-50.

Taking Canterbury's speech on the Salic Law (1.2.33-95) as her starting point, Eggert argues that *Henry V* is "deeply concerned" with the *opposite* of what the Archbishop stipulates—that is, "how an English king might legitimately claim political power without having derived any of that power from a woman" (524). She links this matter with topical concerns over Elizabeth's female rule and the succession issue, and also with the idea that male rule makes for "compelling theatre" (527), an attitude she finds embedded in Canterbury's imagery describing Edward III. Examining virtually every major episode in the play, she sees its "action, language, and imagery as equally bent on purging England and the English of all that is feminine" (528). Special emphasis is placed on Katherine as not only the "regrettably necessary female component of Henry V's progenitive project" (542), but also as the great-great-grandmother of Elizabeth and the forerunner of the subversive women of the *Henry VI* plays. Eggert sees the play as obscuring Katherine's later career as well as her identity as an independent woman of lusty appetite, thus canceling the woman's part in English history and effectively "erasing Elizabeth, first by shaping England as an entirely male dominant body with France as its female victim, then by eliminating Katherine of France as Elizabeth's female forbear" (542).

221. Gurr, Andrew. "*Henry V* and the Bees' Commonwealth." *Shakespeare Survey* 30 (1977): 61-72.

Gurr notes that Canterbury's fable on the bees' commonwealth (1.2.183-220) derives from Erasmus's *Institutio Principis Christiani* (1516), and that Shakespeare alters Erasmus's pacifist use of it to justify the war in France; he further discusses the climate of opinion in Shakespeare's time regarding the justification of war, arguing that Henry avoids the central question of his responsibility for the deaths of good men in an unjust quarrel. For Gurr, however, the temptation to see the play schematically as an exercise in self-interest is a critical distortion; the war presents a mixture of interests and motives—"societies work contrariously" (72)—and it does unite the nation, if only for a short time.

222. Hillman, Richard. "'Not Amurath an Amurath Succeeds': Playing Doubles in Shakespeare's *Henriad.*" *English Literary Renaissance* 21 (1991): 161-89.

Hillman's aim here is to disassociate the name "Amurath" from any specific historical figure; rather he seeks to "re-historicize the concept of Turkish tyranny" in the second tetralogy by displacing the historical "Amurath" with a genericized notion of the "Turk," who "speaks" through a "complex set of intertexts, written and unwritten" as a "powerful subversive emblem of the shadow-side of English monarchy" (167). Hillman surveys several Renaissance treatises on the Turks relating to their military adventures, emphasizing how these works celebrate the exploits of one Scanderbeg, a valiant *adversary* of the Turks who was often compared both to Alexander the Great and to Henry V. For Hillman, these historical narratives contain many "doubles" or "shadow likenesses" (177) suggesting figures in the *Henriad*, most notably Henry V; and this ironic doubling points to "the self-subversion of panegyric" (179) in the second tetralogy, and particularly in *Henry V*, where intertextual comparisons suggest that no conqueror can be anything but an Amurath. The essay concludes by demonstrating how the ironic analogy of the "Turkish double" (182) may be extended to plays like *Othello* and *Hamlet*.

223. Mossman, Judith. "*Henry V* and Plutarch's *Alexander.*" *Shakespeare Quarterly* 45 (1994): 57-73.

Mossman contends that Plutarch's *Life of Alexander* sheds light on the construction of *Henry V* as well as the character of Henry. Her essay is a counter to ironic readings of the play like those of Gould (no. 237), for she sees Shakespeare exploiting the parallel between Alexander and Henry much to the king's advantage; in each of the many implied or stated comparisons between Alexander and Henry in the play, Henry emerges as morally superior—more devout, more capable of self-control, and more inspirational. Mossman amasses much detail from Plutarch's *Alexander* in arguing that structurally Shakespeare's play resembles a classic Plutarchan life, particularly in its attention to "one central figure, with scenes and set pieces contrived so as to reveal the complex features of that dominating character" (73).

224. Smith, Gordon Ross. "Shakespeare's *Henry V*: Another Part of the Critical Forest." *Journal of the History of Ideas* 37 (1976): 3-26.

Smith argues for "an extraordinary diversity of opinion" (6) in Renaissance moral, political, scientific, and religious thought, and maintains that such opinion is the real background of Elizabethan drama. He sees *Henry V* not as the embodiment of Tudor political orthodoxy, but rather as the locus for contradictory and unresolved attitudes toward the king and his war in France.

Smith discusses virtually every major episode in the play, claiming that these undercut the surface heroism and rectitude of Henry; the play thus reflects the contradictory opinions inherent in Renaissance politics, and its patriotism is genuine only in the sense that patriotism is a smokescreen to obscure self-serving motives. He finds in the play "a truthful picture of Renaissance warfare" that reveals "the stubborn and irreducible details of ulterior purpose that characterize most wars" (25).

225. Spencer, Janet M. "Princes, Pirates, and Pigs: Criminalizing Wars of Conquest in *Henry V*." *Shakespeare Quarterly* 47 (1996): 160-77.

Seeing Alexander the Great's encounter with the pirate Dionides as central to *Henry V*'s concerns about the morality of war and the origins of power, Spencer traces this episode from Alexander's life in such writers as Augustine, John of Salisbury, Chaucer, Gower, Lydgate, Boccaccio, and Erasmus. She notes that all versions of the story contain two key elements: Dionides' comparison of conquerors to pirates, and Alexander's pardon of that indictment. Spencer sees this dual aspect of the anecdote as clarifying the structure of *Henry V* as well as allowing the play "to voice otherwise unspeakable knowledge about the origins of power" (161). She examines several key scenes in the play, particularly Henry's interview with Williams (4.1), in arguing that *Henry V* "reveals power's capacity to exceed law and to arrogate a fictional difference between subject and sovereign in order to legitimate that excess" (164).

See also nos. 209, 210, 211, 212, 214, 226, 228, 232, 234, 239, 242, 245, 248, 250, 257, 259, 261.

D. Language and Linguistics.

226. Newman, Karen. "Englishing the Other: 'le tiers exclu' and Shakespeare's *Henry V*." In *Fashioning Femininity and English Renaissance Drama*, 97–108. Chicago: Univ. of Chicago Press, 1991.

This study is concerned with gender as a way of "*figuring* social relations in early modern England" (xviii), and includes chapters on *The Taming of the Shrew*, *Othello*, Jonson's *Epicoene*, and *Henry V*, as well as separate chapters on marriage, witchcraft, and dress. Newman observes of *Henry V* that Henry's "linguistic flexibility and virtuosity enables him ... to move among and seemingly *to master* varied social groups" (101), and then explores the rhetorical, sexual, and political implications of the king's relationship to Katherine. For Newman, Henry's rhetoric at Harfleur (3.3), particularly in its images of sexual violence against women, mirrors the language lesson episode (3.4), in which Katherine is verbally dismembered; moreover, in the wooing scene (5.2), the king both denies Katherine's difference by refashioning her into an English wife and reduces her to a medium of exchange that eroticizes the ties between men. Central to Newman's discussion is her appropriation of Michel Serres's notion of the "tiers exclu" (the excluded third in a two-party conversation) to apply to the female, making the female what Serres calls the "noise" that must be suppressed by men (105-6).

227. Zimbardo, Rose A. "The Formalism of *Henry V*." In *1564-1964: Shakespeare Encomium*, ed. Anne Paolucci, 16-24. The City College Papers I. New York: The City College, 1964. Repr. in Quinn (no. 261).

Zimbardo finds *Henry V* lacking in dramatic conflict and in the qualities of epic, and suggests that the play is best understood when approached from a rhetorical rather than a generic perspective: the "thematic essence" of *Henry V* "is to be found in the formalism of its style and architecture," for "in movement the play resembles a stately, ceremonial dance, each figure of which calls to life a different aspect of the hero's excellence" (16-17). She sees the various "figures" of this pattern (i.e., episodes of the play) as combining to reflect the societal harmony and order of which Henry is the central expression. For Zimbardo, the play is "a system of contrasts and balances" ordered by "stylistic and structural formalism" (21); this process, moreover, extends beyond the play itself "to invest the [second] tetralogy with new meaning and to draw the circle closed" (23).

See also nos. 210, 215, 227, 233, 239, 243, 259.

E. Criticism.

228. Altieri, Joanne. "Romance in *Henry V*." *SEL: Studies in English Literature, 1500-1900* 21 (1981): 223-40.

Identifying *Henry V* as a "generic puzzle" (224) containing mixed elements of comedy, epic, and tragedy, Altieri seeks to affirm the comic perspective on the play by stressing its affinities with romance; she argues that in *Henry V* war serves the same function as the forest or sheepcote of traditional pastoral, leading to a new sense of personal and societal union. For Altieri, however, this sense of romance is seriously modified by the intrusions of the Chorus, which causes us to focus upon the sharp differences between an ideal and a real view of history, and by the disturbing remnants of the old tavern world of the *Henry IV* plays; thus the play presents us with a reformulated vision of romance—"a naturalistic representation of life's seamier qualities under the idealizing umbrella of a comic perspective" (238).

229. Babula, William. "Whatever Happened to Prince Hal? An Essay on *Henry V*." *Shakespeare Survey* 30 (1977): 47-59.

The emphasis here is on the development of Henry V as a character. Babula contends that before the battle of Harfleur (3.1) Henry is seen in ironic terms, his behavior ironically parodied in the debased actions of characters like Nym, Bardolph, and the traitors; after Harfleur, however, the king begins to change, struggling with his earlier insincere and immature rhetoric, which he finally abandons in the wooing scene (5.2). In the wooing scene, Babula contends, we no longer have the Hal of the *Henry IV* plays; for, although the same pattern of the education of a prince that characterized these plays recurs in *Henry V*, in the later drama we have a different prince. For Babula, the unity of *Henry V* does not depend on the other plays of the tetralogy; indeed the play "must stand alone if its dramatic unity is to be appreciated" (59).

230. Battenhouse, Roy W. "*Henry V* as Heroic Comedy." In *Essays on Shakespeare and Elizabethan Drama in Honor of Hardin Craig*, ed. Richard Hosley, 163-82. Columbia: Univ. of Missouri Press, 1962.

Building on the views of critics such as Goddard (no. 55) who take an ironic or satiric approach to *Henry V*, Battenhouse sees the satire in the play as "Chaucerian" in nature, "gently sympathetic," "covertly hilarious," and "grounded in irony" (165); and it is this irony that produces the "heroic comedy" that pervades the play. He argues that *Henry V* depicts a king and a society that are "admittedly illustrious but bounded within the limits of sub-Christian virtue" (168), and sees ironic readings even in the chronicles (particularly Holinshed), suggesting that these are incorporated into the play "within a fuller context" (172). Particular emphasis is placed on the role of the clergy and Henry's relationship to them, but virtually all major episodes in *Henry V*, which Battenhouse regards as a "pitiful history of 'foiled' cupidity" (182), receive close inspection. Similar views on the play and its protagonist are expressed in two of Battenhouse's later articles: "The Relation of Henry V to Tamburlaine" *Shakespeare Survey* 27 (1974): 71-79; and "*Henry V* in the Light of Erasmus," *Shakespeare Studies* 17 (1985): 77-88.

231. Berry, Edward I. "'True Things and Mock'ries': Epic and History in *Henry V*." *Journal of English and Germanic Philology* 78 (1979): 1-16.

Berry sees *Henry V* as exploring the genre of epic and the view of reality it implies, and argues that the Chorus's apology for the inadequacy of the stage to represent a realm of epic ideals suggests that "not merely the stage is imperfect, but audience and author as well" (4). He detects a conflict in *Henry V* between two radically different notions of truth (one relating to the ideals of the imagination and the other to the facts of history) that comprises the basic rhythm of the play. For Berry, both the play and its hero never cease to remind us that the idealized world of epic can exist only outside of time: the play "is epic history only if we accept the phrase as oxymoron" (16).

232. Bradshaw, Graham. "Being Oneself: New Historicists, Cultural Materialists, and *Henry V*." In *Misrepresentations: Shakespeare and the Materialists*, 34-124. Ithaca: Cornell Univ. Press, 1993.

Bradshaw's study, which also includes extensive treatments of *Othello* and *The Merchant of Venice* in addition to the essay on *Henry V*, is an assault on the critical practices of British cultural materialists like Dollimore and Sinfield (no. 235) and American New Historicists like Greenblatt (no. 29) and Tennenhouse (no. 34). "Being Oneself" is essentially an analysis and critique of Greenblatt's "Invisible Bullets," in which Bradshaw argues that the "powerful logic" that for

Greenblatt "governs the relation between orthodoxy and subversion" in the Henriad as well as in Thomas Harriot's *Brief and True Report* is in fact a "logic" not produced in the Henriad at all but instead a product of Greenblatt's own reading (98). Bradshaw finds this to be particularly true of Greenblatt's depiction of Henry as a hypocrite (with this reading's attendant potential subversiveness), which Bradshaw sees as deriving from Greenblatt's anti-monarchical attitudes rather than from Shakespeare's play. Bradshaw disparages Greenblatt's theoretical position by claiming that to argue, as Greenblatt does, "that 'power' produces and contains the Shakespearean subversion is to argue that the 'historical and ideological situation' produces and *governs* the literary text; in other words, old historicism with a Foucauldian facelift" (85). A second purpose of Bradshaw's essay is to argue against oversimplified, either/or readings of the play, and to emphasize instead the presence of unresolved energies essential to its complexity.

233. Brennan, Anthony S. "That Within Which Passes Show: The Function of the Chorus in *Henry V*." *Philological Quarterly* 58 (1979): 40–52.

After claiming that we cannot identify the Chorus with Shakespeare and that very little in the speeches of the Chorus has a strictly narrative function, Brennan argues that the figure represents the English nation as well as a romantic, patriotic attitude associated with national tradition and the partly mythologized past. He further affirms that the Chorus, through its rhetoric, passes the "cause of battle" from the individual to the nation (43), and also embodies "the rich paradox that reality is a product of the imagination" (41). For Brennan, the Chorus comes to represent the ideal extreme in a broad spectrum of views on patriotism, with Pistol at the other, most debased, extreme, and Henry in the middle holding the balance. Brennan emphasizes throughout the duality of the ideal and the tawdry in *Henry V*, seeing the king as placed "in a central position to mediate the dialectical contrast" (50), with the glories as well as the horrors of war meeting in him.

234. Danson, Lawrence. "*Henry V*: King, Chorus, and Critics." *Shakespeare Quarterly* 34 (1983): 27–43.

Seeing the reference to Essex's campaign in Ireland in the Chorus to act 5 as a "pluckily defiant" attempt to invigorate English spirits, Danson "would like to believe that *Henry V* was the first of Shakespeare's plays to be performed in his new Globe theatre," probably in the fall of 1599—i.e., *after* not before Essex's campaign "was in shambles" (27). He then goes on to explore the mutuality that exists between playwright and audience, locating this in the person of the Chorus, whose virtuosity, "histrionic self-indulgence" (33), and sense of imaginative triumph also parallel Henry's. Danson interprets the many deficiencies attributed to the king (even those apparent in the troubling episode with Bates, Court, and Williams [4.1]) "in the spirit of the Chorus" (36)—that is, as real, but hardly fatal, elements of an essential greatness that we watch being acted out (in all senses of the term) throughout the play. According to Danson, it is in part because of a sort of theatrical mutuality that unites Chorus, king, and audience that sympathy for Henry becomes "a more appropriate response to him than judgmental detachment" (38). The essay is an important counter to many ironic readings of the play.

235. Dollimore, Jonathan, and Alan Sinfield. "History and Ideology: The Instance of *Henry V*." In *Alternative Shakespeares*, ed. John Drakakis, 206–27. London: Methuen, 1985. Repr. in Bloom (no. 260) and, in part, in Holderness (no. 85).

This materialist reading of *Henry V* affirms that even anti-Tillyardians, such as Sanders (no. 129), who "oppose the idea that Shakespeare believed in and expresses a political hierarchy whose rightness is guaranteed by its reflection of a divine hierarchy, [are] trapped nevertheless in a problematic of order, one which stems from a long tradition of idealist philosophy" (207). For Dollimore and Sinfield, political ideology is not merely a set of ideas, but a "material practice, woven into the fabric of everyday life" (211); and they see *Henry V* as a play that, while seeming to consolidate dominant ideological structures, actually undermines them. The authors read several key events in the play (the bishops' support for the war; the rebellion of Cambridge, Scroop, and Grey; the subservience of the Irish, Welsh, and Scottish soldiers; Henry's speech on ceremony [4.1.230–84]; the conversation with Bates and Williams [4.1]; the Irish problem; the idea of the monarch as the central power in the state, etc.) as exposing the play's "obsessive preoccupation" (216) with insurrection, and implying the demystification of authority.

236. Erickson, Peter. "Fathers, Sons, and Brothers in *Henry V*." In *Patriarchal Structures in Shakespeare's Drama*, 39–65. Berkeley: Univ. of California Press, 1985. Repr. in Bloom (no. 260).

This book is concerned with gender relationships in Shakespeare, particularly the "conflict between male-female relations and male-male relations" (1) as a dominant motif of the plays. It includes chapters on *As You Like It*; *Hamlet*, *Othello*, and *King Lear*; *Antony and Cleopatra*; and *The Winter's Tale*—in addition to the essay on *Henry V*. Erickson argues that the king in *Henry V* is a far more complex character than has generally been acknowledged, and focuses upon the similarities he shares with his father (in language, attitude, and behavior) as signs of both a mutual resentment and a desire for atonement; ironically, however, his need for atonement is complicated by the political guilt he inherits from Henry IV as well as a competing need to surpass his father's accomplishments. Erickson sees the "heroic impulse" of Henry V as a form of "psychological escapism" (54) that conceals inherited guilt by draping it in the dead spirit of chivalry, and the Dauphin and the French king as a "negative version" (57) of Henry V and his father—an unworthy pair against whom Henry V can legitimately direct his filial hostilities. For Erickson, Henry's wooing of Katherine (5.2) is the triumphant culmination of his rivalry with the Dauphin, as well as a sexually charged incident that gives men of "narrow masculinity" (62) the opportunity to resolve their political differences by joining in erotic humor at a woman's expense.

237. Gould, Gerald. "A New Reading of *Henry V*." *English Review* 29 (1919): 42–55. Repr. in Quinn (no. 261).

Gould maintains that *Henry V* is unmistakably ironic: the play is a satire on monarchy, imperialism, debased patriotism, and war. He sees Hal/Henry V as essentially unchanging throughout the *Henry* plays, a coldly successful politician whose harsh pragmatism contrasts sharply with the warm humanity of Falstaff; Shakespeare clearly preferred Falstaff to the self-righteous king, and depicted the latter's behavior throughout *Henry V* as consistently ruthless and insincere. Gould's article is an early and influential study of the perceived deflationary qualities of the play, and the first to affirm its unremitting irony.

238. Granville-Barker, Harley. "From *Henry V* to *Hamlet*." In *More Prefaces to Shakespeare: By Harley-Granville Barker*, ed. Edward M. Moore, 135–67. Princeton: Princeton Univ. Press, 1974. Repr. often.

This is a revised and corrected version of Granville-Barker's essay, first published in *Proceedings of the British Academy* 11 (1924–25), London: Humphrey Milford for Oxford Univ. Press, 1926, 283–309, and often reprinted. Granville-Barker posits two sides to Shakespeare the dramatist, the "complaisant" and the "daemonic"; the former gives the public what it wants and adheres to established conventions, while the latter goes its own way, even to the point of infusing characters at times with a vitality or humanity that is, strictly speaking, inappropriate to the action of the play. He claims that Shakespeare excels in suddenly illuminating "the whole nature of a man" (141) in the latter instance, but that in *Henry V* there is a flatness to the protagonist and the dramatic action that disappoints us and that must have disappointed Shakespeare. Granville-Barker sees the play as the locus of an "artistic crisis" that marks the "dangerpoint" (143) of Shakespeare's career, and further argues that the dramatist's own sense of failure, his deep "disillusion with his art" (145), is reflected in the speeches of the Chorus and in the portrait of Henry as a mere man of action rather than a man of thought. For Granville-Barker, the play has neither distinctive artistry nor a "spirtually significant idea" (146); in writing it Shakespeare acted "complaisantly" rather than "daemonically," a process he reverses in *Hamlet*, which represents "the triumph of dramatic idea over dramatic action and of character over plot" (150).

239. Hall, Joan Lord. *"Henry V": A Guide to the Play*. Westport, Conn.: Greenwood Press, 1997.

This is an extensive critical, scholarly, and performance guide to *Henry V*. It consists of six chapters and a concluding "Bibliographical Essay." Chapter 1 (1–12) examines the textual history of the play, with emphasis upon the differences among the quarto texts (1600, 1602, 1619) and the First Folio (1623); it also briefly describes twentieth-century editions of *Henry V*. Chapter 2 (13–29) gives a description of the historical and cultural contexts of the play as well as of its sources and analogues. Chapter 3 (31–76) provides a detailed analysis of the dramatic structure of *Henry V*, and takes up such questions as the function of the Chorus as a framing device, the handling of plot and subplot, the importance of the minor characters, the character of the king (in particular his development from prince to monarch and his moral ambivalence), and the play's language and style. Hall concludes that *Henry V* is a subtle play, full of contradictions—the site of conflicting versions of kingship, war, and political order. Chapter 4 (77-93), extends these critical remarks in a detailed examination of the play's ambivalent treatment of the themes of order and disorder, war, and kingship; indeed, Hall sees ambivalence as the thematic essence of the play. Chapter 5 (95-122) consists of a summary of critical approaches to the play from 1900 to 1980. Chapter 6 (123-67), treats the play in performance, and includes extensive discussions of the 1975 Royal Shakespeare Company production directed by Terry Hands, Laurence Olivier's 1944 film, Kenneth Branagh's 1989 film, and the 1979 BBC television production, directed by David Giles. The "Bibliographical Essay" (169-76) selectively "outlines the most important critical work on the play, emphasizing books over articles" (169). Hall's volume is a useful compendium of information on all aspects of the play.

240. Hammond, Antony. "'It must be your imagination then': The Prologue and the Plural Text in *Henry V* and Elsewhere." In *"Fanned and Winnowed Opinions": Shakespearean Essays Presented to Harold Jenkins*, ed. John W. Mahon and Thomas A. Pendleton, 133-50. London: Methuen, 1987.

Hammond uses the term "plural text" to refer to the discrepancy between what the Chorus *says* and what actually *happens* in *Henry V*, particularly as regards heroic action; and he links this phenomenon with the issue of the morality of Henry's behavior, which is similarly plural, since Henry seems so unaware of the "ambivalent moral dimensions of the actions he undertakes" (143). Hammond affirms that, since the play insists upon being taken plurally by presenting us with a dramatic action at odds with the views of the Chorus, it cannot be contained by any *single* reading, and thus "interprets and challenges ideology at once" (145). He sees the Chorus's repeated concern with the limitations of the stage as focusing our attention not upon theatrical failure but rather upon theatrical triumph, since the play forces us to "stretch our imaginations ... to meet the challenges of the complexity of the moral action" (149).

241. Jorgensen, Paul A. "Accidental Judgments, Casual Slaughters, and Purposes Mistook: Critical Reactions to Shakespeare's *Henry the Fifth*." *Shakespeare Association Bulletin* 22 (1947): 51-61.

Jorgensen notes the universal praise of Henry by other characters in *Henry V*, and finds that this "unanimous and uncoerced assent toward a character's magnificence is virtually unique in the Shakespearian drama" (52). He surveys criticism of *Henry V* by Samuel Johnson, S. T. Coleridge, Thomas Carlyle, William Hazlitt, John Palmer, G. B. Shaw, W. B. Yeats (no. 78), Frank Harris, John Masefield, Edward Dowden, R. G. Moulton, A. C. Bradley (no. 179), J.W. Cunliffe, G. L. Kittredge, and Mark Van Doren (no. 75), noting the discrepancy between Shakespeare's apparent intention to glorify Henry and the negative responses of many influential critics. He concludes that Shakespeare's conscious attempt to glorify Henry is obvious enough from the choruses, but "the artist in him may have failed to comply" (60). The essay is a useful summary of some major critical responses to the play up to the mid-1940s.

242. McEachern, Claire. "*Henry V* and the Paradox of the Body Politic." In *Materialist Shakespeare*, ed. Ivo Kamps, 292-319. London: Verso, 1995.

Noting the critical emphasis on the *personableness* of the king in *Henry V*, McEachern seeks to alter this focus by discussing the "person-ality" of Henry (293)—that is, his personification as "the nation" and the related critical implications of imagining the state as a person. McEachern argues that for Elizabethans the paradoxical principles of "fellowship" and "hegemony" were "complicit forms of social existence" (296), and locates this duality not only in the theatre but also *literally* in the body of Queen Elizabeth (specifically her "appetite" for the stage), since "royal sponsorship of the theatre was threatening hierarchy precisely in its promise of a common allegiance" (301). She reads Henry V's "personhood" in light of this "dual valence of the monarch's body" (301), seeing England's (i.e., Henry's) fellowship *and* hegemony represented in Fluellen, Gower, Jamy, and Macmorris; the purification of the royal body as a component of the death of Falstaff (2.3); and the antithetical need for both power and pleasure as present in the wooing of Katherine (5.2). She concludes by examining "the discourse of monarchic pleasure and its relations to gender" (307), finding associations between female corporeality and political corruption that makes the ending of *Henry V* a "containment of the 'effeminate'" (311).

243. Mallett, Phillip. "Shakespeare's Trickster-Kings: Richard III and Henry V." In *The Fool and the Trickster*, ed. Paul V. A. Williams, 64-82. Cambridge: D. S. Brewer; Totowa, N.J.: Rowman & Littlefield, 1979.

This assessment of Henry regards him as a trickster who takes *everybody* in, even himself, and stresses the modifying, deflationary, and negative aspects of *Henry V* and its protagonist. Mallett emphasizes the images of the stage and the sun in the second tetralogy, associating these with Henry's alleged insincerity and repeated false appearances, among the most prominent of which are his condemnation of the traitors (2.2), and his nocturnal walk among his soldiers (4.1); the king is a theatrical and impenetrable Machiavel, different from Richard III only in the sense that he never drops his public mask. In Mallett's interpretive scheme Henry emerges not only as "a parody of the true king he claims to be" (80), but also as a man unaware of the distortions he presents to the world.

244. Phialas, Peter G. "Shakespeare's *Henry V* and the Second Tetralogy." *Studies in Philology* 62 (1965): 155-75.

The argument here is that in Shakespeare's political plays, particularly those of the second tetralogy, success depends upon one's ability to reconcile public and private imperatives. Phialas sees the Hal of the *Henry IV* plays as rising above the demands of the private self (Falstaff) and of worldly vanity (Hotspur) without totally rejecting either, and as emerging in *Henry V* as a balanced personality; he also links the rejection of Falstaff in *2 Henry IV* (5.5) with the king's treatment of Scroop in *Henry V* (2.2), since both episodes "underscore the tragic element in Shakespeare's—and King Henry's—conception of the royal dilemma" (168). For Phialas, the public/private duality is especially evident in Henry's conversation with his soldiers (4.1), which he sees as emphasizing the monarch's humanity and the ideal relationship of king to subject, an idea also apparent in the St. Crispin's Day speech (4.2.18-67) and the wooing scene (5.2). Phialas concludes by noting Shakespeare's debt to Holinshed, who also depicts the king as embodying well-balanced humanity.

245. Plotnick, Jerrold. "'Imaginary Puissance': The New Historicism and *Henry V.*" *English Studies in Canada* 17 (1991): 249-67.

Using the arguments of Greenblatt (no. 29) and Dollimore and Sinfield (no. 235) as paradigms of New Historicist approaches to *Henry V*, Plotnick takes such criticism to task for "a readiness to impose on works of literature a priori conceptions of how power operates" (249). His essay consists of a detailed refutation of these critics' ideological readings of the play, with particular focus upon the debate between Henry and Williams on the eve of Agincourt (4.1). Plotnick's intention throughout is to counter what he sees as a New Historicist narrowness of perspective—that is, a kind of interpretive "double standard" (263) that gives the modern critic considerable freedom from "his own culture's signifying practices," while granting "his historical figures virtually no freedom from the signifying practices of *their* time" (263). In so doing, he argues (contrary to the critical belief of Greenblatt, Dollimore, and Sinfield) that Shakespeare "can 'transcend' what we assign as the narrow interests of his class, the political authorities, or the theatre" (264).

246. Rabkin, Norman. "Either/Or: Responding to *Henry V.*" In *Shakespeare and the Problem of Meaning*, 33-62. Chicago: Univ. of Chicago Press, 1981. Repr. in Bloom (no. 260).

Rabkin's aim in this book is to affirm the dynamic complexity and ambivalence of Shakespearean drama, and to stress the "unresolvably problematic sense of human experience" built into its structure (29); this he does in separate chapters on *The Merchant of Venice*, *Henry V*, the tragedies, and the romances. In his discussion of *Henry V* (a revision of his article "Rabbits, Ducks, and *Henry V*," *Shakespeare Quarterly* 28 [1977], 279-96), Rabkin notes that the two opposed representations of Henry in the play, as ideal Christian king and as Machiavellian, are completely irreconcilable, and that Shakespeare prepared for this deliberate ambiguity in *Henry V* by casting negative light in *2 Henry IV* upon elements of Henry's character that seemed attractive in *1 Henry IV*. Rabkin sees this opposition—what he calls the two "rival gestalts" (62) of *Henry V*—as forcing us to come to terms not only with the unsettling fact of the play's inscrutability, but with our own personal and political conflicts as well. The essay has become a highly influential reading of the play.

247. Salomon, Brownell. "Thematic Contraries and the Dramaturgy of *Henry V.*" *Shakespeare Quarterly* 31 (1980): 343-56.

Salomon contends that *Henry V* is "a coherent dramatic work, an imaginative unity with a form totally integral with its meaning" (343), and that we should not rely too heavily on evidence from other plays of the second tetralogy in interpreting it. He gives a detailed scene-by-scene analysis of the play (excepting the prologue and epilogue), illustrating that all scenes are organically integrated by a conceptual framework consisting of "two rival ethical attitudes" (344): private cause versus public good. Those characters who represent self-interest (e.g., Pistol and the French nobility) experience "a diagonal descent to repudiation" (356), while Henry (an endorser of communal goals) moves in just the opposite direction. For Salomon, this "scenic structure" suggests that *Henry V* is "exemplary rather than ironic or satiric" in intent (356).

248. Wentersdorf, Karl P. "The Conspiracy of Silence in *Henry V*." *Shakespeare Quarterly* 27 (1976), 264–87.

Wentersdorf examines the episode at Southampton (2.2) in which Henry condemns the conspirators, focusing upon the light the incident sheds on the king's character as well as on the justice of the war in France. He notes that in this episode Shakespeare (contrary to his usual practice) deliberately omits historical details about the traitors and their scheme, especially those relating to the family ties and political motives of Cambridge, who hoped to make his brother-in-law (Edmund Mortimer) king, and thus enhance his own claim to the crown. Wentersdorf further observes that the conspirators remain silent on the dynastic motives of their rebellion in order to protect their families, and that Henry also skillfully sidesteps the dynastic question as well as Scroop's political idealism because of their obvious applicability both to his own claim to the crown and to the invasion of France. For Wentersdorf, the episode is fraught with subtleties of implication that a sensitive spectator, aware of the unspoken issues involved, could not fail to see.

249. Williamson, Marilyn L. "The Episode with Williams in *Henry V*." *SEL: Studies in English Literature, 1500–1900* 9 (1969): 275–82.

The focus here is on how Henry's visit to his soldiers, particularly the quarrel with Williams and its aftermath (4.1), sheds light on the character of the king as it develops in the second tetralogy. The author finds traces of Henry's habits as Prince Hal in the episode: his disguise evokes those he used to trick Falstaff, and his speech on ceremony recalls his planned reformation. According to Williamson, Henry reverts here to his old Eastcheap habits by trying to pay off Williams with the money-stuffed glove (4.8)—an action she regards as "a travesty of chivalric custom" (281)—and such lingering reminders of his old self seriously modify the official position on his "reformation" expressed by Canterbury (1.1). Williamson concludes that Shakespeare "did not jettison" the old Hal, but instead made Henry V "a more complex and interesting character" than many critics have thought (281–82).

F. Stage History; Productions; Performance Criticism; Film Versions.

250. Arden, John. "Henry V." *New Statesman* 67 (1964): 946–47.

Arden's comments are a response to Ronald Bryden's objection to an allegedly pacifist production of *Henry V* at Stratford-upon-Avon in 1964 (*New Statesman* 67 [1964]: 924–25). Arden suggests that *Henry V* may reflect Shakespeare's disillusionment with the portrait of the king he found in Holinshed, a disillusionment that caused him to embed a "secret play within the official one" (947), critical of the king. He sees contradictions between what is seen and what is said in *Henry V*, and relates Shakespeare's so-called "secret play" to his own dramatic practice: "I myself constantly write secret plays within my ostensible ones" (947). Lewis Casson responds to Arden (*New Statesman* 67 [1964]: 992), endorsing a two-level approach to Shakespeare and citing Gerald Gould's remarks on *Henry V* (no. 237) in support.

251. Beauman, Sally, ed. *"King Henry V." The Royal Shakespeare Company's Production of "Henry V" for the Centenary Season at the Royal Shakespeare Theatre: The Working Text of Shakespeare's Play together with Articles and Notes by the Director, Designer, Composer, Actors and Other Members of the Company, and Comments from the Critics and the Audience. Foreword by HRH the Duke of Edinburgh.* Oxford: Pergamon Press, 1976.

This volume embeds the text of *Henry V* in an extensive commentary on all aspects of a specific production—the highly praised 1975 staging at Stratford-upon-Avon by Terry Hands with Alan Howard as Henry. The text is the acting version, and is accompanied by full notes, mostly by the director, explaining cuts (printed in italics), transpositions, reassignments of speeches, and details of staging. The volume includes some thirty-four pages of illustrations (costume designs and photographs of the production). In the introduction, Hands refers to the drama as "Shakespeare's theatre play par excellence" in which "every aspect of role playing is examined" (16), and sees it as embodying an "alternating pattern of doubt and certainty" (18). Beauman contributes a brief stage history of the play since the eighteenth century, and conducts interviews with the designer (Abdel Farrah), the composer of special music (Guy Woolfenden), and various members of the cast, including Alan Howard. An appendix contains biographies of the Royal Shakespeare Company, an "Afterword" by Ronald Bryden treating the relationship between convention and illusion in the staging of Shakespeare, reprints of newspaper reviews of the production, and letters of response from members of the audience.

252. Berger, Thomas L. "Casting *Henry V*." *Shakespeare Studies* 20 (1988): 89–104.

Berger suggests that the doubling of parts in *Henry V* allows an audience to make thematic, ironic, comic, aesthetic, or otherwise revealing connections among the various roles played by a single actor, and stresses the analogies between this dramatic practice and that of the court masque, which encourages the audience to see *through* the stage characters to the noble personages beneath. He sees the minimum number of actors who could have performed the First Folio text of *Henry V* as thirteen, and examines in detail the thematic implications created *on stage* by the following instances of doubling: 1) Cambridge, Scroop, and Grey doubling as Bates, Court, and Williams; 2) the Boy doubling as Princess Katherine; 3) Pistol, the Chorus, Mountjoy, and the Herald played by the same actor; 4) Exeter doubling as Macmorris; 5) the Dauphin doubling as French Ambassador; 6) the Constable doubling as French Ambassador; and 7) King Henry, Berri, and Grandpre played by the same actor.

253. **Branagh, Kenneth.** "Henry V." In *Players of Shakespeare 2: Further Essays in Shakespearean Performance by Players with the Royal Shakespeare Company*, ed. Russell Jackson and Robert Smallwood, 93–105. Cambridge: Cambridge Univ. Press, 1988.

This essay recounts Branagh's recollections of his performance as the king in Adrian Noble's production of *Henry V* at Stratford-upon-Avon in 1984 and at the Barbican Theatre in London in 1985. Branagh sees the role of Henry as a young man's part, and briefly discusses how his earlier performance as St. Francis of Assisi in Julian Mitchell's *Francis* helped prepare him for the role of the king: both characters have "huge reserves of compassion" and "a genuine visionary quality" (97). For Branagh, the king is an intensely private person who is forced to prove himself under the pressure of public scrutiny, a young man whose genuine sensitivity and piety are wedded to the ruthlessness of a "professional killer" (97), whose contradictions must be embraced rather than explained. Throughout his discussion, Branagh emphasizes the complexities of both Henry and the play, particularly in his discussion of what he sees as the young king's divided response to the execution of Bardolph (3.6.106ff.). Against the grain of much modern criticism, he sees Henry and Katherine actually falling in love during the wooing scene (5.2). Branagh's remarks are often critically astute, and serve as a provocative counter to prevailing ironic or deflationary interpretations of the play and its hero.

254. **Branagh, Kenneth.** *"Henry V" by William Shakespeare: A Screen Adaptation by Kenneth Branagh*. London: Chatto & Windus, 1989.

This is the screenplay of Branagh's 1989 film of *Henry V*. It includes a complete cast list and list of credits for the film (8). In his introduction (9–12), Branagh recounts his interest in the play from his earliest days as an actor until he began work on his film in 1988. He stresses the complexity of the king's character and the "filmic" qualities of Shakespeare's text in arguing that the play is "a political thriller ... a detailed analysis of leadership and a complex debate about war" (10). He also explains his rationale for cutting the script to an appropriate length for film production, his decision to locate the opening Chorus in an empty film studio, his departures from Laurence Olivier's 1944 film of the play, and his inclusion of the Falstaff scenes from the *Henry IV* plays. The book includes numerous black-and-white stills from the film interspersed within the text.

255. **Donaldson, Peter S.** "'Claiming from the Female': Gender and Representation in Laurence Olivier's *Henry V*." In *Shakespearean Films/ Shakespearean Directors*, 1-30. Boston: Unwin Hyman, 1990.

Donaldson sees the prologue to *Henry V* as positing a discrepancy between self and role that relates both to the representation of stage action in cinematic terms and to the issue of gender. He focuses on Olivier's film in examining the problem posed by the "boy actress" as a figure who, like King Henry, can succeed only by "claiming from the female" (4); he also makes a distinction between "downstage" and "upstage" action in the film—the former (the world of the Globe playhouse) reserved for "low" scenes, and the latter (the world of "cinematic space") for more dignified ones (5-6). For Donaldson, these two symbolic locations are also linked to gender, since boys playing women occupy the former and actual women the latter; therefore, just as Henry in the play must claim through the female by virtue of the Salic Law, so in the film "male artistic achievement" also claims from the female by "incorporating the depth, compassion, and sexual presence of 'real' women into the all-male institution of the Shakespearean stage" (14). Donaldson further argues that the softening of Henry's character by Olivier "intimates an integration of the feminine" in the king's own personality (14), particularly in the scene on the eve of battle (4.1) when Henry, appearing as a compassionate nurturer, strokes the head of Court; he even locates the roots of this attitude in Olivier's childhood experience as a student in the English public school system.

256. **Geduld, Harry M.** *Filmguide to "Henry V."* Bloomington: Indiana Univ. Press, 1973.

This is the most comprehensive account of Laurence Olivier's 1944 film of *Henry V* available; it includes a full list of credits (1-3), an outline of the action (4-9), biographical details on Olivier (10-12), and a section on "The Production" (13-25), describing the inception of the film, as well as presenting a detailed account of the production schedule, including artistic, financial, and logistical problems encountered during shooting in frequently bad weather under wartime conditions. The longest section, "Analysis" (26-66), examines in detail the camera work and aesthetic effects of the film by dividing the action into four main parts: 1) the introduction (the sequences in the Globe Theatre); 2) the scenes following the transition from the Globe but before the Battle of Agincourt; 3) the Agincourt sequences; and 4) the scenes after the battle. Geduld emphasizes Olivier's exploitation of the contrast between theatrical conventions and film realism, the use of high and low camera angles to distinguish class levels or contrasts between comic and serious material, the tendency to exaggerate the comedy and emphasize its slapstick rather than verbal content, the distortion and simplification of character (e.g., Henry, the English clerics, the French), and the integration of parts of the Chorus's speeches "into the fabric of the screenplay" (58). He also compares Olivier's text with Shakespeare's original, showing in considerable detail how Olivier refashioned the play to serve the patriotic (even propagandistic) intention of the film. He then takes up the various styles of the film ("anti-illusionistic," "quasi-naturalistic," "illusionistic-stylized"), examining to what extent they conflict or harmonize with each other, and, after surveying various critical opinions on the matter, concludes the section by analyzing William Walton's musical score and its successful integration into the total effect of the film. A "Summary Critique" (67–69) briefly surveys contemporary responses to the production, and a useful annotated bibliography (73–82) completes the volume.

257. Tyler, Sharon. "Minding True Things: The Chorus, the Audience, and *Henry V*." In *The Theatrical Space*, ed. James Redmond, 69–79. Themes in Drama 9. Cambridge: Cambridge Univ. Press, 1987.

Tyler sees the speeches of the Chorus in *Henry V* as a virtual mockery of the dramatic principles expressed by Sir Philip Sidney in *The Defence of Poetry*, and further contends that the Chorus establishes a rapport with the audience that is thematically and dramatically significant. She claims that the Chorus appeals only mildly to the imaginative engagement of the audience in the first two prologues, but becomes far more demanding of it in the last three, even to the point of forcing it to become literally involved in the play and to supply its deficiencies. Tyler sees this latter dynamic occurring in the relationship of the act 4 Chorus to the scenes preceding Agincourt. Here she sees both the Chorus and the stage action compelling the audience (imaginatively *and* successfully) to see the unrealistically small numbers of Henry's army, even as the audience responds (imaginatively *and* successfully) by filling the vacuity created by Henry's missing soldiers. For Tyler, the Chorus and the play do not merely apologize for dramatic limitation; rather they deliberately create the theatrical conditions under which limitation must be "habitually ignored" in order to make a "virtue of it" (76).

258. Willson, Robert F., Jr. "War and Reflection on War: The Olivier and Branagh Films of *Henry V*." *Shakespeare Bulletin* 9 (Summer 1991): 27–29.

This is a thorough examination of the origins, purposes, and techniques of the Olivier and Branagh film versions of Shakespeare's play. Throughout, Willson insists that Olivier's production "is primarily a stage-centered treatment of the material" (28) that seeks to represent on camera the experience of viewing the play in the theatre and to depict the king and the French war in favorable light; Branagh's production, on the other hand, not only presents a darker and more introspective hero, but also exploits a "documentary mode" that stresses an anti-war theme. Willson also compares the use of the Chorus in both productions to underscore his contention that Branagh's *Henry V*, unlike Olivier's, "is a predominantly filmic interpretation" of the play (29).

See also nos. 30, 79, 81, 209, 210, 211, 213, 216, 234, 238, 239.

G. Collections of Essays.

259. Berman, Ronald, ed. *Twentieth Century Interpretations of "Henry V": A Collection of Critical Essays.* Englewood Cliffs, N.J.: Prentice-Hall, 1968.

This collection reprints criticism on *Henry V* by Lily B. Campbell (no. 27), Geoffrey Bullough (no. 14), Charles Williams, E. M. W. Tillyard (no. 35), Una Ellis-Fermor, Derek Traversi (no. 74), A. P. Rossiter (no. 72), M. M. Reese (no. 32), W. B. Yeats (no. 78), A. C. Bradley (no. 179), E. E. Stoll, Caroline Spurgeon, Mark Van Doren (no. 75), J. D. Wilson (no. 195), and Paul A. Jorgensen. Berman's introduction (1-14) begins with a short biographical sketch of Shakespeare, then moves on to brief treatments of Shakespeare's histories and Tudor politics, plot and character in *Henry V*, the play's images and ideas, its themes, and its effect upon audiences.

260. Bloom, Harold, ed. *William Shakespeare's "Henry V."* New York: Chelsea House, 1988.

This volume reprints criticism on *Henry V* by Anne Barton (no. 217), James L. Calderwood (no. 37), Norman Rabkin (no. 246), David Quint, James R. Siemon, Jonathan Dollimore and Alan Sinfield (no. 235), and Peter Erickson (no. 236). In his brief introduction (1-4), Bloom eulogizes Falstaff as one who truly loved Hal, agreed to his own rejection (*2 Henry IV*, 5.5), and willed to die; praises the description of his death by Mistress Quickly (2.3); and argues that Shakespeare's portrait of the king in *Henry V* is both ironic and celebratory.

261. Quinn, Michael, ed. *Shakespeare: "Henry V."* London: Macmillan, 1969.

In part one, "Shorter Critical Extracts" (31-78), Quinn reprints remarks on *Henry V* by twenty-six critics from the eighteenth century to the present day. In part two, "Longer Studies" (81-238), he reprints more extensive comments on the play by Gerald Gould (no. 237), E. E. Stoll, Charles Williams, Mark Van Doren (no. 75), Una Ellis-Fermor, J. H. Walter (no. 212), Derek Traversi (no. 74), Rose Zimbardo (no. 227), Zdeněk Stříbrný, A. C. Sprague (no. 84), Honor Matthews, and L. C. Knights. In his introduction (11-25), Quinn discusses the place of *Henry V* in Shakespeare's histories as well as the backgrounds to the plays. He also takes up Henry's image among Elizabethans as the ideal king and Shakespeare's possibly ambivalent attitude toward this notion, as well as the wide divergence in critical reaction to the play and its protagonist. In delineating this last point, Quinn neatly summarizes many of the critical perspectives anthologized in the volume.

H. Bibliography.

262. Candido, Joseph, and Charles R. Forker, comps. *"Henry V": An Annotated Bibliography.* New York: Garland Publishing, 1983.

This is the most comprehensive annotated bibliography of *Henry V*, containing over 2100 entries covering chiefly the period from 1940 to 1983 but including several items before 1940 as well. The compilers arrange their work under the following headings: I. Criticism; II. Individual Editions; III. Complete and Collected Editions; IV. Adaptations, Parodies, Altered Versions; V. Textual and Bibliographical Studies, Dating; VI. Language, Vocabulary, Prosody; VII. Sources of *Henry V*, Historical and Intellectual Background, Topicality, Influences on the Play; VIII. *Henry V* as a Source for or Influence upon Later Writers and Works; IX. Stage History and Staging; X. Criticism of Films and Other Media, Screenplays and Scripts, Films and Filmstrips, Phonograph Records and Audio Cassettes, Published Music; XI. Translations. In their introduction (ix–xxiv), Candido and Forker trace in broad outline important interpretive, scholarly, and performance-based responses to the play. The work is an indispensable source of scholarly information on *Henry V*.

See also no. 239.

INDEX I: AUTHORS AND EDITORS
(FOR SECTIONS II, III, IV, AND V)

Citations are to item number.

Abrams, Richard, 173
Altick, Richard D., 94, 106, 141, 143, 144
Altieri, Joanne, 228
Altman, Joel B., 216
Arden, John, 250
Auden, W. H., 174, 202, 205

Babula, William, 229
Baker, Susan, 126
Bamber, Linda, 43, 85
Barber, C. L., 151, 158, 202, 203, 204, 205
Barish, Jonas A., 175, 202
Barnet, Sylvan, 94
Barroll, J. Leeds, 62
Barton, Anne, 36, 211, 217, 219, 260
Battenhouse, Roy W., 230
Baxter, John, 107
Beauman, Sally, 251
Belsey, Catherine, 26, 85
Berger, Harry, Jr., 114, 133, 140, 204
Berger, Thomas L., 252
Bergeron, David M., 96, 115, 176
Berman, Ronald, 27, 32, 35, 72, 74, 75, 78, 179, 195, 259
Berry, Edward I., 101, 177, 231
Bevington, David, 35, 40, 45, 50, 75, 147, 150, 158, 163, 174, 179, 184, 187, 191, 195, 200, 202
Black, James, 115, 178
Black, Matthew W., 92, 97, 145
Blanpied, John W., 44, 204
Bloom, Harold, 29, 37, 44, 55, 69, 114, 124, 127, 140, 158, 189, 192, 203, 204, 217, 235, 236, 246, 260
Bogard, Travis, 116
Booth, Stephen, 140
Bradbrook, M. C., 141, 204
Bradley, A. C., 175, 179, 195, 202, 205, 241, 259
Bradshaw, Graham, 232
Branagh, Kenneth, 253, 254. See also INDEX II
Brennan, Anthony S., 233
Brockbank, Philip, 117

Brooke, Nicholas, 35, 66, 72, 78, 100, 106, 134, 135, 141
Brown, John Russell, 134, 141, 144
Bryant, J. A., Jr., 141
Bryden, Ronald, 250, 251
Bullough, Geoffrey, 259
Burckhardt, Sigurd, 45, 202
Burden, Dennis H., 87, 90

Cairncross, A. S., 215
Calderwood, James L., 37, 85, 140, 260
Campbell, Lily B., 27, 86, 161, 259
Candido, Joseph, 262
Carlyle, Thomas, 241
Carr, Virginia M., 46
Casson, Lewis, 250
Chambers, E. K., 144
Champion, Larry S., 47, 48, 88
Charlton, H. B., 205
Cohen, Derek, 85, 180
Coleridge, Samuel Taylor, 141, 144, 202, 241
Cookson, Linda, 142
Cox, John D., 28
Craik, T. W., 209
Crewe, Jonathan, 155, 181
Crowl, Samuel, 79
Cubeta, Paul M., 35, 49, 62, 95, 106, 143, 218
Cumberland, Richard, 202
Cunliffe, J. W., 241
Cunningham, J. V., 107
Cunningham, John E., 142

Danson, Lawrence, 234
Davis, Norman, 167, 171
Dawson, Giles E., 97
Dean, Leonard F., 49, 143
Dean, Paul, 219
DeNeef, A. Leigh, 96
Dessen, Alan C., 159
Devlin, Diana, 142
Dollimore, Jonathan, 34, 85, 232, 235, 245, 260

Donaldson, E. Talbot, 203
Donaldson, Peter S., 255
Donovan, Dennis G., 96
Dorius, R. J., 50, 86, 202
Dowden, Edward, 202, 241
Drakakis, John, 235
Draper, Ronald, 142
Dryden, John, 141
Dutton, Richard, 89

Edwards, Philip, 51
Eggert, Katherine, 220
Elliott, John R., Jr., 118
Ellis-Fermor, Una, 259, 261
Empson, William, 182, 205
Erickson, Peter, 236, 260
Evans, G. Blakemore, 148, 207
Everett, Barbara, 166, 183

Fineman, Daniel A., 191
Fischer, Sandra K., 52
Folland, Harold F., 119
Forker, Charles R., 53, 262
Foucault, Michel, 56, 232.
French, A. L., 120
Friedman, Donald M., 108
Frye, Northrop, 54, 140, 202

Gaudet, Paul, 121
Geduld, Harry M., 256
Gibson, Andrew, 142
Gielgud, John, 135, 141, 144. *See also* INDEX II
Gilman, Ernest B., 98
Gira, Catherine, 206
Goddard, Harold C., 55, 203, 204, 230
Goldberg, Jonathan, 56, 155
Goldman, Michael, 80
Gottschalk, Paul A., 184, 202
Gould, Gerald, 223, 237, 250, 261
Granville-Barker, Harley, 144, 238
Greenblatt, Stephen, 29, 68, 161, 181, 204, 232, 245
Gurr, Andrew, 93, 210, 221

Halio, Jay L., 187
Hall, Joan Lord, 239
Halvorson, John, 122
Hammond, Antony, 240
Hapgood, Robert, 38, 57, 123, 128
Harris, Frank, 241
Harris, Kathryn Montgomery, 109
Harrison, Thomas P., 49
Hartman, Geoffrey, 114
Hawkins, Sherman H., 58, 160, 185
Hazell, Stephen, 142
Hazlitt, William, 141, 202, 209, 241

Hemingway, Samuel Burdett, 148, 149, 207
Heninger, S. K., Jr., 110
Hexter, J. H., 99
Hillman, Richard, 222
Hodgdon, Barbara, 59, 150, 196
Holderness, Graham, 26, 30, 34, 37, 43, 61, 65, 85, 142, 180, 214, 235
Hosley, Richard, 62, 230
Howard, Jean E., 60
Hulme, Peter, 26
Humphreys, A. R., 151, 152
Hunter, G. K., 35, 73, 158, 168, 174, 179, 182, 186, 188, 189, 191, 195, 202, 205
Hunter, Robert G., 187, 202

Iverson, Margaret, 26

Jackson, Russell, 253
Jagendorf, Zvi, 204
Jenkins, Harold, 87, 90, 152, 185, 188, 205, 240
Johnson, Samuel, 141, 195, 202, 205, 212, 241
Jones, G. P., 213
Jorgens, Jack J., 81
Jorgensen, Paul A., 163, 168, 205, 241, 259

Kahn, Coppélia, 61, 85
Kamps, Ivo, 243
Kantorowicz, Ernst H., 100, 141, 144
Kehler, Dorothea, 126
Kelly, Henry Ansgar, 31
Kernan, Alvin B., 62, 143
Kiernan, Michael, 207
Kittredge, G. L., 241
Knights, L. C., 189, 204, 205, 261
Knowles, Richard, 169
Kott, Jan, 143
Krieger, Eliot, 203
Kris, Ernst, 190

Langbaum, Robert, 202
Lanham, Richard A., 39
Leggatt, Alexander, 62
Levin, Richard, 133, 219
Lewis, Wyndham, 203
Liebler, Naomi Conn, 101
Loughrey, Bryan, 142

McAlindon, Tom, 161
McCanles, Michael, 203
Macdonald, Ronald R., 40, 202
McEachern, Claire, 242
McGuire, Philip C., 136
McGuire, Richard L., 184
Mack, Maynard, Jr., 124, 140
MacKenzie, Clayton G., 102

INDEX

Mackenzie, Henry, 202
Maclean, Hugh, 63
McManaway, James G., 97
McMillin, Scott, 125, 197
Mahon, John W., 240
Mahood, M. M., 141
Mallett, Phillip, 243
Manheim, Michael, 64
Manzoni, Alessandro, 144
Martindale, Charles, 103
Masefield, John, 241
Matthews, Honor, 261
Maveety, Stanley R., 111
Melchiori, Giorgio, 153, 162
Metz, G. Harold, 145
Montagu, Elizabeth, 202
Montague, C. E., 141, 144
Moore, Edward M., 238
Moore, Jeanie Grant, 126
Morgann, Maurice, 174, 179, 191, 195, 202, 205
Morris, Corbyn, 202
Moseley, Charles, 142
Mossman, Judith, 223
Moulton, R. G., 241
Muir, Kenneth, 66, 74, 94, 106

Nevo, Ruth, 127, 140
Newlin, Jeanne T., 35, 65, 66, 78, 100, 106, 130, 134, 135, 144
Newman, Karen, 226
Nuttall, A. D., 103, 192, 203

Ornstein, Robert, 65, 85, 144

Page, Malcolm, 137
Palmer, D. J., 163, 202
Palmer, John, 241
Paolucci, Anne, 227
Parker, Francis, 26
Parker, Patricia, 114
Pater, Walter, 66, 94, 141, 144
Patterson, Annabel, 85, 214
Pechter, Edward, 198
Pendleton, Thomas A., 156, 240
Phialas, Peter G., 123, 128, 244
Pilkington, Ace G., 82
Plotnick, Jerrold, 245
Poole, Kristen, 164
Porter, Joseph A., 41
Potter, Lois, 112
Potter, Nicholas, 142
Price, Joseph G., 217
Prior, Moody E., 67, 204
Pye, Christopher, 68

Quinn, Michael, 74, 75, 84, 212, 227, 237, 261

Quinones, Ricardo J., 69, 203
Quint, David, 260

Rabkin, Norman, 70, 246, 260
Rackin, Phyllis, 60, 83, 138
Redmond, James, 257
Reese, M. M., 32, 86, 259
Ribner, Irving, 33, 143, 144
Richmond, H. M., 71
Roberts, Josephine A., 146
Rossiter, A. P., 72, 141, 259
Rumrich, John P., 193

Sajdak, Bruce T., 91
Salomon, Brownell, 247
Samuelson, David A., 136
Sanders, Wilbur, 129, 235
Sandler, Robert, 54
Schell, Edgar, 104
Seeff, Adele, 206
Selden, Raman, 142
Serres, Michel, 226
Shaaber, Matthias A., 154, 208
Shaw, George Bernard, 202, 241
Shewring, Margaret, 139
Sider, John W., 199
Siemon, James R., 260
Sinfield, Alan, 34, 85, 232, 235, 245, 260
Sledd, James H., 49
Smallwood, Robert L., 202, 253
Smith, Gordon Ross, 224
Somerset, J. A. B., 165
Spencer, Janet M., 225
Spivack, Bernard, 202
Sprague, Arthur Colby, 84, 202, 261
Spurgeon, Caroline, 259
Stewart, J. I. M., 73, 205
Stirling, Brents, 130, 141, 143, 144
Stoll, E. E., 259, 261
Storey, Graham, 72
Stříbrný, Zdeněk, 261
Sundelson, David, 203
Suzman, Arthur, 113
Swinburne, Algernon Charles, 141, 144

Tate, Nahum, 141
Taylor, Gary, 133, 155, 156, 157, 164, 211, 215
Tennenhouse, Leonard, 34, 85, 232
Thompson, Karl F., 105
Tillyard, E. M. W., 26, 30, 31, 35, 85, 86, 120, 128, 141, 143, 144, 161, 202, 205, 235, 259
Traub, Valerie, 194
Traversi, Derek A., 74, 86, 94, 143, 259, 261
Tyler, Sharon, 257

Ure, Peter, 93, 95, 120, 131, 143

Van Doren, Mark, 75, 202, 241, 259, 261
Vaughan, Virginia, see Carr, Virginia M.
Velz, John W., 193
Vickers, Brian, 42

Waith, Eugene M., 27, 32, 35, 50, 74, 86, 195, 212
Walter, J. H., 86, 212, 261
Watson, Robert N., 202
Watts, Cedric, 142
Webber, Joan, 76
Wells, Stanley, 89, 144, 215
Wells, Susan, 140
Wentersdorf, Karl P., 248
Wharton, T. F., 200, 202
Wiles, David, 201
Williams, Charles, 259, 261
Williams, George Walton, 167, 170, 171

Williams, Paul V. A., 242
Williamson, Marilyn L., 249
Willoughby, Edwin E., 97
Willson, Robert F., Jr., 167, 172, 258
Wilson, J. Dover, 86, 97, 144, 165, 182, 195, 202, 205, 259
Winny, James, 77
Winters, Yvor, 107
Womersley, David, 166
Woodbridge, Linda, 101
Worsley, T. C., 144
Wright, W. Aldis, 212

Yeats, William Butler, 78, 141, 144, 241, 259

Zagorin, Perez, 99
Zimbardo, Rose A., 227, 261
Zitner, Sheldon P., 115, 132

INDEX II: SUBJECTS
(FOR SECTIONS II, III, IV, AND V)

Texts (including Shakespeare's works but excluding the plays of the second tetralogy) are listed under the authors' names. The only exceptions to this rule occur in the case of anonymous works or works by multiple authors; these are listed by title. The plays of the second tetralogy are listed in the Index only when a specific act and scene from them has been cited or discussed; act, scene, and line references (if relevant) are given sequentially under each play. Characters from the plays are also listed individually. Citations are to item number.

Abel, 54, 111
Ackland, Joss, 196, 200
acting styles, 79, 201
Adam, 111
Agincourt, Battle of, 31, 32, 36, 42, 166, 211, 245, 256, 257
Alexander the Great, 222, 223, 225
Alighieri, Dante, 69
ambivalence, 46, 47, 64, 70, 72, 83, 98, 121, 147, 182, 216, 224, 232, 239, 240, 246, 250, 253, 261. See also indeterminacy
Amurath (Turkish ruler), 222
anachronism, 83
anamorphic art, 98
anamorphosis, 68
Andrews, Harry, 196, 197
antanaclasis, 210
Apocrypha (Shakespearean), 91
archetypal criticism, see critical approaches
archetypes, 54
Aristotle, 58, 160
Armin, Robert, 201
Arnold, Matthew, 30
ars moriendi, 28, 218. See also death

artifice, see role-playing *and* theatricality
Ascham, Roger, *The Schoolmaster*, 150
audience response, 46, 47, 60, 80, 83, 99, 121, 133, 134, 137, 138, 156, 179, 184, 195, 196, 198, 201, 213, 216, 231, 233, 238, 248, 251, 252, 257, 259
Augustine, Saint, 225
Aumerle (*Richard II*), 94, 115, 132
auxesis, 108

bad quartos, 209, 215
Bagot (*Richard II*), 121
Bakhtin, Mikhail, 194
ballads, 66, 151, 217
Bardolph (*Henry V*), 229, 253
Barton, John, 137, 139, 200
Bates (*Henry V*), 166, 234, 235, 252
Baxter, Keith, 197
BBC, see British Broadcasting Company
Beattie, Rod, 137
Benson, Frank, 139
Berners, Lord, see Bourchier, John, 2nd Baron Berners
Berri (*Henry V*), 252

INDEX

Bible, the, 147, 163, 168, 195; *Book of Genesis*, 111; *Epistle to the Ephesians*, 163
bibliographies, 92, 94, 148, 154, 196, 197, 239. See also filmographies *and* subsection F for section II, and subsection H for sections III, IV, and V.
blood, 106, 111; blood sacrifice, 180
Boccaccio, Giovanni, 225
Bodin, Jean, *Six Books of a Commonweale*, 117
body, the, 50, 56, 80, 100, 106, 166, 172, 183, 187, 193, 194, 199, 220, 242. See also King's Two Bodies, the
Bogdanov, Michael, 196, 197; *The Wars of the Roses*, 79
Bolingbroke, *see* Henry IV
Bordin, Joannes de (presumed author), *Henrici Quinti Angliae Regis Gesta*, 212
Bottom (*A Midsummer Night's Dream*), 183
Bourbon (*Henry V*), 210, 211, 215
Bourchier, John, 2nd Baron Berners, (translation of Froissart's *Chronicles*), 93, 95
Boy (*Henry V*), 252
boy actors, 68, 255
Bradford, William, 56
Branagh, Kenneth (film of *Henry V*), 30, 60, 79, 239, 254, 258; (stage performance in the role of Henry V), 79, 253. See also INDEX I
Brecht, Bertolt, 30, 59
British Broadcasting Company (BBC), 30; production of *Richard II*, 82, 139; production of *1* and *2 Henry IV*, 82, 196, 197, 200; production of *Henry V*, 82, 239
Brooke, Sir William, Lord Cobham, 156, 157, 212
Burrell, John, 197
Burton, Richard, 196, 197
Bushy (*Richard II*), 121, 125

Cain, 54, 98, 111
Caldwell, Zoe, 137
Calvin, John, 187
Cambridge (*Henry V*), 235, 248, 252
Canterbury (*Henry V*), 220, 221, 249
carnivalesque, 30, 34, 164, 187. See also saturnalia *and* subversion
Castiglione, Baldassare, *The Courtier*, 177
Castle, John, 196
Castle of Perseverance, The (Anon.), 104
Catholicism, 166. See also religion
censorship, 155, 162
ceremony, 35, 39, 44, 46, 62, 76, 93, 100, 115, 117, 122, 123, 126, 135, 158, 227, 235, 249. See also ritual
Chapman, George, *Conspiracy and Tragedy of Charles Duke of Byron*, 186; *Seven Books of the Iliads of Homer*, 211
Chaucer, Geoffrey, 225, 230
Chelidonius, Tigurinus, 212
chivalry, 30, 32, 147, 150, 162, 168, 195, 236, 249
Chorus (and choruses) (*Henry V*), 32, 39, 47, 55, 65, 80, 210, 211, 213, 214, 228, 231, 233, 234, 238, 239, 240, 241, 247, 252, 254, 255, 256, 257, 258
Christ, 100
Christian kingship, *see* kingship
Christianity, *see* religion; church and church-state relations; Catholicism; *and* Protestantism
chronicle play (as a genre), *see* history play (as a genre)
Chronicque de la Traïson et Mort de Richart Deux (Anon.), 95, 97
church and church/state relations, 27, 28. See also religion
Cicero, 160
Clarence (*Henry V*), 215
class, 42, 60, 83, 150, 182, 183, 210, 214, 226, 245, 256
Cleaver, Robert, *see* Dod, John
clergy, 27, 55, 230, 235, 249, 256
closure, 59, 198, 242
clown, *see* fool
Coleville, (*2 Henry IV*), 191
comedy and the comic, 28, 34, 43, 44, 53, 55, 60, 72, 81, 115, 122, 132, 151, 153, 158, 164, 169, 174, 175, 179, 187, 189, 191, 195, 198, 201, 203, 205, 217, 218, 219, 228, 230, 252, 256
Constable (*Henry V*), 252
Court (*Henry V*), 166, 234, 252, 255
court performances, 213
Créton, Jean, *Histoire du Roy Angleterre Richard*, 95, 97
critical approaches
- archetypal approaches, 54
- feminist and gender studies approaches, 30, 43, 56, 60, 61, 83, 126, 150, 183, 194, 220, 226, 236, 242, 255
- gay theory approaches, 56
- Marxist approaches, 26, 30
- metadramatic approaches, 37, 44, 114, 153
- mimetic approaches, 192
- New Critical and formalist approaches, 50, 62, 63, 69, 74, 77, 106, 109, 110, 111, 113, 136, 169, 189, 192, 216, 227, 247
- New Historicist and cultural materialist approaches, 28, 29, 30, 34, 60, 68, 150, 155, 161, 164, 194, 214, 216, 225, 232, 235, 242, 245
- postmodern approaches, 26, 30, 79
- psychological approaches, 61, 73, 114,

177, 181, 190, 194, 203, 236
— speech-act theory approaches, 41, 133
— structuralist approaches, 192
Crompton, Richard, *The Mansion of Magnanimitie*, 210
Cronin, Michael, 196
cuckoldry, 61
cultural materialism, *see* critical approaches
Curtain Theatre, 153

Dalton, Timothy, 200
dance, 227
Daniel, Samuel, *Civil Wars*, 31, 93, 95, 97, 147, 150, 151, 152
Dante, *see* Alighieri, Dante
dating of plays, 92, 93, 94, 95, 96, 147, 148, 149, 151, 152, 153, 154, 206, 208, 209, 210, 211, 212, 213, 262
Dauphin (*Henry V*), 210, 211, 215, 236, 252
death, 42, 54, 73, 105, 108, 119, 124, 132, 136, 174, 178, 180, 183, 186, 191, 218, 221, 242, 260; Death (allegorical personification), 102; regicide, 105, 119, 124, 130, 139, 190. *See also ars moriendi*
debt, 163. *See also* money
deceit, *see* hypocrisy
Dekker, Thomas, *Of Lantern and Candlelight*, 150
democracy, 55
deposition, 27, 31, 40, 45, 65, 67, 68, 77, 95, 96, 98, 99, 101, 109, 112, 113, 114, 115, 119, 120, 124, 130, 131, 133, 138, 139
Dionides, 225
disease, 32, 50, 71, 77, 106, 152, 153, 159, 200
disorder, 35, 38, 45, 67, 101, 117, 165, 198, 239. *See also* order
divine right, 33, 48, 54, 55, 67, 70, 74, 94, 122
Dod, John, *A Godly Form of Household Government* (with Robert Cleaver), 150
Doll Tearsheet (*2 Henry IV*), 60, 189
Dolphin (*Henry V*), *see* Dauphin
Don Giovanni (Mozart), 174
Dotrice, Roy, 197, 200
doubling of parts, 153, 209, 252
Dougall, John, 196
dramatic structure, *see* structure
Drayton, Michael, *see Sir John Oldcastle*
dress, 226
drunkenness, *see* gluttony and drunkenness
duality, *see* ambivalence
Du Bartas, Guillaume Saluste, 95; *Creation du Monde*, 108. *See also* Sylvester, Joshua; *and* Eliot, John
Duchess of Gloucester (*Richard II*), 114, 128

Duchess of York (*Richard II*), 98, 117, 132
Dudley, Craig, 137
Duke of York (*Richard II*), 94, 98, 99, 101, 107, 114, 117, 118, 125, 128, 132, 137, 138
duplicity, *see* hypocrisy

earth, *see* land
economy and economics, 50, 52. *See also* debt *and* money
Eden, Garden of, 53, 102
Edinburgh, Duke of, 251
Edmund Ironside (Anon.), 48
Edward III, 123, 128, 220
Edward III (Anon.) (partly Shakespearean?), 48, 162, 219
Eliot, John, *Ortho-Epia Gallica*, 95; as translator of Du Bartas, 108
Elizabeth I, 27, 28, 34, 60, 68, 83, 92, 95, 139, 144, 159, 214, 220, 242
Elmham, Thomas of (Pseudo-Elmham), *Vita et Gesta Henrici Quinti*, 212
Elyot, Sir Thomas, 212; *The Book of the Governor*, 152, 177
emblem books, 147
emblematic meaning, *see* symbolism and emblematic meaning
England's Parnassus (multiple authors), 93
English Shakespeare Company, 196, 197
Enlightenment, the, 99
epic, 28, 228; epic history, 27, 32, 35, 58, 62, 200, 209, 211, 212, 213, 231. *See also* history play (as a genre)
Erasmus, Desiderius, 212, 225, 230; *Institutio Principis Christiani*, 221
Erastianism, 151
Essex, Earl of, 27, 28, 92, 93, 95, 211, 234; the Essex Rebellion, 27, 93, 95, 96, 214
Evans, Maurice, 139
excess, 50, 69, 71
Exeter (*Henry V*), 252
Exton (*Richard II*), 130

Fabyan, Robert, 212
Fall of Man, 41, 102, 111
Falstaff (in the *Henry IV* plays), 27, 28, 30, 32, 33, 35, 36, 42, 43, 44, 47, 50, 54, 55, 56, 57, 60, 61, 67, 69, 70, 71, 73, 74, 75, 77, 79, 80, 132, 147, 150, 151, 152, 155, 156, 157, 158, 159, 162, 163, 164, 165, 166, 167, 170, 171, 172, 173, 174, 176, 182, 183, 184, 186, 188, 189, 190, 191, 192, 194, 195, 196, 197, 199, 200, 201, 203, 205, 218, 237, 244, 249, 254, 260; rejection of in *2 Henry IV*, 55, 59, 70, 152, 159, 165, 175, 176, 177, 179, 187, 188, 190, 195, 201, 205, 244, 260; death of (as described) in *Henry V*, 32, 42, 73, 157,

218, 242, 260; absence from *Henry V*, 72, 182, 212; in *The Merry Wives of Windsor*, 42, 157, 162, 170; in Shakespearean film and television productions, 79, 81, 196, 197, 200
family relationships, 61, 69, 236. *See also* father-son relationships
Famous Victories of Henry the Fifth, The (Anon.), 48, 147, 150, 151, 152, 153, 209, 210, 212
Farrah, Abdel, 251
Fastolf, Sir John, 167, 171, 172
Fastolf (*1 Henry VI*), 162, 170
father-son relationships, 35, 43, 44, 54, 58, 59, 61, 73, 77, 79, 114, 128, 147, 153, 163, 174, 180, 181, 190, 192, 200, 201, 236
feminist criticism, *see* critical approaches
fertility myths, 73
Festival of Britain, 30
feudalism, 30, 74, 108. *See also* medievalism
film versions of Shakespeare, 59, 60, 79, 81, 82, 89, 94, 146, 196, 197, 206, 209, 210, 239, 254, 255, 256, 258, 262
filmographies, 82, 146
Finch, Jon, 196, 197, 200
first tetralogy, 30, 43, 58, 61, 67, 79, 91, 120, 185
Fluellen (*Henry V*), 242
fool, the, 35, 100, 102, 147, 151, 174, 201, 243. *See also* Armin, Robert; Kemp, Will; *and* Tarlton, Richard
form, *see* structure
formalism, *see* critical approaches
Fortinbras (*Hamlet*), 78
Foxe, John, 105, 166; *Book of Martyrs* (also *Acts and Monuments*), 105, 150
Francis of Assisi, Saint, 253
French Ambassador (*Henry V*), 252
Freud, Sigmund, 190, 194
Froissart, Jean, 97. *See also* Bourchier, John, 2nd Baron Berners
Fulwell, Ulpian, *Like Will to Like*, 165

Gardener, the (*Richard II*), 55, 136
gardening and gardens, 43, 50, 69, 95, 106, 111
Gaunt (*Richard II*), 107, 108, 114, 118, 124, 128
gay theory, *see* critical approaches
gender, 183, 255. *See also* critical approaches
Genesis, Book of, 111
genre, *see* history play (as a genre)
Gentili, Alberico, *De Jure Belli*, 210
Gielgud, John, 139, 197. *See also* INDEX I
Giles, David, 196, 197, 200, 239
Globe Theatre, 99, 234, 255, 256
gluttony and drunkenness, 172, 174, 191

Gorboduc (Sackville and Norton), 32
Gosson, Stephen, *The School of Abuse*, 150
Gower, John, 225
Gower (*Henry V*), 242
grace (divine), 161; (human), 183
Grandpre (*Henry V*), 252
Green (*Richard II*), 121
Greene, Robert, *Friar Bacon and Friar Bungay*, 219; *James IV*, 219
Greville, Fulke, *Mustapha*, 107
Grey (*Henry V*), 235, 252
Griffith, Hugh, 197, 200
guilt, 55, 79, 114, 119, 133, 138, 173, 236
Gwillam, David, 196, 197, 200

Hal, *see* Henry V
Hall, Edward (all references to Hall are either explicitly or implicitly to *The Union of the Two Noble and Illustre Famelies of Lancastre & Yorke*), 31, 32, 45, 58, 97, 117, 150, 166, 210, 211, 212
Hall, Peter, 197, 200
Hamlet, 78, 190
Hands, Terry, 137, 196, 197, 200, 239, 251
Hannen, Nicholas, 197
Harfleur, Battle of, 229
Harpsfield, Nicholas, *Dialogi Sex*, 166
Harriot, Thomas, *A Brief and True Report of the New Found Land of Virginia*, 29, 232
Harrison, William, *The Description of England*, 150
Hathaway, Richard, *see Sir John Oldcastle*
Hayward, Sir John, *The First Part of the Life and Reign of King Henry IV*, 93, 95, 214
health, *see* disease
Henry IV (as Bolingbroke), 26, 28, 32, 33, 34, 37, 39, 41, 47, 48, 54, 55, 57, 59, 61, 64, 66, 67, 71, 74, 76, 77, 93, 94, 95, 99, 101, 104, 107, 108, 109, 110, 111, 112, 113, 114, 115, 117, 118, 119, 120, 123, 124, 125, 126, 129, 130, 133, 134, 137, 138; (as king), 28, 32, 33, 35, 43, 44, 46, 47, 51, 55, 57, 58, 63, 66, 67, 71, 73, 74, 75, 77, 79, 152, 163, 173, 178, 180, 181, 189, 190, 192, 196, 197, 200, 201, 236
Henry IV, part one (act and scene),
– (1.2.41-42), 156
– (1.2.217), 163, 168
– (1.2.195-217), 168, 192
– (2.2), 191
– (2.2.81-111), 195
– (2.4), 36, 184, 195
– (2.4.529ff.), 80
– (3.1), 150
– (3.2.129-59), 180

- (4.1), 217
- (4.1.104-110), 193
- (5.4), 180, 191
- (5.4.77-86), 180
- (5.4.127-29), 183

Henry IV, part two (act and scene),
- (1.2), 42
- (4.1), 152
- (4.2), 45, 152
- (4.3.1-23), 191
- (4.3.26-29), 191
- (4.4), 152
- (4.5), 152, 173, 192, 195
- (5.4.77-86), 180
- (5.5), 54, 59, 152, 159, 165, 173, 175, 176, 177, 179, 187, 188, 190, 195, 201, 205, 244, 260

Henry V (as Hal), 27, 28, 29, 32, 33, 34, 35, 37, 39, 41, 42, 43, 44, 45, 47, 48, 49, 50, 51, 52, 54, 55, 56, 57, 61, 63, 65, 67, 69, 70, 71, 74, 75, 76, 77, 79, 147, 151, 152, 158, 159, 160, 162, 163, 165, 168, 173, 174, 175, 176, 177, 179, 180, 181, 182, 184, 186, 188, 190, 192, 194, 195, 196, 197, 200, 201, 203, 205, 212, 229, 232, 237, 244, 249; (as king), 26, 27, 28, 32, 33, 34, 35, 36, 37, 41, 45, 46, 47, 48, 49, 51, 52, 55, 56, 57, 58, 60, 61, 63, 64, 65, 66, 67, 68, 70, 71, 72, 75, 76, 77, 78, 79, 80, 81, 83, 124, 160, 166, 177, 179, 182, 187, 210, 214, 216, 217, 219, 221, 222, 223, 225, 226, 229, 230, 231, 232, 233, 234, 236, 237, 238, 240, 241, 242, 243, 244, 245, 246, 247, 248, 249, 250, 252, 253, 255, 256, 257, 260, 261

Henry V (historical figure), 166

Henry V (act and scene),
- (Chorus, 1), 254, 255, 257
- (1.1), 28, 249
- (1.2), 212
- (1.2.33-95), 220
- (1.2.183-220), 221
- (Chorus, 2), 157
- (Chorus, 2.41-42), 211
- (2.2), 243, 244, 248
- (2.3), 32, 42, 73, 218, 242, 260
- (2.3.16), 211
- (Chorus, 3), 257
- (3.1), 229
- (3.3), 226
- (3.4), 60, 226
- (3.6.106ff.), 253
- (3.7), 210, 211
- (Chorus, 4), 257
- (4.1), 26, 27, 32, 42, 166, 217, 225, 234, 235, 243, 244, 245, 249, 255
- (4.1.35-63), 36
- (4.1.1-100), 211
- (4.1.230-84), 235
- (4.1.290-93), 211
- (4.2), 210, 211
- (4.2.18-67), 244
- (4.5), 210, 211
- (4.8), 249
- (Chorus, 5), 234, 257
- (Chorus, 5.39-40), 211
- (5.2), 42, 43, 45, 56, 68, 80, 217, 226, 229, 236, 242, 244, 253

Henry VI (*Henry VI* plays), 31
Henry VIII (historical figure), 161
Herald (*Henry V*), 252
heroism, 27, 33, 35, 43, 49, 58, 65, 71, 78, 127, 162, 165, 180, 198, 224, 227, 230, 236, 240, 253
Heywood, Thomas, *Edward IV*, 219; *An Apology for Actors*, 150
historiography, 27, 30, 67, 83
history play (as a genre), 33, 43, 53, 60, 71, 86, 117, 118, 122, 132, 137, 158, 162, 176, 193, 205, 217, 219, 227, 228, 230, 231. See also epic
Holbein, Hans, *The Ambassadors* (anamorphic painting), 98
Holinshed, Raphael (all references to Holinshed are either explicitly or implicitly to the *Chronicles*), 31, 48, 52, 93, 94, 95, 97, 99, 104, 117, 147, 150, 151, 152, 153, 166, 209, 210, 211, 212, 230, 244, 250
Holm, Ian, 197, 200
homilies, 32, 168; *Homily Against Disobedience*, 93, 150
homosexuality, *see* sexuality
honor, 41, 60, 67, 77, 150, 162, 168, 195
Hooker, Richard, 212
horses and horsemanship, 63
Hostess, *see* Mistress Quickly
Hotspur, 32, 35, 47, 54, 56, 57, 60, 63, 67, 69, 71, 74, 75, 77, 147, 159, 168, 173, 180, 188, 195, 197, 200, 244
Howard, Alan, 137, 196, 197, 200, 251
Howell, Jane, 30
humanum genus, 165
hypocrisy, 29, 40, 71, 77, 104, 112, 130, 232, 237, 243

identity, 26, 28, 39, 43, 53, 54, 61, 63, 67, 76, 77, 79, 80, 100, 103, 109, 122, 125, 127, 131, 140, 143, 147, 175, 177, 184, 193, 220, 229, 242, 255. *See also* self-consciousness, role-playing, *and* theatricality
imagery and metaphor, 37, 50, 52, 53, 62, 69, 74, 77, 93, 95, 106, 109, 110, 111, 113, 126, 148, 153, 193, 195, 220, 243, 259
imagination and the imaginative, 36, 44, 55,

INDEX

58, 77, 78, 106, 117, 124, 133, 151, 152, 178, 183, 203, 213, 216, 231, 233, 234, 240, 245, 247, 257
incest, 53
indeterminacy, 26, 40, 53, 155. *See also* ambivalence
inheritance, 45, 60, 61, 104, 106, 111, 160, 181, 210, 220, 248; inheritance rights, 99; inheritance of personal attributes, 191
Irons, Jeremy, 139
irony, 32, 49, 53, 55, 63, 64, 65, 66, 70, 77, 83, 98, 112, 124, 126, 136, 172, 173, 178, 189, 199, 209, 210, 222, 223, 229, 230, 234, 236, 237, 247, 252, 253, 260; ironic view of history, 49, 83
Isabel (*Richard II*), 43, 125, 126
Isolde (Wagner), 174

Jacobi, Derek, 139
James I, 27, 34
James, Emrys, 196, 197, 200
Jamy (*Henry V*), 242
Jerusalem, 210
jester, *see* fool
jig, the, 162, 201
jingoism, 72
Joan of Arc (*Henry VI*, part one), 43
Jonson, Ben, 153; humors comedy, 153; *Bartholomew Fair*, 164; *Epicoene*, 226; *Masque of Blackness*, 213

kabuki drama, 137
Katherina (*The Taming of the Shrew*), 60
Katherine (*Henry V*), 43, 45, 56, 60, 83, 194, 220, 226, 236, 243, 252, 253
Kean, Charles, 139
Kemp, Will, 195, 201
King of France (*Henry V*), 236
King's Two Bodies, the, 59, 67, 68, 100, 217; the "two bodies" of *Richard II*, 98. *See also* body, the
kingship, 26, 30, 31, 32, 33, 34, 35, 37, 40, 42, 44, 46, 50, 61, 64, 65, 66, 67, 69, 71, 74, 76, 77, 78, 95, 100, 115, 118, 119, 124, 131, 160, 163, 188, 212, 216, 217, 222, 225, 232, 237, 239, 242, 244, 246, 261
Kyd, Thomas, *Soliman and Perseda*, 151
Kyle, Barry, 139

Lacan, Jacques, 194
Lady Percy (*1* and *2 Henry IV*), 43, 60
Lambarde Document, 139
land, 106, 108, 111, 193
Launce's dog (*The Two Gentlemen of Verona*), 183
law, 33, 45, 99, 165, 193, 195, 225, 255; natural law, 45, 53; Salic Law, 220

Layamon, *Brut*, 150, 212
Le Fèvre, J., Seigneur de Saint-Remy, 212
lineation, 211
Lord Chief Justice (*2 Henry IV*), 33, 42, 67, 153, 195
Lord of Misrule, 147, 158, 174. *See also* misrule
love, 174, 191, 203, 253, 260; self-love, 103. *See also* marriage and wooing *and* sexuality
Lucan, 58
Lupton, Thomas, *All for Money*, 165
Luther, Martin, 187
Lydgate, John, 225
lying, 40, 147, 170, 171, 179, 191. *See also* hypocrisy
Lyly, John, *Campaspe*, 219

Machiavel, the, 44, 243
Machiavelli, Niccoló, *The Prince*, 150; Machiavellianism, 46, 48, 64, 71, 178, 182, 192, 243, 246. *See also* Machiavel, the
McKellen, Ian, 139
Macmorris (*Henry V*), 242, 252
McQueen, Jim, 137
magic, 60
majesty, *see* kingship
Maradan, Frank, 137
Marlowe, Christopher, 56, 58, 140; *Doctor Faustus*, 129; *Edward II*, 64, 129, 140; *The Jew of Malta*, 129; *The Massacre at Paris*, 129; *Tamburlaine*, 33, 36, 186, 230
marriage and wooing, 43, 45, 56, 60, 61, 68, 83, 212, 217, 220, 226, 229, 242, 244, 253. *See also* love *and* sexuality
Marston, John, *Antonio and Mellida*, 186
Martin Marprelate, 164
martyrdom, 105
Marxist approaches to literature, *see* critical approaches
Mason, Brewster, 196, 197, 200
masque, the, 115, 213, 252
May Game, the, 158
medieval drama, 28, 104, 115. *See also* morality play *and* Vice, the
medievalism, 35, 41, 46, 53, 62, 71, 81, 83, 100, 103, 128. *See also* feudalism
memorially reported texts, 210, 215
metadrama, *see* critical approaches
metaphor, *see* imagery and metaphor
metaphysical wit, 98; metaphysical style, 107
middle ages, *see* medievalism
miles gloriosus, 147, 151, 191, 195
military profession, 27, 60, 147, 150, 191, 195, 222, 235, 257; military trades, 150. *See also miles gloriosus*

Milton, John, 69
mimesis, 37, 114, 192, 203
Mirror for Magistrates, The, 32, 95, 151, 152
mirrors, 33, 100, 103, 110, 116, 125, 126, 131
misogyny, 56
misrule, 32, 34, 158. See also Lord of Misrule
Mistress Quickly (*Henry V*), 42, 60
Mitchell, Julian, *Francis*, 253
Mnouchkine, Ariane, 137, 139
moderation, see excess
monarchy, see kingship
money, 29. See also debt *and* economy and economics
monopoly, 99
Montaigne, Michel de, 69
moral play, 159. See also morality play
morality play, 28, 33, 35, 104, 151, 153, 165, 195, 201. See also moral play *and* Vice, the
Mortimer, Edmund (historical figure), 248
Mountjoy (*Henry V*), 252
Mowbray (*Richard II*), 48, 94, 112, 114, 191
Munday, Anthony, *Two Italian Gentlemen*, 162. See also Sir John Oldcastle
murder, see death
Murphy, Gerard, 196, 200
music, 117, 145, 207, 208, 262; in stage performances, 251; in Olivier's film of *Henry V*, 256; musicality of Shakespeare's verse, 135
myths (historical and political) and myth-making, 28, 31, 39, 59, 67, 102, 195, 218, 233; fertility myths, 73. See also Tudor Myth *and* providential view of history

names and naming, 26, 41, 150, 155, 156, 157, 163, 164, 167, 168, 170, 171, 172, 183, 210, 211, 214, 215
narcissism, 53, 140
Narcissus, 103
Nashe, Thomas, *Summer's Last Will and Testament*, 158
National Broadcasting Company (NBC), 139
nationalism, see patriotism
natural law, see law
nature of man, 50, 55
Neptune, 102
New Criticism, see critical approaches
New Historicism, see critical approaches
Noble, Adrian, 79, 253
noise, 169, 226
Northern Rebellion, 27, 161
Northumberland (*Richard II*), 129; (*2 Henry IV*), 189

nostalgia, 26, 81, 83, 124, 128, 220
Nunn, Trevor, 196, 200
Nym (*Henry V*), 229

oaths, see swearing
O'Connell, Patrick, 196, 197
old age, 73, 77, 152, 163, 174, 189, 192, 199
Oldcastle, Sir John, 147, 151, 153, 155, 156, 157, 162, 164, 166, 171, 183; Oldcastle controversy, 147, 150, 152, 155, 156, 157, 164, 170, 171, 212
Old Vic Theatre, 197
Olivier, Laurence, 197; (film of *Henry V*), 30, 60, 79, 81, 82, 239, 254, 255, 256, 258
order, 26, 38, 41, 45, 53, 60, 65, 67, 69, 74, 101, 110, 117, 150, 186, 195, 198, 227, 235, 239. See also disorder
Order of the Garter, 162
Ovid, *Metamorphoses*, 103

pageants and pageantry, see ceremony
Paradise, see Eden, Garden of
parasite, the (theatrical type), 151
Pasco, Richard, 137
pastoral, 53, 153, 228
pathos, 189
patriotism, 72, 75, 182, 205, 210, 211, 224, 233, 237, 256
Paul, Saint, *Epistle to the Ephesians*, 163
Pennell, Nicholas, 137
Pennington, Michael, 196, 197
perspective (in art), 98
Petrarch, Francesco (and Petrarchanism), 34, 69; Petrarchan style, 107
Petruchio (*The Taming of the Shrew*), 60
picaresque hero, 147
Pigott-Smith, Tim, 197, 200
pilgrimage, 161, 178. See also processioning *and* walking
Pilgrimage of Grace, 161
piracy, 225
Pistol, 168; (*Henry V*), 36, 233, 247, 252
Plato, 39, 58, 160
plot, 47, 65, 81, 83, 149, 151, 169, 200, 219, 238, 239, 259
Plutarch, 58; *Life of Alexander*, 223
Poins (*1 Henry IV*), 195
Ponet, John, *A Short Treatise of Political Power*, 150
Porter, Eric, 197, 200
postmodernism, see critical approaches
poststructuralism, 30
power (political), 26, 28, 29, 34, 43, 44, 48, 52, 54, 56, 67, 68, 133, 150, 162, 214, 219, 224, 232, 242, 245
Price, John, 197
Prince Hal, see Henry V

Prince John (*2 Henry IV*), 45, 67, 191; (*Henry V*) as "Bedford," 215
processioning, 193. *See also* pilgrimage *and* walking
profanity, 211. *See also* swearing
Prologue (to *Henry V*), *see* Chorus
property, 99, 193
prose, 42
Protestantism, 104, 156, 166, 187. *See also* religion *and* Puritanism
providential view of history, 31, 32, 35, 45, 48, 53, 67, 120. *See also* myths (historical and political) and mythmaking *and* Tudor Myth
prudence, 50, 69
psychological criticism, *see* critical approaches
psychology, 177, 178, 187, 216. *See also* critical approaches
puns and punning, 170
Puritanism, 99, 164

Quayle, Anthony, 139, 196, 197, 200
Queen Isabel (*Richard II*), *see* Isabel

Rabelais, François, 69
rebellion, 27, 33, 95, 99, 118, 138, 150, 161, 186, 235, 247
Redgrave, Michael, 196, 197
Reformation, the, 28, 161
regicide, *see* death
religion, 28, 29, 53, 67, 71, 94, 100, 102, 105, 124, 129, 151, 156, 161, 163, 164, 166, 168, 174, 187, 212, 224, 230. *See also* Catholicism, church and church-state relations, *and* Protestantism
Respublica, 35
rhetoric, 37, 38, 39, 40, 41, 42, 66, 107, 108, 110, 112, 114, 115, 119, 122, 133, 135, 136, 177, 210, 216, 226, 227, 229, 233
rhyme, 94
Rich, Barnaby, *A Pathway to Military Practice,* 150
Richard II, 26, 27, 32, 33, 36, 37, 39, 40, 41, 44, 45, 46, 47, 48, 50, 51, 52, 54, 55, 59, 61, 63, 64, 65, 67, 68, 70, 71, 74, 75, 76, 77, 78, 93, 94, 95, 99, 100, 101, 102, 103, 104, 105, 107, 109, 110, 111, 112, 113, 116, 117, 118, 119, 120, 121, 122, 123, 124, 125, 126, 127, 128, 129, 130, 131, 133, 134, 135, 136, 137, 139, 140, 190
Richard II (act and scene),
– (1.1), 48, 98, 101, 113, 114, 117
– (1.2), 114
– (1.3), 98, 101, 112, 113, 114, 117
– (2.1), 57, 104, 108
– (2.1.201-4), 99
– (2.2.14-27), 125
– (3.2), 100, 120, 133
– (3.3), 100, 113, 119, 120, 130
– (3.3.147-53), 101
– (3.4), 43, 55, 95
– (3.4.104-7), 136
– (4.1), 36, 95, 98, 100, 101, 109, 112, 113, 115, 117, 119, 120, 124, 130, 133
– (4.1.154-318), 96
– (4.1.265-67), 131
– (4.1.275ff.), 100, 103, 124
– (4.1.288), 116, 125
– (5.1), 117
– (5.1.40-45), 136
– (5.2), 115, 125, 132
– (5.2.23-36), 101
– (5.2.12-20), 125
– (5.3), 98, 115, 117, 132
– (5.4), 98
– (5.5), 98, 117, 127
– (5.5.1-66), 125
– (5.5.31-41), 124
– (5.6), 98, 130
Richard III, 58, 67, 183, 242
Richardson, Ian, 137
Richardson, Ralph, 197
rise and fall, 113
ritual, 62, 68, 73, 101, 114, 158, 180, 218. *See also* ceremony
robbery, *see* thievery
Rodway, Norman, 197
role-playing, 39, 48, 51, 64, 67, 76, 77, 80, 124, 147, 177, 184, 217, 243, 249, 251, 255; by the audience, 138, 257. *See also* identity, self-consciousness, *and* theatricality
romance, 39, 211, 217, 219, 228, 233
romantic comedy, 28, 34
Royal Cockpit (theatre), 213
Royal Shakespeare Company, 79, 137, 139, 196, 197, 200, 239, 251
Rumor (*2 Henry IV*), 169, 173, 176, 196
Russell, Richard, 137

sacraments and sacramentalism, 51, 216
Salisbury, John of, 225
saturnalia, 151, 158. *See also* carnivalesque *and* subversion
Scanderbeg, 222
Scroop (*Henry V*), 235, 244, 248, 252
Segar, Sir William, *Honor Military and Civil,* 150
self, the, *see* identity
self-consciousness (on the part of characters) 39, 40, 103, 112, 127; (on the part of Shakespeare), 44, 176. *See also* identity, role-playing, *and* theatricality

128 INDEX

Serres, Michel, 226
sexuality, 56, 60, 61, 68, 150, 162, 170, 172, 194, 220, 226, 236, 242. See also love and marriage and wooing
Shakespeare, William (works)
- All's Well That Ends Well, 159
- Antony and Cleopatra, 54, 127, 179, 189, 236
- As You Like It, 158, 194, 236
- Coriolanus, 36, 51, 61, 70, 71, 80, 127, 168, 189, 192
- Hamlet, 54, 78, 80, 124, 127, 134, 143, 168, 190, 194, 214, 222, 236, 238
- Henry VI plays, 43, 48, 60, 67, 68, 220
- Henry VI, part one, 43, 60, 162, 170
- Henry VI, part two, 60
- Henry VI, part three, 60
- Henry VIII, 34, 35, 44, 78
- Julius Caesar, 51, 70, 71, 127, 192
- King John, 47, 48, 60, 71
- King Lear, 36, 51, 54, 80, 127, 143, 189, 214, 236
- Love's Labor's Lost, 36, 158
- Macbeth, 35, 61, 68, 107, 124, 127, 129, 189
- Measure for Measure, 54, 70
- The Merchant of Venice, 158, 183, 192, 232, 246
- The Merry Wives of Windsor, 42, 157, 162, 170
- A Midsummer Night's Dream, 34, 54, 98, 132, 158, 183, 214
- Much Ado About Nothing, 168
- Othello, 127, 168, 192, 194, 222, 226, 232, 236
- Pericles, 36
- Richard III, 47, 58, 60, 67, 116, 129, 159, 183, 243
- Romeo and Juliet, 54, 61, 80, 127, 134
- Sonnets, 94, 189
- The Taming of the Shrew, 60, 61, 226
- The Tempest, 36, 54, 80, 191, 214
- Troilus and Cressida, 189, 194
- Twelfth Night, 98, 134, 158, 194
- The Two Gentlemen of Verona, 183
- Venus and Adonis, 61
- The Winter's Tale, 54, 80, 194, 236
Shakespeare Memorial Theatre, 196, 197
Shallow (2 Henry IV), 189
Shylock (The Merchant of Venice), 183
sickness, see disease
Sidney, Sir Philip, Defence of Poetry, 107, 257
Silence (2 Henry IV), 189
Silver, George, The Paradoxes of Defense, 150
Sir John Oldcastle (Michael Drayton, Richard Hathaway, Anthony Munday, and Robert Wilson, joint authors), 48, 150, 155, 210, 217
Slaughter of the Innocents (Fleury), 104
sleep, 80
snakes and serpents, 106, 111
sodomy, 56
soldiers and soldiering, see military profession
sources and backgrounds, 37, 45, 46, 48, 49, 52, 54, 56, 58, 67, 68, 73, 83, 86, 108, 115, 117, 118, 121, 137, 143, 145, 146, 200, 206, 207, 208, 228, 230, 232, 239, 244, 248, 250, 261, 262; of film versions, 79. See also subsection A for section II and subsections A and C for sections III, IV, and V
speech-act theory, see critical approaches
Speed, John, The History of Great Britain, 150
Spenser, Edmund, 56, 58, 69
sprezzatura, 161
stage business (including stage directions), 84, 93, 137
Stanton, Barry, 196
Stewart, Patrick, 196, 200
Stow, John, 147, 152; Chronicles of England, 151; Annals, 151; Survey of London, 150
Stratford Festival (Ontario, Canada), 137
Strecche, John, Chronicle of John Strecche, 212
Strehler, Giorgio, 139
structure, 37, 47, 53, 59, 66, 74, 93, 95, 98, 106, 109, 117, 118, 127, 130, 134, 136, 139, 147, 151, 152, 153, 158, 159, 160, 161, 162, 163, 165, 169, 183, 185, 186, 188, 193, 195, 198, 201, 205, 213, 219, 225, 227, 231, 239, 246, 247; in filmed Shakespeare, 81. See also unity of the second tetralogy
Stubbes, John, Gaping Gulf, 210
style, 39, 42, 66, 72, 75, 107, 108, 148, 152, 153, 198, 239; dramatic style, 159, 227; film style in Olivier's Henry V, 256, 258; in Branagh's Henry V, 258
subversion, 29, 48, 59, 60, 68, 83, 93, 122, 126, 150, 164, 214, 220, 222, 232, 235. See also carnivalesque and saturnalia
succession (royal), see inheritance
Suchet, David, 137
sun, 106, 109, 110, 243
Sutcliffe, Matthew, The Right Practice, Proceedings, and Laws of Arms, 150
swearing, 40, 180
Swetnam, Joseph, The Arraignment of Lewd, Idle, Froward, and Unconstant

INDEX

Women, 150
syllepsis, 210
Sylvester, Joshua, (as translator of Du Bartas), 108; *Deuine Weekes and Workes* (translation of Du Bartas), 95
symbolism and emblematic meaning, 76, 95, 110, 113, 159, 163, 172, 174, 255

Talbot (*1 Henry VI*), 162
Tarlton, Richard, 28, 153, 201; *Tarlton's Jests,* 153.
tears, *see* weeping
television versions of Shakespeare, 82, 137, 139, 196, 197, 200, 209, 210, 239
Théâtre du Soleil, 137
theatre of the absurd, 122
theatricality, 28, 41, 43, 44, 54, 60, 67, 68, 114, 117, 119, 129, 133, 137, 147, 181, 192, 234, 243. *See also* role-playing, identity, *and* self-consciousness
theology, *see* religion
thievery, 57, 191, 195
Thomas, Lord Cromwell (Anon.), 48
Thomas of Woodstock (Anon.), 64, 93, 95, 97, 121, 151
time, 44, 50, 53, 63, 69, 152, 153, 163, 168, 177, 187, 189, 231; theatrical time, 104, 200; Time as a personification in 2 *Henry IV,* 173
topicality, 27, 28, 29, 34, 60, 83, 93, 95, 99, 150, 156, 161, 162, 167, 183, 213, 216, 221. *See also* Elizabeth I; Essex, Earl of; James I; *and* Oldcastle, Sir John
tragedy and the tragic, 43, 44, 47, 49, 50, 53, 58, 67, 70, 71, 72, 75, 95, 107, 118, 122, 124, 126, 127, 131, 132, 143, 174, 189, 198, 217, 228, 244
tragicomedy, 189
Tristan (Wagner), 174
Troublesome Reign of King John (Anon.), 27
Tudor Myth, the, and Tudor views of history, 31, 32, 35, 49, 65, 67, 83, 108, 224. *See also* myths (historical and political) and mythmaking *and* providential view of history
Tyndale, William, 166
tyranny and tyrants, 58, 65, 173, 222

unity of the second tetralogy, 31, 32, 35, 38, 41, 42, 44, 45, 52, 57, 58, 62, 64, 67, 68, 74, 162, 185, 188, 197, 200, 222, 227, 229, 244, 247, 261. *See also* structure
usurpation, *see* deposition

Vanitas, 131
Vergil, Polydore, 31
Vice, the, 35, 147, 151, 159, 165, 201. *See also* morality play
vice, 33, 77, 78, 165
Vilar, Jean, 139

Wager, W., *Enough is as Good as a Feast,* 159, 165; *The Trial of Treasure,* 159, 165
walking, 193. *See also* pilgrimage *and* processioning
Walton, William, 256
Wapull, George, *The Tide Tarrieth No Man,* 165
war, 60, 198, 209, 216, 224, 228, 233, 237, 239, 254, 256, 258; (morality of), 27, 32, 221, 225, 248, 254; (practice of), 27, 210, 222, 224; (language of), 168, 233; (violence of), 180. *See also* military profession
Warre, Michael, 197
Wars of the Roses (Royal Shakespeare Company), 139
water, 109
weeping, 60, 106, 109, 126
Welles, Orson, *Chimes at Midnight,* 79, 81, 82, 196, 197
Wever, R., *Lusty Juventus,* 168
Wheel of Fortune, 54
Whitgift, John, Archbishop of Canterbury, 150
Williams (*Henry V*), 26, 166, 214, 225, 234, 235, 245, 249, 252
Williams, Clifford, 200
Wilson, Robert, *see Sir John Oldcastle*
Wilson, Stuart, 197, 200
witchcraft, 226
Woodstock, see Thomas of Woodstock
Woodvine, John, 196, 197
wooing, *see* marriage and wooing
Woolfenden, Guy, 251

Xenophon, 58

York (*Richard II*), *see* Duke of York

Zeal-of-the-Land Busy (Jonson's *Bartholomew Fair*), 164